Keith M. Kilty, PhD
Elizabeth A. Segal, PhD
Editors

The Promise of Welfare Reform
Political Rhetoric and the Reality of Poverty in the Twenty-First Century

Pre-publication
REVIEWS,
COMMENTARIES,
EVALUATIONS . . .

"*The Promise of Welfare Reform* issues a call to arms to everyone interested in the fight for economic and social justice in the United States. The book analyzes historical, social, and globalization influences in the context of gender, race, and class through articles that are written with clarity and passion. The work strips away the mind-numbing political rhetoric of conservatives and neoliberal policy ideologues to reveal the realities of low-income single mothers, the working poor, and the continued insidiousness of racism and sexism.

This is not a book written solely for academics, but is highly readable, instructive, and useful for policymakers, activists, students, politicians, and social work practitioners, as well as teachers at universities. The authors of the articles ask all of us to wake up before the gains won by activists of twentieth-century social movements are stolen by the new 'robber barons.' We felt as though they were speaking directly to us with a warning to take action before it is too late. In some of the most innovative and fresh perspectives in the book, the contributors challenge the conventional and stale progressive strategy, entrenched over the past couple of decades, of fighting over the pathetic 'crumbs' leftover from what was once our safety net; they ask us to think beyond what seems politically possible or expedient and advocate for welfare programs the way they *should* be. We recommend this book not only to American readers but to Japanese as well. This is a book about poverty that gets it right!"

Deborah McDowell Aoki, PhD
Professor, Hokusei Gakuen University, Japan
Osamu Aoki, PhD
Professor, Hokkaido University, Japan

"**T**he Promise of Welfare Reform promises to separate the real impacts of new welfare policies from the falsehoods that politicians used to justify these policies. And the book delivers. The essays in this valuable volume provide a set of honest accounts of the intentions and effects of 'welfare reform,' including accounts of the monumental deceptions at the heart of ending welfare as we knew it. While politicians and policymakers have relied on gaseous hyperbole, racial and gender stereotyping, the authors in this book raise and explore these essential questions in a rich variety of ways: Do poor people have the right to dignity and the right to life?

This book brings together a wonderfully vibrant and interdisciplinary mix of voices. These scholars and activists invite readers to consider practical and visionary matters, from local and global perspectives, from everyday consequences to theoretical analyses. This book is a uniquely important assessment of the ideological and real-life impacts of the late twentieth-century's war against the poor in the United States."

Rickie Solinger, PhD
Historian; Author of *Pregnancy and Power: A Short History of Reproductive Politics in America*

"**T**he Promise of Welfare Reform paints a painful picture of the failure of the United States to meet its obligation to its citizens. Justifying cutbacks in state support to the poor through the frames of personal responsibility and independence, the federal government and the states have set up a system that punishes people for the sins of structural inequality in this country. By mapping the political rhetoric of public officials and popular discourse that blames the poor for their poverty against the realities of poor peoples' lives, the editors and contributing authors reveal the human costs of political irresponsibility. Most important, the collection centers the experiences of those whose voices have been left out of the welfare reform debates, such as the working poor, low-income rural residents, people of color, immigrants, and battered women. Kilty and Segal and the contributors to *The Promise of Welfare Reform* provide a strong foundation for a challenge to the contemporary rhetoric of welfare reform that masks racism, sexism, and class oppression. The authors challenge the call to marriage as a solution to poverty and reframe the role of the state in preventing and mitigating poverty, homelessness, racism, and domestic violence as a matter of human rights. *The Promise of Welfare Reform* makes clear that it is time to wage a new war on poverty, one that recasts poverty as a violation of economic human rights and redefines personal responsibility as a collective obligation of the U.S. government to its citizens."

Nancy A. Naples, PhD
Professor, Sociology and Women's Studies; Advisor, Women's Studies Graduate Certificate, University of Connecticut

More pre-publication
REVIEWS, COMMENTARIES, EVALUATIONS . . .

"*The Promise of Welfare Reform* is an impressive compilation of essays regarding one of the most disturbing social welfare experiments in the recent past. Kilty and Segal bring together both well-known authors on this topic and emerging scholars to the field to accomplish their task of providing a comprehensive analysis of the mismatch between political and media rhetoric and the reality of 'welfare reform' for impoverished families. One stated goal of the book is to be accessible to a broad readership, beyond academicians—the editors succeed in this goal by offering relatively short, focused chapters that are compelling and readable.

The organization of the book makes sense. Each of the five topic areas is essential to understanding the full meaning and impact of the Personal Responsibility and Work Opportunity Reconciliation Act. The multiple chapters under each heading offer unique information and analysis, thereby providing the reader with an in-depth and many-layered accounting of the larger topic covered. In its entirety, the book will provide the reader with a broad and rich examination of the social and political context that produced the 1996 welfare law, how the law has profoundly impacted some of the most vulnerable and oppressed members of our population, and what the prospects are for progressive change in the future."

Sandra S. Butler, PhD, MSW
Interim Director and Associate Professor,
School of Social Work,
University of Maine

"This book will provide students of welfare and poverty policy a breadth of understanding of welfare reform and its less than positive impact on impoverished families in our country.

Welfare reform may be a political success because of the significant drop in public assistance caseloads, but it has not been a human success—needy families have not found good jobs that would lift them out of poverty. This volume provides those concerned about alleviating poverty in the United States with an in-depth understanding of the political context and aims of Clinton-era welfare reform policies. Chapters by nationally known scholars such as Abramovitz, Blau, and Reisch provide insight into the history and context of welfare policy in the United States. Authors such as Mink explain the rhetoric of welfare reform and why ending single motherhood was targeted more than alleviating poverty. Other chapters explain why immigrants, victims of domestic violence, and African-American women have been particularly affected by the sanctions imposed by the new law and are less likely to find and keep jobs. Those concerned about economic justice will find Neubeck's analysis of American reluctance to support economic human rights insightful but disheartening."

Wynne Sandra Korr, PhD
Dean and Professor,
School of Social Work,
University of Illinois
at Urbana-Champaign

More pre-publication
REVIEWS, COMMENTARIES, EVALUATIONS . . .

"I love this book. The editors of the *Journal of Poverty* have brought together an outstanding group of authors to 'separate the reality from the rhetoric of welfare reform.' The resulting book will be valuable to students, academics, and practitioners in a variety of fields. From its splendid foreword to the final chapter, this book is eminently readable and well researched. It offers a rich collection of insights and perspectives for those who care about the country's treatment of its most vulnerable. I will certainly be using it in my social policy classes!

Some of my favorite chapters consider the broad social and economic context of the 1996 welfare 'reforms.' For example, Mimi Abramowitz explains that marriage promotion affects all women, just as workfare weakens the bargaining position of all who work for a wage. Joel Blau puts the 1996 act in the context of other moments in U.S. history when social welfare policy has been used to regulate the workforce during major economic transitions. Several authors suggest that the proposed privatization of Social Security can be understood as the natural sequel to PRWORA, as corporations and employers continue to advance their economic advantage. Thus, welfare reform is understood as part and parcel of a broad transformation of American society characterized by growing power imbalances between rich and poor, employers and labor, institutions and individuals. In this context, as Bart Miles and Patrick Fowler explain, the goal of the 1996 legislation was not to reduce poverty or suffering, but to reduce government responsibility for poverty and promote family forms that enjoy the approval of conservatives.

The book also provides practical guidance for emerging advocacy efforts. Joel Blau prescribes a social movement. The roots of this might be found in global efforts to promote fair trade and rein in the World Trade Organization. Of course, as Michael Reisch points out, social workers are not at the forefront of these efforts. Margaret Nelson offers practical goals for advocates, focusing on the needs of low-wage workers, on real tax reform, and on the right of mothers to care for their children. Kenneth Neubeck caps off this approach, advising that advocates frame their efforts in terms of human rights."

Amanda S. Barusch
Associate Dean for Research
and Doctoral Studies,
College of Social Work,
University of Utah

The Haworth Press
New York • London • Oxford

The Promise
of Welfare Reform
Political Rhetoric
and the Reality of Poverty
in the Twenty-First Century

THE HAWORTH PRESS
Titles of Related Interest

Rediscovering the Other America: The Continuing Crisis of Poverty and Inequality in the United States edited by Keith M. Kilty and Elizabeth A. Segal

The Transition from Welfare to Work: Processes, Challenges, and Outcomes edited by Sharon Telleen and Judith V. Sayad

Health and Poverty edited by Michael J. Holosko and Marvin D. Feit

Welfare, Work, and Well-Being edited by Mary Clare Lennon

Beyond Altruism: Social Welfare Policy in American Society by Willard C. Richan

Changing Welfare Services: Case Studies of Local Welfare Reform Programs edited by Michael J. Austin

Child Welfare in the Legal Setting: A Critical and Interpretive Perspective by Thomas M. O'Brien

Children's Rights: Policy and Practice, Second Edition by John T. Pardeck

Behind the Eight Ball: Sex for Crack Cocaine Exchange and Poor Black Women by Tanya Telfair Sharpe

The Promise
of Welfare Reform
Political Rhetoric
and the Reality of Poverty
in the Twenty-First Century

Keith M. Kilty, PhD
Elizabeth A. Segal, PhD
Editors

The Haworth Press
New York • London • Oxford

For more information on this book or to order, visit
http://www.haworthpress.com/store/product.asp?sku=5608

or call 1-800-HAWORTH (800-429-6784) in the United States and Canada
or (607) 722-5857 outside the United States and Canada

or contact orders@HaworthPress.com

PUBLISHER'S NOTE
The development, preparation, and publication of this work has been undertaken with great care. However, the Publisher, employees, editors, and agents of The Haworth Press are not responsible for any errors contained herein or for consequences that may ensue from use of materials or information contained in this work. The Haworth Press is committed to the dissemination of ideas and information according to the highest standards of intellectual freedom and the free exchange of ideas. Statements made and opinions expressed in this publication do not necessarily reflect the views of the Publisher, Directors, management, or staff of The Haworth Press, Inc., or an endorsement by them.

The Haworth Press, Inc., 10 Alice Street, Binghamton, NY 13904-1580.

Cover design by Kelly E. Fye.

Library of Congress Cataloging-in-Publication Data

The promise of welfare reform : political rhetoric and the reality of poverty in the twenty-first century / Keith M. Kilty, Elizabeth A. Segal, editors.
    p. cm.
Includes bibliographical references and index.
ISBN-13: 978-0-7890-2921-8 (hard : alk. paper)
ISBN-10: 0-7890-2921-9 (hard : alk. paper)
ISBN-13: 978-0-7890-2922-5 (soft : alk. paper)
ISBN-10: 0-7890-2922-7 (soft : alk. paper)
    1. Public welfare—United States. 2. Poor—Government policy—United States. 3. Welfare recipients—United States. 4. United States—Social policy—1993- I. Kilty, Keith M. (Keith Michael), 1946- II. Segal, Elizabeth A.

HV95.P7372 2006
361.6'8'0973—dc22

                2005023076

CONTENTS

PART II: POVERTY AND WELFARE REFORM

**PART III: FAMILY CONSTRUCTION
AND DESTRUCTION: MARRIAGE,
FATHERHOOD, AND DOMESTIC VIOLENCE**

**Chapter 20. Weaving a Safety Net for Immigrants
Post-PRWORA**   **249**

> *Susan F. Grossman*
> *Maria Vidal de Haymes*
> *Jami Evans*
> *Lawrence Benito*
> *Choua Vue*
> *Susan Wilkie*

PART V: LOOKING TO THE FUTURE

**Chapter 21. Welfare As We *Should* Know It:
Social Empathy and Welfare Reform**   **265**

> *Elizabeth A. Segal*

**Chapter 22. Establishing Respect for Economic
Human Rights**   **275**

> *Kenneth J. Neubeck*

ABOUT THE EDITORS

Keith M. Kilty, PhD, is a professor in the College of Social Work at Ohio State University in Columbus. He is co-editor of the *Journal of Poverty: Innovations on Social, Political & Economic Inequalities*. Dr Kilty chaired the Poverty, Class, and Inequality Division of the Society for the Study of Social Problems (SSSP) and continues to be active in the SSSP, and in the Social Welfare Action Alliance (SWAA).

Elizabeth A. Segal, PhD, is an associate dean of the College of Public Programs and a professor in the College of Social Work at Arizona State University in Tempe. She is co-editor of the *Journal of Poverty: Innovations on Social, Political & Economic Inequalities* and is a member of the Social Welfare Action Alliance (SWAA).

doi:10.1300/5608_a

CONTRIBUTORS

Mimi Abramovitz is a professor of social policy, Hunter College School of Social Work and The Graduate Center, City University of New York. She is the author of *Regulating the Lives of Women: Social Welfare Policy from Colonial Times to the Present* (1996, 2nd ed.); *Under Attack, Fighting Back: Women and Welfare in the United States* (2000, 2nd ed.); and *The Dynamics of Social Welfare Policy* (with Joel Blau) (2004).

Joan Acker is a professor emeritus in sociology at the University of Oregon. She has been awarded the American Sociological Association's Career Distinguished Scholarship Award and its Jessie Bernard Award for feminist scholarship. Her research interests involve class, women and work, gender and organizations, gender and the welfare state, and feminist theory.

Lawrence Benito is a community organizer with the Illinois Coalition for Immigrant and Refugee Rights in Chicago.

Joel Blau is a professor of social policy in the School of Social Welfare at Stony Brook University. He is the author of many articles and three books on social welfare policy, including most recently, with Mimi Abramovitz, a new social welfare policy text, *The Dynamics of Social Welfare Policy.*

Lisa D. Brush is an associate professor of sociology and women's studies at the University of Pittsburgh. She has published findings from her research on gender, status, social policies, and violence against women in numerous journals and book chapters. She is the author of *Gender and Governance* (2003).

Nakeina E. Douglas is a doctoral candidate at the Center for Public Administration and Policy at Virginia Tech.

Jami Evans is an MSW student in the School of Social Work at Loyola University Chicago.

© 2006 by The Haworth Press, Inc. All rights reserved.
doi:10.1300/5608_b

Patrick J. Fowler is a graduate student in the clinical psychology program at Wayne State University, where he studies children living in poverty. Prior to starting graduate school, he advocated for families leaving welfare in Tennessee and Illinois.

Lynn Fujiwara is an assistant professor in the Women's and Gender Studies Program and the Department of Sociology at the University of Oregon. Other related publications include "Immigrant Rights are Human Rights: The Reframing of Immigrant Entitlement and Welfare" in *Social Problems* (2005) and "Asian Immigrant Communities and the Racial Politics of Welfare Reform" in *Whose Welfare,* edited by Gwendolyn Mink (1999). She is currently finishing her manuscript *Sanctioning Immigrants: Asian Immigrant Women and the Racial Politics of Welfare Reform.*

Christine C. George is a senior research fellow at the Loyola University Chicago Center for Urban Research and Learning. Her recent research has included work on domestic violence and South Asian immigrants, and an ongoing National Institute of Justice-funded evaluation of the City of Chicago's Domestic Violence Help Line. She has also been following welfare reform both as a public policy advocate in the late 1980s and early 1990s, and more recently as a researcher and scholar.

Sarah Allen Gershon is a PhD candidate in political science at Arizona State University.

Lisa Gonzales is a doctoral student in sociology at the University of Oregon.

Susan Tinsley Gooden is an associate professor in the Wilder School of Government and Public Affairs at Virginia Commonwealth University, where she conducts research in the areas of social policy and social equity.

Susan F. Grossman is an associate professor in the School of Social Work at Loyola University Chicago.

Alfred L. Joseph Jr. is an associate professor in the Department of Family Studies and Social Work at Miami University (Ohio). His research focus is primarily in the area of school policies that negatively impact at-risk children. He is particularly concerned with the educational practice of tracking or ability grouping and how it impacts the lives of poor and minority school children.

Nancy C. Jurik is a professor of justice and social inquiry at Arizona State University. She teaches courses on "Women and Work" and "Economic Justice." Her publications focus on gender, work organizations, and economic development programs. She has published books titled *Doing Justice, Doing Gender: Women in Law and Criminal Justice Occupations* (1996) and *Bootstrap Dreams: U.S. Microenterprise Development in an Era of Welfare Reform* (2005).

Bart W. Miles is an assistant professor in the School of Social Work at Wayne State University and is affiliated faculty with the Research Group on Homelessness and Poverty at Wayne State University. His research interests are in urban at-risk youth and issues of homelessness and poverty.

Gwendolyn Mink is the Charles N. Clark Professor at Smith College in Northampton, Massachusetts. She is co-editor, with Rickie Solinger, of *Welfare: A Documentary History of U.S. Policy and Politics* (2003).

Sandra Morgen is the director of the Center for the Study of Women in Society at the University of Oregon.

Margaret K. Nelson is the Hepburn Professor of Sociology at Middlebury College, Middlebury, Vermont. Her most recent book is *The Social Economy of Single Mothers: Raising Children in Rural America* (2005).

Kenneth J. Neubeck is a professor emeritus at the University of Connecticut, where he was a director of the university's undergraduate human rights minor, and currently resides in Eugene, Oregon. He is co-author of the award-winning *Welfare Racism: Playing the Race Card Against America's Poor* (2001). He recently authored the book *When Welfare Disappears: The Case for Economic Human Rights* (2006).

Jessica W. Pardee is a doctoral student in sociology at Tulane University. She is doing research on community power relations under federal housing policy.

Laura R. Peck is an assistant professor in the School of Public Affairs at Arizona State University. Her research focuses on the effects of U.S. social policy and on program evaluation methodology.

Ellen Reese is an assistant professor in the Department of Sociology at the University of California, Riverside. She is the author of *Backlash Against Welfare Mothers: Past and Present* (2005).

Michael Reisch is a professor and director of the Multicultural Social Welfare History Project at the University of Michigan. He is the author or editor of more than twenty books and monographs and more than eighty articles and book chapters on the history and philosophy of social welfare, community organization theory and practice, the nonprofit sector, and contemporary policy issues, particularly welfare reform.

Sanford F. Schram teaches social theory and policy in the Graduate School of Social Work and Social Research at Bryn Mawr College.

Eric Swank is an associate professor of social work at Morehead State University. He has published several articles on peace movements, media portrayals of poor people, the racial elements of American welfare attitudes, homophobia in rural populations, and perceptions of unions among college professors.

Maria Vidal de Haymes is a professor in the School of Social Work at Loyola University.

Choua Vue is the program coordinator for the Outreach and Interpretation Project Associate of the Illinois Coalition for Immigrant and Refugee Rights in Chicago.

Jill Weigt is an assistant professor of sociology at California State University San Marcos. She is currently working on a book with Sandra Morgen and Joan Acker which examines welfare reform from multiple perspectives.

Susan Wilkie is an MSW student in the School of Social Work at Loyola University Chicago.

Ann Withorn is a professor of social policy at the College of Public and Community Service, University of Massachusetts Boston. She has long been actively involved in research, writing, and advocacy on welfare rights issues. She is co-editor of *For Crying Out Loud: Women's Poverty in the U. S.* (1968).

Foreword

For nearly a decade, the press has carried reports announcing the extraordinary success of the legislative enactment known as "welfare reform," the Personal Responsibility and Work Opportunity Reconciliation Act (PRWORA) of 1996. Story after story tells what is ostensibly the good news: The welfare rolls are down by more than half, and many more poor mothers are working for wages. In fact, it takes little in the way of policy innovation to drive the welfare rolls down and to coerce women into low-wage work. All that is required are regulations and administrative practices that make welfare benefits exceedingly difficult to get, which is what the 1996 legislation accomplished. But the press is satisfied. Few reporters probe behind the claims of success to find out just what has happened to poor women and their families. If they did, a deeply troubling picture would emerge, of exhausted women struggling to survive on paltry earnings while trying to keep their children safe in troubled environments, of people striving to shake off the insult of the welfare stigma against impossible odds, of vulnerable people made more vulnerable by official government policy justified by the slogan of "personal responsibility."

The essays that follow go far toward illuminating the dark side of welfare reform that is usually ignored. They examine the impact of restrictive income support policies on the most vulnerable groups in American society, including immigrants, most of whom simply are denied welfare; African Americans, always the butt of conservative assaults; and, more generally, of single mothers raising children on their own. They document the unmet needs of these families, and they also show the travails of mother-headed families trying to survive on low-wage work. In other words, Keith Kilty and Liz Segal have compiled the record that documents the human travesty produced by welfare cutbacks in the richest and most powerful nation on earth. They have done a service to the long-term cause of restoring a measure of humanity to American social policy.

doi:10.1300/5608_c

That long-term goal cannot be accomplished by the poorest of the poor unless they find allies among other Americans. Hopefully, honest accounts of the impact of current welfare policy will serve in that cause. But Americans have been told, again and again, that programs such as welfare are funded at the expense of hardworking taxpayers like themselves. The conservative propaganda machine has thus succeeded in pitting the majority of middle- and working-class Americans against the very poor, most of whom are also by any reasonable definition working class.

This is a monumental deception. It is a deception in part because the overall costs of programs that support the poor have always been small compared to other budget expenditures, and have grown steadily more miniscule. True, federal budget deficits have grown astronomically, but that is the result of repeated tax cuts for the affluent and corporations, along with new subsidies for pharmaceutical and energy companies, and a huge military buildup. Ironically, however, the Republican political machine is turning the inevitable pressure to reduce those deficits into a political club to further slash the programs that reach the poor.

The popular view that the welfare poor are somehow taking from the rest of us is a deception for another and perhaps more important reason. The campaign to cut welfare, and food stamps, and subsidized housing programs, and now Medicaid, is transforming American society in ways that will make life harder, more brutish, for all of us. Partly this is simply the result of the withdrawal of income supports which, as some of the essays within reveal, increases the insecurity of low-wage workers generally, making them more vulnerable to whatever terms their employers dictate.

But it is not simply a matter of the direct economic consequences of restricted income supports. The campaign against welfare is a campaign to transform American culture. It is an effort to stamp out the belief that people have a political right to a minimal level of income security to allow them to weather the exigencies of biology or of unstable labor markets. The PRWORA was passed by Congress after a multi-year campaign against that idea. The campaign was conducted by politicians who insulted and cariacatured those who received government support, helping to create excruciating social pressure on all working people, and especially low-wage working people, to keep their shoulders to the wheel, no matter the exhaustion, the injuries, the personal trauma, and losses they endure.

The harsh and arbitrary administration of welfare reinforces that message. Think of the difference between the treatment of social security recipients or, for that matter, agricultural subsidy recipients, and the treatment that people receive at the hands of the welfare program. In fact, this has always been the case. Welfare offices have always been unpleasant; lines have always been long; the application process has always been insulting. Many mothers shunned welfare for just this reason. Now with the new "work first" agenda, it is worse. The lines are longer, people are shuffled into job-readiness classes instead of being allowed to file an application, the bureaucratic rigamarole is endless, and if they succeed in making a formal application, the chances they will be rejected are much higher. All this means that the humiliation of welfare, and the message that ritual humiliation sends, is heightened, not only for those who find themselves entangled in the system but also for those on the periphery who observe the spectacle.

The impact of this kind of welfare system on our culture goes beyond enforcing work. It desiccates what we have of a culture of democratic solidarity. To be fully appreciated, it has to be viewed in the context of other recent political developments. While the screws are tightened in the programs which once helped the poor, and wages fail to keep up with inflation, the Republican-business propaganda has created an almost Orwellian celebration of individualism, hard work, an "ownership society," and the shimmering illusion of fabulous wealth that can be earned by meager pensions invested in the stock market. *Every Man a Speculator* is the title of a new book about Wall Street. Every man and woman a speculator is the theme of the Bush administration proposal to divert Social Security taxes into private accounts that would be invested in market securities. It's an old American dream, that pot of gold. And while we nod-off, the programs won by the social movements of the twentieth century, programs that protected the old, the feeble, and the poor, are stolen away.

We have to hope that Americans will shake themselves awake. This bracing collection is a contribution to that effort.

Frances Fox Piven
Distinguished Professor of Political Science and Sociology
Graduate Center of the City University of New York

Introduction

When President William Clinton signed into law P. L. 104-193, the Personal Responsibility and Work Opportunity Reconciliation Act (PRWORA), on August 22, 1996, he brought to conclusion his 1992 campaign promise "to end welfare as we know it." More important, he brought to conclusion a process begun many years earlier by many other politicians in both major U.S. political parties: an assault on poor women and their children. That is the reality—rather than the rhetoric—of "welfare reform." Bill Clinton and far too many Democratic politicians played into this process, but it was an assault led by conservative Republicans, from the very beginning of Aid to Dependent Children (and the later Aid for Families with Dependent Children program) as a provision in the Social Security Act of 1935 (originally titled the Economic Security Bill). After six decades of public assistance gradually evolving into an entitlement, "public aid" to mothers and children had once again become a privilege for those identified as being deserving rather than a right—a privilege to those deemed worthy through being subjected to working far below minimum wage and who would be subject to lifetime time limits on how long they would be provided a public "helping hand."

Calling the PRWORA "welfare reform" is a misnomer. To reform something means to improve it, not to eliminate it. The rhetoric of the welfare reform movement has focused on "personal responsibility" and the need for individuals to engage in "hard work." Yet the reality of the welfare reform movement has been to do away with the little bit of public assistance that the ADC and AFDC programs provided for poor families. The reality of welfare reform for a decade now has been the purging of the welfare roles through a punitive program called Temporary Assistance for Needy Families (TANF)—not the elimination of poverty. Millions of people are still mired deep in poverty in America. But it is apparently their personal responsibility to remove themselves from that state—not the responsibility of their

doi:10.1300/5608_01

government. And so the rich get richer and the poor get poorer—which is the history of this country.

We created this book in order to separate the reality from the rhetoric of welfare reform. For years now, government officials and politicians have insisted that welfare reform has been a monumental success. The evidence to support these claims is virtually nonexistent. The journal we co-edit, the *Journal of Poverty: Innovations on Social, Political & Economic Opportunities,* was born the same year as TANF: 1997. During that time, we have seen several hundred manuscripts, very few of which have provided support for the claims of our nation's leaders. Year after year, we have documented the plight of the poor in America—people who receive less and less support from their government, people who for the most part are on their own to survive in an increasingly harsh world. Help for the poor has rarely been a major priority for our society. Even at the height of the AFDC program, barely a third of those below the official poverty line received so-called public assistance. Now, though, the crisis for those at the bottom of our society just gets worse and worse.

It is time to challenge the rhetoric that led to welfare reform and to restore some sense of reality to the claims of those who run our country. In the twenty-three chapters that follow, the disengagement between reality and rhetoric is glaringly exposed. We asked a variety of scholars to help us in this expose. Some of the names of contributors are well-known, while others are new participants in the continuing rediscovery of poverty that reflects our history. All of them bring not only empathy and concern to their work on poverty and the poor but also passion. We asked our contributors to transcend conventional academic writing. We asked them, while maintaining an analytic approach, to put welfare reform or some aspect of it into perspective and to take a position, to present a point of view. We know that many people are concerned about the direction that our society has been going during the conservative "revolution" of the past quarter century. Therefore, we asked our contributors to write in a way that would be accessible to a broad audience, including not only academics but also social welfare workers, decision makers and policymakers, and the general public. Congress will once again be taking up reauthorization of the 1996 legislation, and it is imperative that the narrow ideas adopted by legislators at the national, state, and local levels a decade ago be confronted.

A number of connecting themes may be found in the pages that follow, including the fact that what passes for a "welfare state" in this country has always been under attack, that underlying conservative images of welfare recipients revolve around racial representations (especially now with a growing hostility toward immigrants) about who is lazy and who is poor, about the fact that economic rights are (or should be) human rights, and about the persistent disconnect between the problem of poverty and the issue of public assistance.

The book is organized into five parts. The first part presents a context for why welfare reform came about, including the important fact that welfare reform efforts have historically followed periods when public welfare was expanded. Images of who is at the bottom and why they are there have been consistently negative throughout our history as a nation. The second part focuses on the connection (or lack of connection) between poverty and welfare reform. Since the development of neo-liberalism in the 1970s, efforts to privatize public programs have escalated. Is poverty a problem that is a public responsibility and affects the common welfare, or is it a problem that simply represents the irresponsible behavior of some individuals, a sentiment that neo-liberalism would lead us to believe? The third part deals with family issues, especially marriage and fatherhood. For many conservatives, the way out of welfare for mothers and children is marriage. Yet many women find themselves as well as their children in abusive situations. If we just ignore those problems, will they simply disappear? That seems to be the perspective of those advocating marriage as a solution to poverty. The fourth part brings up a reality that many now deny still exists in our society: the impact of racism on poverty and treatment of the poor. Race and ethnicity have been major forces throughout the history of the United States, and they continue to be. That racism is no longer the blatant province of bigots does not mean that it has faded away. It has become more subtle but still infuses concerns about welfare and public assistance recipients. This is a growing problem, too, since the provisions of the PRWORA directly affect immigrants, many of whom are people of color from Latin America, Asia, Africa, and the Middle East. Finally, the fifth part takes a look to the future. What can we do? How can we think about welfare in a way that might change public misconceptions about it? Are economic rights fundamental human rights? How do we bring about change? Are there effective alternatives to the conventional political process?

We firmly believe that our country started down the wrong path many years ago. We live in a society in which there is an ever-widening gap between rich and poor, where the rich get increasing assistance from their government through tax breaks while the poor get increasing demands that they take care of themselves. That is wrong. We also believe that many others in our society are deeply compassionate individuals who have been overwhelmed by a strident rhetoric that gives a false picture of the poor and of welfare. We hope that this volume will help in bridging the chasm between rhetoric and reality.

PART I:
THE CONTEXT OF WELFARE REFORM

Chapter 1

Looking Up the Slippery Slope: Lessons from a Lifetime of Trying to Figure Out and Fight Poverty

Ann Withorn

LEARNING BEGINS AT HOME

As long as I can remember, poverty and its consequences have taught me important lessons.

Born in 1947, my earliest memories are of living in Atlanta, Georgia, in a cramped three-room apartment. My grandmother's even smaller place was next door. She had raised my mother as well as my aunt and uncle on nothing but unreliable veterans' benefits. My grandfather had been hospitalized since 1933 with PTSD from World War I. Because of this situation the whole family had a hard life with tough consequences. As a child Mother was taunted when neighbors found out her father was a "crazy man." Relatives viewed them as "poor city kin with no daddy"—as kids who could neither refuse the raggediest hand-me-downs nor the most demeaning chores when staying with country cousins because Grandmother was herself sick.

Later, when we made our monthly three-hour drive to the VA hospital in Augusta, these country relatives sometimes came along. Their teasing humor was cruel, while my grandfather's quiet muttering to voices only he could hear seemed gentle. He hated violence and would tear all the war pictures out of magazines in the visitors' room. An early lesson for me was that even when people acted crazy they might be nicer than a whole lot of normal people.

Mother's voice remained the constant background noise. The lesson she drew from her lifetime of being poor, moving around to avoid

doi:10.1300/5608_02

evictions, and living with cruel relatives, was that people would betray you so you shouldn't trust anybody, especially anybody poor. For me, the lesson was that being poor *had* hurt Mother, but the fear of being thought poor had messed her up even more. She never connected to other people's pain; she was too focused on denying and/or projecting her own.

Mother's big way of proving her personal progress was, whenever we had a little money, to hire a black woman to come into the house to iron for a half day a week. One woman, called "Nancy" (although white women were always Mrs. or Miss to me) clearly didn't like Mother—which made me appreciate her. Once I went with Daddy to bring the pay to Nancy's house. No one would answer the door. Daddy said it was because he was "a white man with a hat." He had me get out of the car, and when she saw me she came out. Driving home I asked again why no one had come, and he said, "Because they thought I was a bill collector."

So began a lifelong process of learning how it was even harder to be poor *and* black. All Nancy said about it later was that "you never know who is at your door. You have to be careful." I knew that some of my poor relatives would have answered the door yelling, with a beer in hand. So it seemed that lots of people were poor, but black poor people had to be careful.

My family also showed me how poverty's lessons get passed on. Once we were driving through a "bad" part of town. My little sister peered out the window of our old Studebaker and asked, "why don't Negroes live in nice houses?" My mother answered easily, "Because they don't know how to save, so they don't have money for nice things." My relatives in the country didn't have nice houses either, but you couldn't see them from the road. Mother never said *they* weren't smart with their money. Or in Charlotte I was injured on Sunday so we had to go to the county's emergency clinic. Usually we went to our doctor's nice office, not a clinic that was big, noisy, and had no special painted playroom. Mother said the clinic was mainly for white trash who "didn't bother to find their own doctors but waited until they were really sick to get free medicine." The lesson that poor people got what they deserved was one of the many things about my world that never made sense.

So I grew up in rebellion, saying out loud what seemed true and getting in trouble for it. I hated the snap judgments, constant cynicism, and petty cruelty that permeated the southern white culture. Now I see it as indoctrination, aimed at making everyone into what I now name as "libertarian fascists." This world was one where adults teased kids, older kids bullied younger ones, and the weak like my grandfather and eggheads like me were ridiculed. It was a world where bad things were supposed to happen mainly to people who made stupid choices. Somehow I gradually learned to reject the notion that there was no moral vision, and no hope that people could behave better if given other options.[1]

POLITICAL LESSONS

During the mid-1950s I watched Little Rock on the TV, thinking how brave the kids were, and secretly admiring Eisenhower for sending troops. I identified with kids wanting to go to school and saw my relatives and neighbors in the jeering adults. Indeed, TV was my most immediate source for examples of alternative action until I was in college. Much as the local stations tried to hide them, the civil rights struggles and the body counts in Vietnam were national news. And if I didn't get the message about what was wrong immediately, all I had to do was listen to my parents' comments and take the other side.

In the fall of 1964, I went to college and volunteered at the Tallahassee Goldwater for President office. I had been a Republican for a long time because Southern Democrats were corrupt. Besides, Goldwater's proclamation that "extremism in defense of liberty" was "no vice" made sense to me. My relatives said Goldwater couldn't be trusted because he was really Jewish, so I knew he must be good.

At Goldwater headquarters a man who proclaimed himself the "oldest Leon County White Republican" held forth daily about how bad the United Nations was, among other rants. "Why was working for world peace so bad?" I asked. The OLCWR pointed his knobby tobacco-stained finger at me: "Little girl, supporting the United Nations makes you a liberal, and a liberal is just a cowardly socialist, and a socialist is just a sneaky communist. All of them want a world government to confiscate hard-earned money and give it to lazy poor people. Go read the *Communist Manifesto* and you'll see." At the library, I read the *Communist Manifesto* even though I had to get special permission to read it in the University Reading Room. It was soon clear. My aged would-be mentor was right. "Workers of the world unite, you have nothing to lose but your chains" made sense. I *was* a communist all right, not a Republican, so I never went back to Goldwater headquarters.

For the rest of my undergraduate years I was an autodidact communist who hid out in libraries like Marx did. Although I attended some rallies and meetings, went to Washington in the fall of 1967, mourned King and Kennedy in 1968, I was too much the serious student to be a committed activist—mainly I was just a geek who wrote an honors thesis on "how the Gilded Age Robber Barons created wealth and politicians protected it."

After winning a fellowship to graduate school and then leaving in dismay over Harvard's profound intellectual elitism, I needed to bring my ideas into action, for the first time since my Goldwater days. Cambridge, Massachusetts, was a great place to do this. I could combine my Marxism with a newfound feminism and help make connections between local and global issues—especially in regard to the problems of poverty, which still haunted me.

Needing my wages as a temporary typist to support political work, I kept trying to find ways to practice my politics personally, as well as in meetings and demonstrations. After being fired from one temporary job for putting up announcements of a meeting to discuss "our issues as women," this seemed imperative. Soon I learned that by teaching women's labor history to garment workers and then to other trade unionists through the Catholic Labor Guild and community schools I could make a difference, if not a revolution. There were older Italian women who could still recall the funeral march for Sacco and Vanzetti, along with younger working-class lesbians who had been in the "union business" for a long time—fighting for basic rights within electrical, postal, and communications unions.

It was exciting to learn something that my relatives had tried so hard to deny—that jobs *were* important to women and that most women were employed despite the barriers. My family had looked down on "mill girls," with their loose morals, but Grandmother *had* taken in sewing in her home. She had been ashamed to talk about it, because it wasn't ladylike and also because she had never told Veterans' Affairs, who would have cut her benefits for working. It all began to link together.

Still, teaching labor history raised doubts as well as hopes. Sure, unions helped those who could work at full-time jobs in big industries. But what about single mothers like my grandmother? Or people whose families had problems that prevented them from earning a living wage no matter what, at least some of the time? Labor activists were understandably concerned with workplace problems, but the visible and invisible effects of women's poverty remained unaddressed.[2]

WELFARE AND WELFARE RIGHTS: REMEMBERING WHAT WE HAVE LOST AND LEARNED

While trying to find answers in the labor movement, I accidentally discovered the roots for an activism that seemed more grounded—in the Cambridge Welfare Rights office, next door to the SDS antiwar office. Their mimeograph machine worked better than ours, so I was there often. Besides, the "welfare moms" were nicer than the radical men in the SDS office. They were full of earthy wit and every bit as sharp in their analysis of the systems that oppressed them as the Gramsci-quoting men next door. Gradually I spent more and more time helping out in their office and then tutoring some of the kids in the nearby housing projects. It was a politics that made personal sense, connected to issues that both felt right and still were central to real radical change.

In 1971, the parent-controlled board of a local five-town Head Start program hired me as a service coordinator. With amazing luck this everyday paying job offered focus, and a way to be angry and be loving—if I just listened hard and stayed really well connected to the women, several of whom became lifelong mentors and friends. I went with folks to welfare offices, to welfare rights meetings, and to statewide poverty program and legal services briefings—as well as learning deeply about the challenges faced daily in the hidden corners of semi-urban neighborhoods. I reported back at parent meetings where the mothers went from one agenda item dealing with proper bathroom policy to another deciding how to fight for increases in clothing allowances. We saw such "special needs" income supplements as important in themselves and as essential steps in expanding universal benefits.

Significantly, no one I knew then, even those of us most pessimistic about *Amerika,* thought that "welfare" would ever be taken away as a basic income maintenance right. Our concerns were to expand it—by getting more benefits added, such as child care to cover education and employment time; such as recognition that men should be acknowledged as deserving too rather than hidden away; such as obtaining cost-of-living increases and transportation vouchers. We tried hard to counter stereotypes of "lazy welfare queens." We also fought against abuse by workers within the system as well as to improve it by allowing more graduated paths out of welfare as people found part-time employment or sought educational advancement.

Sure, some people in the Nixon administration might want work incentive programs that were punitive, or some southern politicians might yell about "accountability" from both recipients and community agencies such as our Head Start. But we simply did not think that we could lose what we saw as a right established in the Social Security Act. Lots of people hated welfare and the people on it, and wanted more punishments in the system, but we did not imagine that within twenty-five years the Aid to Families with Dependent Children program would be ended. It was just impossible to think that in thirty years we would be fighting only to keep the remaining crumbs of programs we then assumed were the baseline, not-good-enough foundation of the underdeveloped American welfare state.

Of course, as we agitated to change the system, we seldom had made a case for why it should remain. When Nixon's welfare reform—the Family Assistance Program (FAP)—died, we celebrated a victory, because it did not guarantee the higher national income floor and recipient rights of the NWRO plan. We didn't realize that shifting income guarantees for people with disabilities into an all-federal program (SSI-D) would be the end, not the continuation, of federal welfare rights expansion. By 1975, the talk among policy activists and welfare rights folks shifted to how we would expand Medicaid into national health care—which we saw as the next likely way to expand benefits to poor people. We could come back to federal income guarantees for all later.

Now I see that we should have been paying more attention to the rhetoric of the right-wing congressmen who fought FAP. We failed to recognize their discovery, that "welfare" could serve as a successful code word to use without directly attacking blacks, cities, liberals, and Big Government. If we thought harder we might have paid more attention to those old leftists who warned that our "community-based, participatory" politics were good but not enough—that we should think harder before we glibly chanted about "smashing the state."

Indeed, now it seems that failing to fight *for* welfare as part of a responsible state back in the early 1970s was the beginning of the slide down the slippery slope that landed us where we are today.[3]

LESSONS LEARNED

Building on this early base, and despite such a fundamental mis-cue, I have learned a lot as we slid down to what I hope is the bottom of the slippery slope of the past quarter century. Continuing my welfare activism (with ebbs and flows due to family obligations), I began to grasp the complexities of organizing and agitating about poverty. Writing and speaking about poverty have humbled me regarding the profound limits of information and theory and yet forced me to see the necessity of continued effort. And twenty-five years of being a university teacher with adult students who work in human services, who are or have been on welfare, or who are or want to be activists, have taught me never to underestimate how much remains to be learned, by all of us, by any means necessary.

About Activism

My first and most critical lesson was *You don't have to be on welfare or a mother or even a woman to be for welfare rights—but building a movement means that everyone must learn from and take leadership from women who are or have been "in the system."* This was how I initially learned the limits of the workerism embedded in my labor activism. Head Start mothers argued forcefully that they needed not jobs but *time* for their families and themselves—as well as more education, and access to decent housing and schools. They only wanted employment as a positive option and not another dead end. Even today, as bad as things are, activists, social workers, and legal service workers who work with and for low-income women must learn that the movement for "welfare rights" was just that, a movement, because it was led by poor people and their allies who together gave it radical strategic meaning, not just tactical efficacy. Frances Fox Piven, Richard Cloward, Betty Reid Mandell, Guida West, and many others would never have been helpful if they had not learned this, along with how to work as equals and critics in strategizing.[4]

Coalitions must be formed among allies, but economic human rights activists (as we now seem to be calling ourselves) especially must not be fooled by them. Poor people know they need allies to help "translate" their demands into policy proposals and lawsuits, to show the links between attacks on welfare and attacks on workers' rights, and to make wide and deep arguments for public responsibility. From the *Zap FAP* national coalition through the myriad other state and national coalitions that I know and/or have been a part of, the grounds for unity were deeply if not openly contested. Professional advocates of various types are always fearful of the anger, the image, and the contestation that poor people bring to the table. They often speak condescendingly about political "realities" and seem willing to avoid the central issue of money. Labor leaders may see the links between income rights and workers' rights yet still fear that too much "poverty talk" will scare off their members. Former Representative from Hawaii Patsy Mink and former Senator Paul Wellstone were two of the very few national politicians who listened and could be trusted not to compromise on subsistence issues, but there have been too few across the states and at the national level.

The lesson from the best antipoverty activists is always be very clear and careful about defining the roles of differing organizations and the boundaries of decision making within any coalitions.[5]

Human relationships and personal engagement matter, especially in welfare rights organizing. Personally, I have made rewarding, deep friendships that have helped me learn, prevent, and/or overcome stupid mistakes. Diane Dujon and I have written and spoken together, spent hours working and talking together. I know especially from her and from other friends in the movement how important real "buddying" is, and how hard patience is for all. As many times as I have had to insist that a recipient be included on an academic panel, Diane has had to argue with her comrades about including academic or professional allies in strategy sessions. There is nothing to it but to do it, and the connection must be both deep and wide—not just joining forces at meetings but sharing sandwiches in the car, talking about music, TV, and children, as well as the "serious stuff." Such bonds make the difference between being foolish and being heard, between winning an argument once and keeping discussion open. When welfare activist Dottie Stevens ran for Massachusetts governor in 1990 (because in part as a welfare mother she considered herself "beneath reproach"), there were many hard, honest struggles over abortion, among other things. The result was she found positions that both expressed her doubts and kept crucial feminist endorsements for her campaign, as well as increased respect about critical class differences on the issue.[6]

There are Real Enemies who are worse than weak allies or an unconcerned public. Looking up the slippery slope now it is easy to find times when we fought and were frustrated with would-be allies, or with cowardly coalitions. But we know that none of these folks would have invented the increasingly hostile "welfare reform" policies and rhetoric. It took the hard, self-conscious Right to create a conventional wisdom that "welfare had failed," to link it to fears of immigrants and crime, to turn "trying to help" into inevitable public failure.

This is a huge lesson to learn. It takes study and constant vigilance to anticipate and accept that the ever-smarter right wing *must* keep opposing welfare. A neoconservative right that wants a dependent global workforce must discredit hopes for a dependable state and a Christian right that wants to maintain a fantasy of patriarchal "family values" cannot abide a meaningful income program which allows women to live without men. Welfare undermines the core fear sustaining both sides of an interlocked right wing. Our activism, our advocacy, and our writing cannot ever retreat from repeating this at every turn. By the time Clinton called for an "end to welfare as we know it" and was not defeated by his own party, it was too late. And his success makes it more reasonable to think that Bush can win his goal of an "ownership society" by privatizing Social Security.

We must now admit that there is no limit to how far this nation can slip away from social responsibility. I do hope that we *are* at the bottom of the slippery slope and that the Right has gone too far, what with the combined whammy of welfare reform, immigration reform, prison reform, education reform, and the PATRIOT Act. All we can do now is keep naming the lies, whether they be "any job is a good job," or that "no child is being left behind" by the race to test and punish, or that "Social Security is bankrupt." We've got to get it right this time. We must face that we can lose, be vigilant in naming the lies, and be demanding in our call for "freedom from want" at home, not freedom to bomb worldwide.[7]

Lessons About Advocacy and Overall Strategy

Research, writing, and documentation matter but cannot make the critical difference. As writers such as Linda Gordon (1994), Wendy Mink (1998), Alice O'Connor (2001), Dorothy Roberts (2002), and Sandy Schram (1995) explain, it wasn't social science or historical research that justified right-wing reforms nor that stopped it. Of course activists need information, and advocates have to pretend to make a case that isn't *just* morally grounded. And it does help ordinary citizens to know how little people receive through benefits, and how many are children. Still we have to be careful. After all, what *did* it mean that advocates kept defending welfare by saying that most people in the system were white? Once academic researchers got into the picture, with their obscenely well-funded "persistent poverty projects" or devolution initiatives, then the pressure was on especially more progressive researchers to write without an "advocacy tone," or to treat everyone "professionally" by inviting a Charles Murray or a Lawrence Mead to hear their results but not to "overwhelm" a welfare recipient by inviting her to their briefings.

The message to researchers has to be that all research on poverty and antipoverty programs is political and contested at the deepest levels of the culture. To deny that any research on right-wing policy effects must have an advocacy frame is to deny the basic historical purpose of social research—to help protect society from harm, and to use evidence to show society what ways to move forward.[8]

Workers and agencies in the system make a difference, for better and for worse. Low-income women have complicated relationships with the workers and agencies that "serve" them. In the past state workers were often the "enemy" who imposed punitive rules and usually meant trouble. Community-based agencies with their less professionalized and more activist approach could be both friends and potential models for future career roles.

Over the years the structure of social support has changed for the worse in many places. The contracting of state services to nonprofit organizations has spread the control tasks to agencies that don't want to acknowledge that mission. The employment-centered goal for most "devolution" funding has limited the advocacy role of community agencies, so families for whom services, education, and general support would seem the best option have few places to go. Community-based agencies have therefore become yet another place where pressures and punishments are either experienced or feared. And "faith-based initiatives" threaten not to spread options for help, but rather to leave low-income families with truly "no place to run, no place to hide." To start, social workers and activists need to face this new reality honestly and not pretend that the network of "community support" is anything like it used to be, nor that workers within the system, whether they are from the community or not, see activism as part of their jobs. And we need to try to figure out what new structures might be helpful, even if it is a return to the state as the place where responsibility cannot be avoided.[9]

Racism is central still to everything about poverty in this country and must always be named. Just as Frederick Douglas, W.E.B. Dubois, Malcolm X, and Martin Luther King Jr. knew, poverty, racism, and militarism come together wrapped in a package to reinforce one another and to hide their deadly interactive effects. If the welfare rights movement and the triumphant right wing have taught us anything, it is this. We must always say it, always make sure it is said by white people as well as by black, brown, and non-European people. Because any issue related to racism is complicated in language and meaning, it is especially critical always to be both direct and complex in how it is discussed and framed.[10]

Still we can specialize, if we make links. The best activism and advocacy around welfare and poverty often grew out of more specific campaigns, against homelessness, for educational access, for public health options. One of the remaining strengths of our system—that people can still name what hurts them and demand regress—remains a powerful tool. The task of everyone with a broader critique is to name the connections between issues and people. Diane Dujon has written and said in hundreds of speeches to fellow union members, "You're next: if there is no welfare system then you will have no place to go after unemployment runs out, if you are lucky enough to get unemployment." To fellow educators and social workers she said, "You're next: if they cut everyone off education benefits and privatize the system you will lose your jobs in the next round." And to home-lessness or domestic violence advocates who want to focus only on "their issues" she has said, "You are next: if we don't defend the right of everyone to have a decent income for her or his family, then what will give you any reason to think that anyone will understand your is-sues? We're all in this together."

Of course, it is easy to say people need to link everything. We all need to learn to make connections without preaching or professing too much. We must still talk about universal benefits, and still target our activism within such dialogue. It is hard. But not to do so is to al-low people to think that putting money in a can for tsunami victims, or that holding benefits to "end family violence" allows them to think they are being responsible citizens.[11]

A FINAL PERSONAL LESSON: WHY IT ALL STILL MATTERS

For me, in the end as in the beginning, the deepest lessons about poverty were learned in the home—this time in the one I created in-tentionally as an adult. Not willing to risk having children until my mid-thirties (out of fear of reproducing the type of pernicious parenting I experienced), I found that being a mother was both the most rewarding *and* the most unnatural learning experience of my life. Personally I relied most for advice on the mothers I knew best, women on welfare. Almost everybody helped me with humor and good advice.

Never sure of what to do, I was as emotionally vulnerable as any mother without familial role models. All I knew desperately was that I had to let myself love my daughters, to allow myself whatever time and attention it took to care for them. Mostly that meant that I couldn't walk out the door unless I thought somehow that I was doing right by them. No job, no personal pain could justify hurting them. And nothing was clearer to me as I raised my daughters (even with the privilege of a job and a reliable husband) than that I and every woman needed what the welfare system, degraded as it was, once of-fered—the right to income just for caring for my children, whenever that's what I felt they required.

All women, all mothers, all families are not the same. All poverty is not the same, with the same depths and the same meanings. No economic system has ended all poverty—either with "full employment" or a "fully developed" welfare state. The only policy solutions imaginable come from insisting on real discussion of real issues, from listening hard with respect for those really trying and from fighting hard against those who want others to "live free or die." Today just as much as when I was a kid asking questions, the paths out of poverty cannot force parents to deny all their needs nor to pretend that one path will work for all families. As I start to face life without the necessities imposed by day in day out motherhood, I can only remember one of the radical slogans that has not failed me, that "the truth will be found in the struggle."

The personal, as we used to say, is political and the political is also personal. I am still learning all these lessons, over and over again. I am still who I was, but older, with daughters, students, colleagues, and comrades who are still both outraged and troubled by the consequences and persistence of poverty. We all still try to figure out why rich people need tax cuts, and why family poverty has remained so acceptable, why there is still money for missile launchers but we still have bake sales to help homeless children.

NOTES

1. I have written more about the lessons from this southern culture in "Why Mother Slapped Me," *For Crying Out Loud: Women's Poverty in the United States,* 1996, edited by Diane Dujon and Ann Withorn. The South's critical role as seedbed for libertarian fascism is discussed in my article "Facing Fears and Fantasies: The Role of Welfare in Right Wing Thought and Politics" (1998).

2. Since those early days the labor movement has changed, due largely to the increasing role of women and "service workers" in state organizations and nationally. In Boston we founded a labor welfare coalition, "Working Mass: For the Welfare of All Workers," to do training of union members about welfare and benefits as well as of low-income groups about unions. See Dujon and Withorn 1996 (1) for more full treatment of this change.

3. The best treatments of this history and the questions of strategy and tactics surrounding FAP are Frances Piven and Richard Cloward (1992) *Poor Peoples Movements* and Guida West (1991) *The National Welfare Rights Movement: The Social Protest of Poor Women.*

4. Betty Reid Mandell and I have been involved together in many areas of Boston welfare rights activism for thirty years. She taught me and many others key lessons about how to integrate one's whole life into the movement.

5. Low-income activists write about this issue frequently. See an unpublished dissertation by Paula Georges (2003), "The Influence of Welfare Coalitions on Massachusetts Welfare Policy" for a full treatment of such efforts in Massachusetts.

6. See Dottie Stevens, "Welfare organizing changed my life," as well as other articles in *For Crying Out Loud* 1996 (Dujon and Withorn, 1). For a cautionary warning about what happens when relationships are not deep and real see Teresa Funicello (1993), *Tyranny of Kindness.*

7. There is an extensive literature on the Right and welfare reform. For a good summary see Lucy Williams, "The Rights' Attack on Families with Dependent Children" (1996).

8. The best source is Alice O'Connor's *Poverty Knowledge* (2001).

9. I have been researching this for years mainly in unpublished reports. For my summary of the issues see "Friends or Foes: Nonprofits and the Puzzle of Welfare Reform" in *Lost Ground,* 2002, edited by Randy Albelda and Ann Withorn. I have learned a great deal about how all this works from James Jennings's extensive writing on urban community and poverty. Currently I am turning all this into a book for Temple University Press, to be titled, "Still Working for Justice? Community Based Agencies Face the Post Welfare Reform Era."

10. Obviously there has been extensive writing about this. I rely most on Gary Delgado and the consistently useful work of the Applied Research Center in Oakland, California.

11. Scholars and activists have been debating this question since the Reagan years. Harvard sociologist Theda Skocpol (1985), whose writing on "bringing the state back in" to social policy is important to this discussion, wrote an especially influential piece about the value of a strategy for "targeting within universalism." I and others objected at the time because we felt she (as an influential academic close to the Clinton administration) was sacrificing income-maintenance priorities to more middle-class issues, and undervaluing the role of social movements, but now I am not so sure we were right.

BIBLIOGRAPHY

Albelda, Randy and Ann Withorn (eds.) 2002. *Lost Ground: Welfare Reform, Poverty and Beyond.* Boston: South End Press.

Dujon, Diane and Ann Withorn (eds.) 1996. *For Crying Out Loud: Women's Poverty in the United States.* Boston: South End Press.

Funicello, Teresa. 1993. *The Tyranny of Kindness: Dismantling the Welfare System to End Poverty in America.* Boston: Atlantic Monthly Press.

Georges, Paula. 2003. The Influence of Welfare Coalitions on Massachusetts Welfare Policy. Unpublished dissertation, University of Massachusetts, Boston.

Gillens, Martin. 1999. *Why Americans Hate Welfare.* Chicago: University of Chicago Press.

Gordon, Linda. 1994. *Pitied But Not Entitled: Single Mothers and the History of Welfare.* New York: Free Press.

Gordon, Rebecca. 2001. *Cruel and Unusual: How Welfare Reform Punishes Poor People.* Oakland, CA: Applied Research Center.

Mink, Gwendolyn. 1998. *Welfare's End.* New York: Cornell University Press.

Neubeck, Kenneth and Noel Casenave. 2001. *Welfare Racism: Playing the Race Card Against America's Poor.* New York: Routledge.

O'Connor, Alice. 2001. *Poverty Knowledge.* Princeton, NJ: Princeton University Press.

Piven, Frances Fox and Richard Cloward. 1993. *Regulating the Poor,* Updated Edition. New York: Vintage.

————. 1992. *Poor Peoples Movements.* New York: Vintage.

Roberts, D. 2002. *Shattered Bonds: The Color of Child Welfare.* New York: Basic Civitas Books.

Schram, Sanford S. 1995. *Words of Welfare: The Poverty of Social Science and the Social Science of Poverty.* Minneapolis: University of Minnesota Press.

Skocpol, Theda. 1985. "Bringing the State Back In: Strategies of Analysis in Current Research." In Peter B. Evans, Dietrich Rueschemeyer, and Theda Skocpol (eds.), *Bringing the State Back In* (pp. 3-44). Cambridge, UK: Cambridge University Press.

Soss, Joe. 2000. *Unwanted Claims: The Politics of Participation in the U.S. Welfare System.* Ann Arbor: University of Michigan Press.

West, Guida 1991. *The National Welfare Rights Movement: The Social Protest of Poor Women.* New York: Praeger.

Williams, Lucy A. 1996. "The Right's Attack on Families with Dependent Children." *Public Eye* 10(3-4).

Withorn, Ann. 1998. "Facing Fears and Fantasies: The Role of Welfare in Right Wing Thought and Politics." In *Unraveling the Right: New Conservativism in American Thought and Politics* (pp. 126-147). Boulder, CO: Westview Press.

Chapter 2

Neither Accidental, Nor Simply Mean-Spirited: The Context for Welfare Reform

Mimi Abramovitz

Neither the appearance of Aid to Dependent Children (ADC) in 1935 nor its dramatic transformation sixty years later into the program called Temporary Assistance for Needy Families (e.g., welfare reform) were accidental. Both developments are best understood as part of historically specific strategies adopted by the powers-that-be to manage crises in the workings of the economy that disrupted the conditions necessary for economic profitability and political stability. The most recent crises of profitability occurred in the 1930s and the 1970s. The collapse of the economy in the 1930s and the crisis of capital formation in the mid-1970s signaled that the policies in place for the prior forty to fifty years—including social welfare policies—had unraveled. They no longer worked for the elite and had to be "reformed."

However, national leaders responded to each crisis quite differently. In the 1930s business and government blamed the collapse of the economy on the failures of the market and called for a New Deal based on greater public spending as the way out. In sharp contrast in the 1970s, the economic and political leaders blamed their economic woes on public spending and the "personal irresponsibility" of social welfare program recipients. Their solution, known as neoliberalism

---

*Neoliberalism represents an updated and more extreme version of the "classical liberal" theory developed in the eighteenth and nineteenth centuries by Adam Smith and David Ricardo. They argued that market forces self-regulate the capitalist economy thereby limiting the need for government. Viewed as conservative today, the theory was considered economically liberal when developed (Kotz, 2003).

doi:10.1300/5608_03

23

(aka Reaganomics and supply-side economics),* called for a self-regulated economy, limited government, and a smaller welfare state.

BACKGROUND:
THE RISE OF THE WELFARE STATE

The U.S. welfare state emerged in 1935, some fifty years after those in Western Europe. Until then cities and states provided what little social welfare provision existed in the United States. However, the 1929 stock market collapse made it clear that the prevailing laissez-faire structures that had fueled economic growth since the 1890s no longer worked. The deterioration of these earlier institutional arrangements led the elite to conclude that a more active state was needed to end the Great Depression. Faced with extreme material hardship during the Depression, the dispossessed—both middle and working class—took to the streets. They too demanded a new and stronger governmental response (Piven & Cloward, 1977).

Pressed by both economic disaster and social movements, the nation turned to the federal government for a New Deal—one that would restore profits, economic growth, and political stability while addressing the needs of the masses. The resulting New Deal programs ushered in a major restructuring of the political economy, including the 1935 Social Security Act. Generally viewed as the birth of the modern welfare state, the Social Security Act transferred social welfare responsibility from the states to the federal government—but not without considerable controversy. It also created an entitlement to income support: social insurance programs for the middle class and means-tested public assistance—including Aid to Dependent Children (ADC)—for the poor. The Supreme Court legalized the new institutional structure by ruling that federal responsibility for the general welfare was constitutional. Officialdom implemented the programs by accepting the economic theory of John Maynard Keynes, the British economist who called for greater government spending to increase aggregate demand and otherwise stimulate economic growth.

From 1935 to 1975 the welfare state grew in response to population growth, the emergence of new needs, the liberalization of program rules, and the victories of the increasingly militant trade union, civil rights, women's liberation, and other movements. The expansion of government programs partially addressed the unmet needs of many but not all households *and* helped get the economy back on its feet. Its programs did so by carrying out a complex set of social, economic, and political functions that simultaneously mediated poverty, enforced work and family ethics, and underwrote business profits. The same programs also muted the social unrest generated by market inequality by negotiating informal "accords" with the trade union (1940s), civil rights (1960s), and women's movements (1960s) (Abramovitz, 1992b).

DISMANTLING THE WELFARE STATE

The U.S. welfare state has been under attack from both sides of the aisle since the mid-1970s when major shifts in the political economy set off another crisis of profitability. The changes—third world revolutions, less access to cheap raw materials, the loss of international dominance, mounting economic competition from abroad, and the victories of U.S. social movements at home—slowly weakened the institutional arrangements set up in the 1930s to promote profits, political stability, and personal well-being (Abramovitz, 1992a). With this the national elite reversed its earlier support for the programs of the New Deal and the Great Society. It concluded that the welfare state was now part of the problem and argued for its demise. The question is why?

For one, deindustrialization at home and the exportation of production abroad left corporate America less reliant on U.S. workers (Amott, 1993). With this, business became less and less willing to support the welfare state programs that previously helped them to maintain the current and future workforce and to appease social movements. The elite also concluded that if the welfare state had once helped to underwrite business profits, it no longer did. Ignoring military costs and corporate welfare (Abramovitz, 2001), they incorrectly laid near-exclusive blame on welfare state spending for the enlarged deficit, rising interest rates, the cost of borrowing, and other fiscal barriers to investment and economic growth (Weisskopf, 1982). Finally, the effort to keep cash benefits extremely low began to falter, leading employers to fear that rising AFDC and unemployment insurance benefits increasingly functioned as alternative sources of income that could undercut profits by enabling women and men to avoid the lowest-paid, most dangerous and dirty jobs (Piven, 1999).

The postwar gains of social movements—especially higher wages and more generous welfare benefits—raised both the standard of living and the political costs to business and government of maintaining the social peace (O'Connor, 1973). Access to cash benefits reduced workers' fears of unemployment which in turn strengthened their bargaining power vis-à-vis employers (Piven, 1999). Income supports also made it possible for women to choose welfare over work or marriage and to decide to raise children on their own, while civil rights gains undercut white racial hegemony (Orloff, 1993).

By the early 1980s, the New Right also gained a strong grip on U.S. public policy. Troubled by changes in the racial and gendered status quo, its leaders blamed the welfare state for creating a "crisis" in the family (i.e., employment of women, high rates of divorce, single motherhood, greater female autonomy, and gay rights). They called for restoring the "traditional" heterosexual, one earner-one breadwinner household by dismantling the welfare state which they hold undermines "personal responsibility," usurps parental authority, weakens so-called family values, and enhances civil rights for persons of color (Klatch, 1987).

The resulting attack on the welfare state is part of the broader neoliberal/New Right strategy designed to restore profitability by downsizing the state, redistributing income and wealth upward, from the have-nots to the haves, and advancing "moral values." The modern version of neoliberalism first surfaced in the mid-1970s when President Carter campaigned for the Democratic Party's nomination on an anti-Washington platform. Launched in full by the Reagan Administration in 1981, every administration since then has pursued the same laissez-faire policies in varying degrees. They have sought to raise profits by

1. lowering the cost of labor,
2. shrinking the welfare state,
3. limiting the role of the federal government, and
4. weakening the political influence of social movements.

Meanwhile, the New Right called for restoring patriarchal "family values" and a color-blind social order.

Regarded as a barrier to cheap labor and cheap money, the welfare state became an early target of neoliberal "reform" which for the past two decades has called for

1. tax cuts (lower and less progressive taxes),
2. social program retrenchment,
3. devolution (the shift of social welfare responsibility from the federal government to the states), and
4. privatization (the transfer of responsibility for social welfare from the public to the private sector).

Advocates promised that the benefits of this pro-market/"pro-family" strategy would trickle down to the average person. Instead the gap between the rich and the poor widened historically. Prior to the late 1970s, economic growth in the United States was rather evenly shared. From 1947 to 1979, the family income of the bottom fifth of the population rose by 116 percent compared to 99 percent for the top fifth. The next two decades reversed this trend. From 1979 to 2001 the income of the bottom 20 percent grew by only 3 percent compared to 53 percent for the top 20 percent (Inequality.org, 2004). In 2000, in forty-five states the gap between the incomes of the richest 20 percent of families and the incomes of the poorest 20 percent of families grew wider than it had been in the late 1970s. The distance between the average income of middle-income families and the average income of high-income families also widened in most states (Bernstein, Boushey, McNichol, & Zahradnik, 2002). The data on control of the nation's wealth shows even greater concentration at the top (Inequality.org, 2004).

WELFARE REFORM

Attacks on the program for single mothers date back to the early 1800s. The powers-that-be typically "reformed" welfare when the expansion of the welfare rolls reduced the supply of cheap labor, challenged patriarchal arrangements, or otherwise interfered with the workings of the wider social order (Abramovitz, 2000). As in the past, the most recent reforms have sought to (1) enforce work, (2) promote marriage, and (3) weaken the welfare state. These goals meshed well with the neoliberal plan to shrink the role of government and to raise profits by redistributing income upward from the have-nots to the haves.

Work First

The work-first provisions of welfare reform—time limits, stricter work rules, harsh sanctions—enforced work. The stringent rules forced recipients off welfare and into the labor market as time limits ended receipt of welfare forever after sixty months, as stiffened work requirements channeled more women into low-paid jobs, and as sanctions cut off benefits for even minor violations of welfare's new rules (http://www.financeprojectinfo.org/win/work/asp). To make sure no one missed the point, Congress changed the name of the nation's welfare program from Aid to Families with Dependent Children (AFDC) to Temporary Assistance for Needy Families (TANF).

This strategy of using the rules of welfare to supply employers with cheap labor dates back to the colonial poor laws which routinely set public aid below the lowest prevailing wage so that only the most desperate person would choose assistance over low-paid work. Today welfare reform's harsh work-first policies help to raise profits by flooding the labor market with thousands of new workers. The increased competition for jobs makes it easier for employers to keep wages down and harder for unions to negotiate good contracts. Along with deindustrialization, globalization, and the well-documented attack on organized labor, welfare reform's work-first program forced workers to accept inferior wages and benefit packages. Indeed, wages for the bottom 10 percent of workers fell by 9.3 percent from 1979 to 1999 (EPI, 2002). In 2002, nearly 40 percent of low-wage workers lived in families with incomes below 200 percent of the poverty line (less than $29,000 for a family of three) and often could not afford basic necessities (Chapman & Ettinger, 2004). *The New York Times* recently reported that the large influx of women into low-wage jobs in the 1990s, caused in part by the overhaul of welfare, depressed the median wage of women as a whole (Utichelle, 2005). Business clearly benefits from falling or stagnant wages. In the late 1990s, Alan Greenspan, the head of the Federal Reserve Board, explained that the economy's "extraordinary" and "exceptional" performance during the late 1990s was in part due to "a heightened sense of job insecurity" which helps to subdue wage gains (Piven, 1999).

Family Values

After pushing "work first" about as far as it could go, the "reform-ers" turned to welfare reform's second main goal—restoring the "tradi-tional" one-earner, one-homemaker, heterosexual family unit. Reflect-ing the "family values" agenda favored by the New Right, the 1996 welfare law hailed marriage as the foundation of society and as a path out of poverty (U.S. Congress, 1996). You did not have to listen too hard during the long welfare reform debate to hear the unspoken but ra-cially coded message—that crime, drug use, school drop-outs, and teenage pregnancies are all transmitted from one generation to the next by husbandless women heading their own families (Roberts, 1997).

Welfare reform contains at least four rules that regulate the marital, childbearing, and parenting choices of poor women and otherwise promote marriage by stigmatizing single motherhood as deviant. The family cap denies financial aid forever to children born while their mother receives welfare even though the average welfare family in-cluded a mother and two children, the same as the national average. The "illegitimacy" bonus divided $100 million a year among the five states that reported the largest decrease in nonmarital births with no increase in abortion rates even though a shortage of data supports the idea that access to welfare benefits encourages women to have chil-dren. The abstinence-only sex education grants earmarked $250 mil-lion for school programs that teach children to postpone sex until marriage but prohibited discussion of contraception or safe sex.

These provisions became part of the welfare law despite counter-vailing data. It was well-known at the time that about one-third of all U.S. births were to unmarried mothers, a ratio that had become rather constant by the early 1990s—long before welfare reform. Referring to the icon of welfare politics in the 1990s—teenage mothers—the Alan Guttmacher Institute (1995) reported that while 70 percent of all teen births were nonmarital, teenagers actually accounted for a smal-ler proportion of such births than they did in the 1970s. Nonmarital births have risen even faster among older women. Like teen *births*, teen *pregnancy rates* also began their now steady decline prior to wel-fare reform. They dropped from 116.3 per 1,000 female teens aged fifteen to nineteen in 1990 to 84.5 per 1,000 female teens in 2000—the lowest rate reported since 1976 (http://www.childtrendsdatabank. org/indicators/14TeenPregnancy.cfm). Since 2000 Congress has devoted hundreds of thousands of government dollars to marriage-promotion programs that favor moral and patriarchal mandates over economic support for poor women. In 2003, the administration vowed to provide at least $1.5 billion for training to help couples develop interpersonal skills that sustain "healthy marriages" (Pear & Kirkpatrick, 2004). The 2006 federal budget proposed $200 billion a year for each of five years for such programs. Among others, feminists point out such welfare policies represent race- and class-driven calls for the control of poor women's sexuality and fertility. According to Pollitt (1998), the 1996 federal welfare law began "with a hymn to marriage and is based on the theory that poverty and social dysfunction are caused by the untrammeled sexuality of poor women" (p. 9).

Last but not least, welfare reform reflected a deep distrust of parenting by single mothers, especially single mothers of color. The states variously "sanction" women (reduce or eliminate their benefits) viewed as not cooperating with paternity identification and child support rules; dock the check of mothers with truant children ("Learnfare"), lower the grants of mothers whose children do not get their immunization shots on time ("Healthfare"), and otherwise wrongly assume that poor women on welfare *choose* to keep their kids uneducated and unvaccinated. Instead of creating good schools, adding more doctors in poor neighborhoods, and fostering other conditions that make for effective parenting, welfare reform penalizes poor women. It revived the long-discredited practice of defining homes as "unfit" simply because they were headed by a poor, black, or single mother (Gordon, 1997).

Like the emphasis on work, the "family value" regulations also have a long history. From the start U.S. social welfare programs have defined women as "deserving" and "undeserving" of aid based on their class, race, and marital status, and treated women who complied with prescribed wife and mother roles better than the others (Abramovitz, 1996). However, such moralistic welfare rules cannot reverse current marriage and childbearing trends which reflect powerful social forces having nothing to do with public assistance. Instead they exploit poor women's dire financial situation by forcing them to trade their marital, childbearing, and parenting preferences for a welfare check. In the name of promoting personal responsibility, they endorse deep government intrusion into private life.

Although welfare reform harms poor women first and foremost, it threatens the well-being of all women. The weakened program deprives women from all walks of life of this potential economic back-up should they fall on hard times. Targeting caregiving by women on welfare also devalues the work done by all women in the home. Further welfare reform legitimizes limiting abortion rights, outlawing same-sex marriages, authorizing state supervision of women in general, and otherwise supports regulating the lives of women.

Weaken the Welfare State

Welfare reform also furthered the neoliberal goal of smaller government by shifting responsibility for social welfare from the federal government back to the states. The 1996 law achieved this by stripping welfare of its entitlement status, converting the program into a state-run block grant, and capping federal funding of the program. These changes, also known as devolution, weakened support for single mothers. As an entitlement program the federal government automatically backed up recipients by guaranteeing funding to the states for every person who applied and qualified for welfare benefits under the state's already strict rules. The guarantee of federal backing represented the government's philosophical as well as financial commitment to the downtrodden. In contrast, the capped block grant provides the states with a fixed amount of federal dollars and allows the chips to fall where they may. During good times when welfare rolls dropped many states used the welfare surplus for programs that did not necessarily serve the poor. When the economy sags and welfare rolls rise, the states have a harder time footing the bill without raising taxes, cutting benefits, or turning people away.

By granting states more control over welfare spending, devolution also opened the door to racialized welfare policymaking. Brown (2003) argues that the federal-state partnership that governed social welfare programs since the 1935 Social Security Act has held "federal policy hostage to the potentially pernicious inclinations of local [white] majorities" (p. 56) which tend to oppose the redistributive policies needed to reduce poverty while tolerating, if not practicing, racial discrimination as well as anti-unionism. The seemingly racially neutral TANF block grant also resulted in racialized outcomes when the states used their increased control of the program to channel TANF dollars away from impoverished persons of color toward working-poor whites regarded as both more deserving and a potential electorate.

Since entitlement programs strengthen the infrastructure of the welfare state, the conversion of AFDC from an entitlement program into a block grant also posed a threat to the social welfare programs serving the middle class. With hindsight it is clear that the elimination of the unpopular welfare entitlement was just the first step on a slippery slope to undoing the more popular and more generous entitlement programs. Following welfare reform, the nation's leaders set their sights on ending an individual's entitlement to Social Security and Medicare by privatizing the programs all or in part. The Bush administration and many in Congress hope to transfer responsibility for these programs from the federal government to individuals and the private sector. There is also talk of turning Medicaid and Section 8 housing vouchers into a block grant. In the name of "reform" these changes promise both to increase the economic insecurity of millions of people and to erode the foundation of the U.S. welfare state. The attack on the welfare state advances still another neoliberal goal—discrediting the general regulatory powers of the federal government and reducing its scale and scope. When allowed to operate, government regulations usefully protect families, consumers, workers, and the environment from the various negative impact of the profit- driven practices of corporate America.

THE RACE CARD

The welfare reformers built public support for welfare reform that threatened the well-being of the middle class as well as the poor by, among other things, playing the race card. Aided and abetted by the media, the reformers tapped into decades of invidious racial stereotypes to turn poverty and welfare into a "black problem" which effectively divided the public along race lines (Gilens, 1999).

The practice has a long history. In 1935 the landmark Social Security Act excluded farm laborers and domestic workers with impunity—the two main occupations open to blacks and Latinos at the time. In the 1940s and 1950s southern welfare offices shut down during the cotton and tobacco harvests to ensure a steady supply of black labor. In the early 1960s more than a few states with large black welfare caseloads threw women off welfare for having children on their own (Abramovitz, 1996).

By the late 1960s the victories of the civil rights movement checked such overt racial discrimination only to see racialization become more covert. Nixon's "southern strategy" invoked fear of the gains made by the civil rights movement to woo white working-class Democrats to the Republican party. In the 1980s Ronald Reagan called forth the stereotype of an African-American "welfare queen" to imply again that the Democrats unreasonably supported government programs. Similarly, in his 1988 campaign for the presidency, George H.W. Bush implied that the Democrats were "soft" on social spending by featuring Willie Horton—an African-American man who raped a woman while on a prison work release-program in Massachusetts—Bush's opponent's home state. By 1992 when the term "welfare" itself had become a code word for race, Bill Clinton urged America "to end welfare as we know it." In 1996 "reformers" from both sides of the aisle regularly evoked racial stereotypes by portraying women on welfare as lazy, Cadillac-driving "welfare queens," who had "kids for money," "lived high on the hog," and "cheated the government" (Delgado & Gordon, 2002).

The racialization of welfare goes beyond winning support for welfare reform. A growing body of research reveals that seemingly race-neutral procedures lead to racialized outcomes. We now know that the racial composition of a state's AFDC caseload turns out to be the strongest and most consistent predictor of the use of waivers. Waivers exempted states from federal public assistance regulations and encouraged them to "experiment" with highly restrictive provisions, including time limits, work requirements, the family cap, learnfare, and healthfare (Fording, 2003). States with larger black populations and larger AFDC caseloads generally offered lower benefits, made deeper cuts in welfare programs (Johnson, 2003), and adopted the strictest welfare reforms (Soss, Schram, Vartanian, & O'Brien, 2003). Gooden (1998, 1999) reports that both welfare department case managers and local employers treated white women more favorably than black women. Case managers were more likely to offer white than black welfare clients educational opportunities and work-related supports (i.e., child care and transportation expenses), while employers were more likely to hire white over black applicants with similar personal backgrounds, work experience, and welfare histories. As a result, since welfare reform, more white than black women have exited welfare. For the first time in the program's history the majority of recipients are of color.

FIGHTING BACK

The fifth goal of the overall agenda aimed to reduce the power of social movements that are best positioned to resist the attack on the welfare state. Since the 1980s, each administration has tried, with some success, to undo the hard-won gains made by the trade union, civil rights, women's liberation, gay rights, and other movements. The good news is that the targets of these assaults have not taken the pain or the punishment lying down. Instead, throughout the 1990s the attack on poor women and welfare unleashed waves of local and state activism. Not always visible on the national front, and not always victorious, hundreds of welfare mothers and community organizations joined forces around welfare reform issues to defend their gains and to advance new ones.

The current economic and political climate may leave little room for victories, but there have been some, especially in the states—and the struggle continues. In the end will the neoliberal strategy followed during the past thirty years unravel as others have done? Profits may soar in the short term, but as in the past, will they be undone by the very conditions that created them? It is too soon to tell, but there are signs of possible troubles. Tax cuts combined with military spending have created a soaring budget deficit and a staggering national debt leading the International Monetary Fund to warn U.S. capital:

> The recent emphasis on cutting taxes, boosting defense and security outlays, and spurring an economic recovery may come at the eventual cost of upward pressure on interest rates, a crowding out of private investment, and an erosion of longer-term U.S. productivity growth. (Shapiro & Friedman, 2004)

The 1990s alone witnessed two jobless recoveries*—the only times since the end of World War II that the number of jobs did not surge to

---

*Jobless recovery: When employers cut staff or froze hiring during recessions and continued to do so into ensuing recovery. In recessions prior to the 1990s, recessions invariably ended in hiring surges (Utichelle, 2004).

prerecession levels nearly three years after the onset of the downturn. With a thinner and thinner safety net, the falling standard of living leaves families less able to adequately sustain themselves, putting family stability and the quality of the domestic workforce at risk. Historically, when left unchecked rising poverty and glaring inequality often became a fertile breeding ground for the rise of social movements that disrupt the status quo. Perhaps it will be as Gandhi predicted: "First they ignore you. Then they laugh at you. Then they fight you. Then you win."

REFERENCES

Abramovitz, M. (1992a). Poor Women in a Bind: Social Reproduction Without Social Supports. *Affilia: A Journal of Women and Social Work* 7(2)(Summer): 23-44.

Abramovitz, M. (1992b). The Reagan Legacy: Undoing Class, Race, and Gender Accords. *Journal of Sociology and Social Welfare,* 19(1), 91-110.

Abramovitz, M. (1996). *Regulating the Lives of Women: Social Welfare Policy from Colonial Times to the Present.* Boston: South End Press.

Abramovitz, M. (2000). *Under Attack, Fighting Back: Women and Welfare in the United States.* New York: Monthly Review Press.

Abramovitz, M. (2001). Everyone Is On Still On Welfare: The Role of Redistribution in Social Policy. *SocialWork,* 46(4)(October): 297-308.

Alan Guttmacher Institute (1995). Teenage Pregnancy and the Welfare Reform Debate. Washington, D.C. Reprinted in G. Mink & R. Solinger (eds.), *Welfare: A Documentary History of U.S. Policy and Politics.* New York: New York University Press, pp. 624-635.

Amott, T. (1993). *Caught in the Crisis: Women and the U.S. Economy Today.* New York: Monthly Review Press.

Bernstein, J., H. Boushey., E. McNichol, & G. Zahradnik (2002). *Pulling Apart: A State by State Analysis of Income Trends.* Washington, DC: Center on Budget and Policy Priorities and the Economic Policy Institute.

Brown, M. (2003). Ghettos, Fiscal Federalism, and Welfare Reform. In S.F. Schram, J. Soss, & R.C. Fording (eds.), *Race and the Politics of Welfare Reform.* Ann Arbor: University of Michigan Press, pp. 47-71.

Chapman, J., & M. Ettinger (2004, August 6). The Who and Why of the Minimum Wage. Issue Brief # 201. Economic Policy Institute. Retrieved December 29, 2004, from <http://www.epinet.org/content.cfm/issuebrief201>.

Delgado, G., & Susan Gordon (2002). From Social Contract to Social Control: Welfare Policy and Race. In G. Delgado (ed.), *From Poverty to Punishment.* Oakland, CA: Applied Research Center, pp. 25-52.

Economic Policy Institute (2002). November Facts at a Glance: Living Wage. Retrieved December 29, 2004 from <http://www.epinet.org/content.cfm/ issueguides_livingwage_livingwagefacts> .

Fording, R.C. (2003). Laboratories of Democracy or Symbolic Politics? The Racial Origins of Welfare Reform. In S F. Schram, J. Soss, & R.C. Fording (eds.), *Race and the Politics of Welfare Reform.* Ann Arbor: University of Michigan Press, pp. 72-100.

Gilens, M. (1999). *Why Americans Hate Welfare: Race, Media, and the Politics of Anti-Poverty Policy.* Chicago: University of Chicago Press.

Gooden, S. (1998). All Things Not Being Equal: Difference in Caseworker Support Toward Black and White Welfare Clients. *Harvard Journal of African American Public Policy,* 4: 232-31.

Gooden, S. (1999). The Hidden Third Party: Welfare Recipients' Experiences with Employers. *Journal of Public Management and Social Policy,* 5(1): 69-83.

Gordon, L. (1997). *Pitied But Not Entitled: Single Mothers and the History of Welfare.* New York: The Free Press.

Inequality.org (2004). How Unequal Are We Anyway: A Statistical Briefing Book. July. Retrieved January 1, 2005, from <http://www.inequality.org/facts.html>.

Johnson, M. (2003). Racial Context, Public Attitudes, and Welfare Effort. In S.F. Schram, J. Soss, & R.C. Fording (eds.), *Race and the Politics of Welfare Reform.* Ann Arbor: University of Michigan Press, pp. 151-170.

Klatch, R.E. (1987). *Women of the New Right.* Philadelphia: Temple University Press.

Kotz, D. (2003). Neoliberalism and the U.S. Expansion of the 1990s. *Monthly Review,* 54(11)(April): 15-33.

O'Connor, J. (1973). *The Fiscal Crisis of the State.* New York: St. Martin's Press.

Orloff, A.S. (1993). Gender and the Social Rights of Citizenship: The Comparative Analysis of Gender Relations and Welfare States. *American Review,* 58*(June): 303-328.*

Pear, R., & D.D. Kirkpatrick (2004). Bush Plans $1.5 Billion Drive for Promotion of Marriage. *New York Times,* January 14, sec. A, p. 1.

Piven, F.F. (1999). The Welfare State As Work Enforces. *Dollars and Sense,* September-October, p. 34.

Piven F.F., & R.M. Cloward (1977). *Poor People's Movements: Why They Succeed, How They Fail.* New York: Vintage.

Pollitt, K. (1998, April 13). Did Someone Say Hypocrites? *The Nation,* p. 9.

Roberts D. (1997). *Killing the Black Body: Race, Reproduction and the Meaning of Liberty.* New York: Pantheon Books.

Shapiro, I., & J. Friedman (2004). *Tax Returns: A Comprehensive Assessment of the Bush Administration's Record on Cutting Taxes.* Center on Budget and Policy Priorities. Retrieved December 20, 2004, from <http://www.cbpp.org/4-14-04tax-sum.htm>.

Soss, J., S. Schram, T.P. Vartanian, & E. O'Brien (2003). The Hard Line and the Color Line. In S. F. Schram, J. Soss, & R.C. Fording (eds.), *Race and the Politics of Welfare Reform.* Ann Arbor: University of Michigan Press, pp. 225-253.

U.S. Congress (1996). Personal Responsibility and Work Opportunity Reconciliation Act of 1996. 104th Cong., 2nd Sess. Reprinted in G. Mink & R. Solinger (eds.), (2003), *Welfare: A Documentary History of U.S. Policy and Politics.* New York: New York University Press, pp. 654-647. Also available at <http://www.thomas/loc.gov>.

Utichelle, L. (2004, December 31). Gaining Ground on the Wage Front. *The New York Times,* pp. C1, C2.

Weisskopf, T. (1981). The Current Economic Crisis in Historical Perspective. *Socialist Review,* #57, pp. 9-54.

Chapter 3

Welfare Reform:
Forward to the Past

Alfred L. Joseph Jr.

INTRODUCTION

Most of the pundits of the mass media, both conservative and not, agree that one of the strengths of the so-called conservative movement is their ability to address social issues and state their vision for the country in a simple, clear, and concise way. Media pundits proclaimed that "people know where they stand" on a variety of domestic and international issues. It is widely agreed that this was at least partially responsible for winning George W. Bush a second term in the White House. Presumably people knew where he stood, and at least 51 percent of the people who bothered to vote voted for him. I would like progressives to consider borrowing a page from the other side's playbook. I am not advocating the spouting of mindless and simplistic solutions to complex social problems such as poverty, health care, drug addiction, homelessness, and crime. I am, however, for developing a simple, clear, and concise message that would stand in stark contrast to the message of the other side.

The message of progressives should be that we refuse to go back to the past. We do not live in the stone age; we live in the twenty-first century. Maybe in antiquity survival depended on the size of your club or biceps or how fast you could run. More recently, the amount of wealth and power accumulated along with your religion or race dictated your quality of life, or if you would survive at all. Those days should be behind us. I thought we had advanced to another level of social organization where your quality of life is based solely on your humanity and not on some "attribute" that is valued by whatever

doi:10.1300/5608_04

group or groups hold state power. Our simple message should be that we reject selfishness and embrace the idea of collective responsibility for one another. Conservative commentator Pat Buchanan, speaking at the 1992 Republican National Convention, surprised many viewers when he stated that a "culture war" was raging across America. He said that this "culture war" would determine what kind of country the United States would become. I agree with this statement, though of course I disagree with his analysis. Mr. Buchanan's "culture war" had to do with the profound life-threatening issues of school prayer, homosexuality, and a woman's right to control her body's reproductive processes. The "culture war" I see being waged about the direction of the country has to do with the survival of people not born to power and privilege. It has to do with access to resources such as cash, housing, medical care, and education. I, like Mr. Buchanan, am also concerned about the country's direction. In one direction lies a culture of greed and selfishness that uses words and phrases such as "tough love," "playing by the rules," "self-reliance," "fiscal responsibility," and "accountability" to mask efforts to de-fund and dismantle social programs designed to meet the needs of the poor and disenfranchised. In the other direction lies a culture of giving and acceptance where all people are equally valued. They are not left to their own devices to survive as somehow society had deemed them unworthy of assistance. You have to pass no tests, meet no requirements for survival here. You are assisted, helped, and nurtured because you are a human being, period. The choices are clear: We can proceed further down the path to the past, where the laws of the Social Darwinist jungle govern civil life, or we can change directions toward a more inclusive and collective future.

WELFARE "REFORM" AND BEYOND

President Bill Clinton's signing of Public Law 104-193, also known as the Personal Responsibility and Work Opportunity Reconciliation Act (PRWORA), was a clear political and physical defeat for poor people. It was also an ideological defeat for people who have a progressive-left vision for the future. Let us make no mistake about this; welfare reform is a step backward. It represents social regression, not progress as its advocates claim. In fact, welfare reform is more than just a step backward; it is a stalking horse. A stalking horse as defined by *Webster's New Collegiate Dictionary* as "something used to mask a purpose." The real agenda, the real purpose of the opposition is not hard to detect. By using liberal amounts of racist, sexist, and anti–working-class disinformation and propaganda, these forces of reaction want to turn back the clock on social progress. They want a return to the good old days of little or no so-called safety nets and the taxes that are used to fund them. In the good old days people were motivated (by starvation and homelessness) to work hard and to shun laziness as if it were a sin. In the good old days there were no pesky labor unions and other advocacy groups to raise concerns over working conditions, job discrimination or if there were jobs at all, and benefits such as health care. In the good old days you could make a profit without interference from outside forces. People were grateful for the opportunity to do an honest day's work for an honest day's pay. These reactionary voices have been present for years; they date back to the founding of the United States (Albelda & Tilly, 1997). In their book titled *Glass Ceilings and Bottomless Pits,* the authors describe how in some colonial villages recipients of relief would have to wear the letter "P" for pauper on their clothes. They could also be denied the right to marry, they could be jailed, and their status could be downgraded to that of indentured servant or slave. Clearly those opposed to the public use of funds to address the needs of poor people were making their voices heard from the earliest of times. Rank (2004) has identified this perspective. He refers to it as "the old paradigm." He writes:

> This paradigm begins with the key assumption that the American economic system generates abundant economic prosperity and well-being for all . . . the assumption is not that everyone will be rich, but that with enough hard work and initiative, nearly everyone is capable of achieving and sustaining a modest and comfortable lifestyle. Given this assumption, poverty becomes understood largely as a result of individual failure. (p. 171)

Of course those who subscribed to this paradigm spent little time discussing slavery and its aftermath, the 100 plus years of legal racial discrimination and oppression and the continued denial of opportunities because of institutional racism that is directed at African Americans and other racial minorities. How might this reality impact a person's chances of securing "economic opportunity"? I also suspect that the "old paradigm-ers" did not give much thought to the status of women and how historic legal and current sexist practices hamper many women in their efforts to secure a "modest and comfortable lifestyle." Lastly, I am fairly sure the question of class was never fully addressed. How might inherited wealth and class privilege influence one's chances in their paradigm? Does the ability to significantly impact this country's economic, political, social, and cultural institutions give one an ever so slight advantage in this paradigm? Could one use this influence and power to create an environment that favors people like you and that disadvantages others? The proponents of the "old paradigm," then and now, leave too many questions unanswered and issues unaddressed as they seek to blame the victims for their inability to prosper in this Garden of Eden.

HISTORY OF HOSTILITY TO ASSISTANCE

Sometimes to understand the present and have some insight into the future it is often useful to study the past. The hostility to the poor, especially the non-white female poor, is embedded in much of this society's antipoverty legislation. To get a better understanding of this hostility we need only look at some New Deal legislation passed in the 1930s. During the social and economic crisis of the Great Depression millions of Americans (some under the leadership of the Communist Party and other radical groups) demanded that the federal government take serious measures to address the needs of those experiencing hardship. For relatively better-off white males there were programs such as the Works Progress Administration (WPA), the Civil Works Administration (CWA), and the Civilian Conservation Corps (CCC). These programs were designed to closely resemble real work. The work was useful, the wages were based on the type of work done, and people were paid in cash. A tremendous amount of racial discrimination occurred: African Americans were paid less and ushered into menial jobs no matter their skill level (Rose, 1994). Despite their flaws, these programs represented a relatively progressive response to poverty and unemployment.

When it came to addressing the needs of the poorest part of the population, women and children (especially African-American women and children), we saw a slightly different response. First, according to Goldberg and Collins (2001), assisting poor women and children was an afterthought. They state that ADC (Aid to Dependent Children) "rode into the social security act on the coattails of popular movements of the elderly and unemployed" (p. 30). The program was intended to be kept small, populated mainly by "virtuous" white women who had children only through marriage. These were mothers who were primarily widowed or had been abandoned (Abramovitz, 1996). White women who were seen as "immoral" or "unfit mothers" had a very difficult time securing assistance, and their children were often placed in orphanages or other institutions. Pervasive racist ideology saw to it that virtually all African-American women were seen in a bad light and therefore unworthy of public assistance. Racist ideology supports a racist (and sexist) labor market. There was concern, particularly in the South, that assistance would interfere with "local economies." This is a euphemism for an agricultural economy characterized by depressed wages made even lower by racist segregation. The South was dependent on cheap and abundant African-American agricultural and domestic labor. The trick is not just getting people to work; it is getting them to work at a particular wage and under conditions dictated by the employer. Goldberg and Collins (2001) are quite clear on this issue:

> Meager mothers'-aid benefits, concludes historian Stephanie Coontz, contributed to a "system that did not so much subsidize domesticity as endorse low-paid, part-time, irregular work for women in marginal labor markets." This description of mothers' aid also fits ADC and, to an even greater extent, its replacement, TANF.

For even virtuous women, ADC hardly guaranteed them an easy existence. Goldberg and Collins (2001) write that

> ADC benefits remained low. Benefits were paltry, even with Washington sharing the costs of the programs with the states. . . . Low benefits thus meant that large numbers of needy families were excluded from coverage because their incomes were above the benefit levels. They were thus obliged to depend on the labor market or other sources of income. (p. 40)

ADC, public assistance for poor women and children, was never popular. It became even more unpopular and became the focus of even more virulent attacks as the programs began to assist more and more women and children of color. National and local politicians thought nothing, then and now, of publicly spewing the most vile racist and sexist slanders as they sought to destroy that program. The most famous slander of all was offered up by Senator Russell Long of Louisiana in 1967 when he referred to poor women as "brood mares." That was almost forty years ago. More recently an Indiana politician compared welfare recipients with alligators who have grown lazy because people feed them and do not let them fend for themselves. In a similar vein, an administrator of human services in Riverside, California, "wonders" if bag women are actually former welfare recipients who can no longer have children for money. These attacks were relentless and, unfortunately, for the most part they have been extremely successful.

Though the programs described previously varied in a number of ways, one of the factors they had in common was opposition from conservatives who were very concerned about the direction of the country. Even the programs that were directed mainly at white males caused alarm in some quarters and generated quite a lot of hostility from many segments of society, especially the community. From the very beginning many in the business community made the CWA, WPA, ADC, and other programs targets of ridicule and strident ideological attacks. While progressives were urging expansion of the programs to cover millions more destitute and unemployed workers, critical voices on the other side of the political spectrum kept applying pressure to keep the programs small and underfunded with elimination seen as the ultimate goal (Rose, 1994).

If left to their own devices, conservatives of that time would have scaled back or done away with all of those relief programs. They would have been willing to sacrifice the health, well-being, and indeed the very lives of vast numbers of people in order to remove all threats to their "right" to make a profit, to make a buck. What was of concern to these folks was more than just the programs that put people to work or gave poor women some cash. What really concerned them were the ideas these programs represented. These programs were seen as alternatives to commodity production and the private wage system. If production for profit meant that at times goods could not or would not be produced because little or no profit was to be made, then maybe production for use made more sense. A 1934 *Business Week* article clearly states the concern of those supportive of private enterprise. Capitalists, the article explained, are worried about "the uncomfortable thought that government manufacture might become permanent" (Rose, 1994, p. 79). The existence of public assistance provides very poor women with options—options about family structure and options having to do with entry into the job market. Options for poor people are seen as a threat to those with wealth and privilege.

THE STRUGGLE CONTINUES: FIGHTING RACISM IS CRUCIAL

The political and ideological attacks on "welfare" are nothing new; they have roots deep in American history. This struggle is about power and who will have power to exert control over the direction and nature of society. This country has never been able to meet the needs of vast numbers of people. Of course through history this number may vary, as does the severity of want and need. Progressives believe that the essential role of the state it to provide assistance to the people with the least power and privilege who for whatever reasons are not able to access resources. The opposite view is that the state should play a limited role in the distribution of resources. The "market" is seen as the primary vehicle for the distribution of resources. Anything that interferes with the free operation of market forces is viewed with great suspicion. Programs that allow people to access to funds, jobs, housing, pensions, etc., outside of the market are of course suspect and immediately called into question. This process will occur, but what is at question is the rate at which the assault will occur. ADC came out of the 1935 Social Security Act, and it took opponents sixty years to realize their dream. They are nothing if not persistent. Progressives need to realize that we are in for a protracted struggle. The other side has tasted victory and they seek more. Racism was used to separate AFDC from other social welfare programs, and its recipients were slandered and degraded and scapegoated. Few came to its defense, not realizing that the goal was not just to "change welfare as we know it" but to change the way we view social welfare and the nature of the state. Goldberg and Collins (2001, p. 111) comment on the strategy of the conservatives:

It was far easier to attack programs that were politically vulnerable, like AFDC. In time, AFDC, though making up only about 1 percent of the federal budget, would become a stand-in for the entire welfare state and the evils of "big government."

If progressives are to build the type of movement necessary to resist these assaults on the social welfare system, central to that movement has to be a vigorous fight against racism. Opposition was present to it from the very beginning of the ADC program. It was when African-American women and children began to appear on the rolls in significant numbers that opposition intensified and took on a particularly vicious nature. Even though most participants through history have not been African Americans, opponents have successfully painted the program as a "black program." Once that happened, because of the prevalence of racism in the general population, no claim was seen as too outrageous. Anything could be believed. The attitude of the average American was that of "don't confuse me with the facts." They don't want to know the actual cost of the system. They don't care to hear about how the actual value of the benefits has been decreasing for over twenty years. They don't care that over 70 percent of the recipients are children. Racism had left them vulnerable to the grossest of lies and distortions. Many of these people, themselves not far removed from the people they despise, were won over to the side of those whose agenda was much more than "changing welfare as we know it." Neubeck and Cazenave (2001), in their thought-provoking book *Welfare Racism: Playing the Race Card Against America's Poor,* make the point that although racism often immediately impacts people of color, sooner or later its impact will be felt by all. I think the words of Jane Addams, social work educator and activist, mean as much today as they did back in her day: "The good we secure for ourselves is precarious and uncertain until it is secured for us all and incorporated into our common life."

REFERENCES

Abramovitz, M. (1996). *Regulating the Lives of Women.* (Rev. Ed.) Boston: South End Press.

Albelda, R. and Tilly, C. (1997). *Glass Ceilings and Bottomless Pits: Women's Work, Women's Poverty.* Boston, MA: South End Press.

Goldberg, G. and Collins, S. D. (2001). *Washington's New Poor Law: Welfare "Reform" and the Roads Not Taken, 1935 to the Present.* New York: The Apex Press.

Neubeck, K. J. and Cazenave, N. A. (2001). *Welfare Racism: Playing the Race Card Against America's Poor.* New York: Routledge.

Rank, M. R. (2004). *One Nation, Underprivileged: Why American Poverty Affects Us All.* New York: Oxford University Press.

Rose, N. E. (1994). *Put to Work: Relief Programs in the Great Depression.* New York: Monthly Review Press.

Chapter 4

Welfare Reform
in Historical Perspective

Joel Blau

It is axiomatic that social welfare policies and programs reflect their political and economic context. By this standard, in 1996, when the age of industrial capitalism was long gone and Temporary Assistance for Needy Families (TANF) replaced Aid to Families with Dependent Children (AFDC), AFDC was already obsolete. Under the regime of industrial capitalism, men worked in large factories, physical strength was a big part of their life on the job, and women stayed at home to take care of the children. In an age when one man's pay was supposed to be enough to support his family, a government welfare program designed to offset part of the loss of that pay made considerable sense.

By 1996, however, none of these conditions existed. U.S. manufacturing had hemorrhaged workers, jobs involving computer technology and most service work no longer required physical strength, and the pay of many male workers had declined. As more women entered low-paid service positions, they looked increasingly askance at AFDC, because it allowed poor women to stay home to take care of their children and therefore offered the poor options that other women did not have. The principle of less eligibility says that even the lowest wageworker must maintain a higher standard of living than any recipient of welfare. As the economy changed and more women worked, the violation of this principle significantly undermined popular support for the program.

The principle of less eligibility establishes a tight link between wages and welfare. Both tend to go up or down together, but whether they rise or fall depends on larger political and economic factors.

doi:10.1300/5608_05

Most recently, global competition and the transition from an industrial to a service economy have pushed down both wages and welfare. For example, the wages of male high school dropouts declined by 30 percent between 1979 and 1997. During the same period, the wages of female high school dropouts declined by 16 percent (Blau, 1999, p. 14). Forced down by this shrinking pay, welfare benefits had to fall in order to maintain the principle of less eligibility. That explains why between 1970 and 2000, the median welfare grant plummeted 47 percent (House Ways and Means Committee, 2000, p. 390).

The 1996 welfare reform bill fits perfectly into this pattern. Historically, when the economy has shifted from one dominant mode of production to another (agricultural to industrial, or industrial to service), employers have always sought to carry out this transition on the most favorable terms. Over time, the elements of this transition have remained remarkably consistent. In the face of declining wages, eligibility rules tightened, and welfare became workfare. Of course, flooding the lower rungs of the labor market with more workers only increases competition for low-wage jobs and exacerbates the decline in wages. From the employers' perspective, however, that is precisely the point: the ideological value of work must be reaffirmed, even as its purchasing power declines. Both the economic and the ideological elements of a workfare regime are bundled together. Without them, employers worry that in the new economic era, they might face a workforce whose militancy grows because it has not been recently disciplined.

The time for AFDC had certainly passed. Born of a different economic era and a different family configuration, AFDC was not sustainable. Yet even as we note the increasing obsolescence of AFDC, we must also acknowledge that its passing constituted an opportunity to depart from the historical pattern. A global labor market and a changing American family structure is going to make many U.S. families much less secure. This prospect could have brought about a new welfare system, one that protected more people from economic insecurity. Such a welfare system would have offered national health care, day care, a family allowance, paid parental leave, easy access to job training, and most of all, a commitment to a full-employment economy. With this list of interventions, the principle of less eligibility might still be maintained, but wages and welfare would rise.

U.S. policymakers missed this historic opportunity. Nevertheless, looking back at this crossroad does sharpen the contrast with what they did do. Ask a mainstream American policymaker to ensure full employment, and most will tell you that it is either inappropriate or counterproductive for the government to intervene so forcefully in the economy. And yet, despite this apparent prohibition, the vast majority of these policymakers welcomed the opportunity to push welfare recipients into a job, where they would be subjected to low wages and the discipline of the labor market. A full-employment economy would have also provided jobs for most welfare recipients. But since it would have pulled rather than pushed people into these jobs, new workers could demand higher wages and better fringe benefits. Without a powerful social movement behind it, full employment will always be rejected for these very reasons.

And so we are left to be both saddened and enlightened by the historical pattern. We can no more change what happened in the 1990s than we can reverse what occurred in the early nineteenth century, when urban economies first began to shift from agriculture to industry, and work was demanded for welfare. Nevertheless, the historical pattern does shed some light on exactly what gave rise to TANF. In order to shape what happens in the future, it is worth recollecting this history.

FROM AGRICULTURAL TO INDUSTRIAL

The early-nineteenth-century transition from an agricultural to an industrial economy offers the first modern evidence of workfare. As industry began to replace agriculture, cities arose that transformed communities, changed the rhythms of daily life, and altered the perception of the poor. In a rural society where agriculture predominated, everyone knew everyone else, nature dictated the rhythms of daily life, and most people saw the poor as an integral part of the community. But the rise of industry and the growth of cities completely upset these traditions. In a city, it was possible to remain anonymous, and work depended not on what season it was but increasingly on whether someone else would hire you.

The new fact of economic life made the poor threatening. No longer were the poor merely neighbors or relatives who couldn't eat or keep warm; now they were people—quite possibly someone completely unknown to you—who lacked the money to survive. Even more ominously, these poor people sometimes acted together as a class. Such new economic and political developments required the use of workfare.

New York City deployed the most advanced version. When New York constructed the Bellevue complex in 1816, it included a workhouse along with an almshouse, a prison, and two hospitals among the buildings. The workhouse, however, did not apparently have a sufficiently deterrent effect, because by the early 1820s, the city was devoting almost one-quarter of its budget to social welfare expenditures. In these circumstances, the city's leaders felt that they had no choice but to intensify the deterrent (Mohl, 1971, p. 90).

The new deterrent was a treadmill, the latest British device for the application of science to the management of the poor. The treadmill consisted of a revolving drum attached to a machine that ground wheat. Sixteen people operated it at any one time, climbing steadily in place for eight minutes until another group replaced them. As its administrator wrote, "[the treadmill] is constant and sufficiently severe: but it is its *monotonous steadiness* and not its *severity* which constitutes its terror, and frequently breaks down the obstinate spirit." Yet with the economy producing an ever greater number of poor people, even this measure failed. Despite grinding forty bushels of grain and saving the city an estimated $1,900 annually, the city halted the treadmill's operation after three years (Schneider, 1938, pp. 152-154).

The 1824 reforms initiated by New York Secretary of State John Yates systematized this new emphasis on work. Yates simply barred any able-bodied male ages eighteen to fifty from receiving assistance. Although the same reforms also ended the old settlement and removal laws, the implications were clear: if you want to survive in the new industrial era, you'd have to work, and in order to work, you'd have to accept whatever employers were willing to offer you. From their perspective during this transition, these were indeed the most favorable terms.

Yates's reforms preceded the British Poor Law Reform Act of 1834 by ten years. Since the 1834 reform is the law that actually popularized the term "less eligibility," it shows both how advanced Yates's reforms were and illustrates that business elites tend to respond to the transition from one mode of production to another in very similar ways. Like Yates, the British Poor Law Reform also prohibited relief in peoples' own homes. This prohibition forced people either to accept the prevailing wages or to enter a workhouse. The 1834 Poor Law Reform, then, performed the function that a work regimen always does. By keeping wages down, it helped the business elite ensure the profitability of the British industrial revolution.

FROM COMPETITIVE CAPITALISM TO MONOPOLY CAPITALISM

A second period that illustrates the uses of work in welfare policy is the transition from competitive to monopoly capitalism that took place after the Civil War. When the first transition occurred from agriculture to industry in the early 1800s, businesses began to use machinery, but these businesses were still relatively small, and competition prevailed. The years between 1870 and 1900, however, witnessed the rise of monopoly capitalism, during which many major industries—oil (John D. Rockefeller), steel (Andrew Carnegie), and railroads (Harriman, Vanderbilt, Stanford)—came to be dominated by just a few firms. These firms and the economy they heralded needed a malleable labor force. A new work regime constituted one method for bringing this workforce into existence.

This new regime sparked a campaign to end outdoor relief—relief in peoples' own homes—and sharply increased the reliance on work tests. Although the 1873 New York State Pauper Act acknowledged a responsibility to care for the transient poor, it qualified this assistance in practice with the demand that the person be disabled. As a result, work was left as the only alternative for the able-bodied. In keeping with this law, Brooklyn and New York (the boroughs were not combined until 1898) ended outdoor relief in the late 1870s, leaving poor people to scramble for any paid employment. Similarly, both the Night Refuge Association and the Charity Organization Society (COS) required work tests as a condition of overnight aid—in the latter case, two meals and a night's lodging were conditioned upon a day's labor in the COS woodyard (Crouse, 1981; Schneider, 1941; Katz, 1986). At a time when unemployment and labor militancy were rising, these workfare policies constituted an essential ingredient of the employers' strategy.

The work policy of the New Deal throws this pattern into clearer relief. Although the American economy collapsed during the 1930s (GDP down 50 percent, unemployment rising to 25 percent), large industries continued to hold sway, and despite the intervention of the government, the predominant mode of production remained the same. Together with the existence of powerful social movements, this continuity elicited an entirely different work policy. Instead of cutting welfare, New Deal social policy rationalized public assistance through the inclusion of ADC in the Social Security Act; instead of forcing people into the labor force, it funneled the unemployed into a variety of well-known work programs such as the Civilian Conservation Corp (CCC) and the Works Progress Administration (WPA).

Admittedly, each of these job programs had limits. These limits—on pay (thirty dollars a month for the CCC), on eligibility (few women or people of color), and on duration (both the WPA and the CCC ended after seven years in 1942)—all served to prevent prolonged competition with the wages or hiring practices of the private sector (Amenta, 1998). Nevertheless, New Deal work policy clearly illustrates the exception that proves the rule. When social movements insisted that the New Deal enact reforms in an existing mode of production, the Roosevelt Administration passed legislation that treated work as an opportunity rather than as a punishment.

Fast forward to the current policy cycle, and the contrast couldn't be sharper. In the aftermath of World War II, the United States was the world's preeminent economy. But this unchallenged position lasted for just twenty-five years. By the early 1970s, Germany and Japan had rebuilt their industrial base and began to undersell the United States. In response, American businesses began to deindustrialize and push down wages. At first, businesses pushed down wages by fighting unions and moving to the South and Southwest—to lower-wage regions of this country. This move was already in full swing when the 1993 passage of the North American Free Trade Agreement globalized the trend. Now, businesses can easily outsource production to Mexico or Southeast Asia, and with the existence of the Internet, computer programs can also be shifted overseas, so that both better-paid technical staff and industrial workers are at risk. Although globalization does not affect service jobs that depend on face-to-face contact—a fast food worker must still hand you your burger, industrialized workers have shrunk to just 15 percent of the workforce, and it is clear that we are far along into the transition toward a service economy.

What has happened in recent social welfare policy hews closely to the historical pattern. In the midst of a transition from one dominant mode of production to another, social welfare policy will usually enforce work norms. Social movements may serve to oppose or modify this tendency, but when they either fade or actually seek to support this enforcement, then, as has happened over the past twenty-five-years, social welfare programs are increasingly going to be tied to work. And so TANF limits assistance to five years; requires recipients to work within two years (many states have even shorter limits); and has been consistently interpreted to favor work—any work—over further education and/or job training. Moreover, with TANF spearheading the way, policymakers have also cracked down on other programs. Since its passage in 1996, they have tightened the eligibility standards for unemployment insurance; obligated the residents of public housing projects to perform eight hours of community work every month; and terminated benefits for people who are disabled due to drug and alcohol addiction (Blau with Abramovitz, 2004; Katz, 2001). In short, work now reigns throughout social welfare policy, and the hallmark of its reign has been reform of the public assistance program.

That modern welfare reform mirrors the historical pattern probably offers little comfort to policy advocates and sympathetic policy analysts. I'm sure they'd choose a better outcome over historical continuity. Yet as always, we ignore history at our peril. The history of welfare reform suggests that what happened should hardly come as a surprise. It also suggests, however, that if we want a different outcome—if we want at a minimum, a new New Deal—history looks favorably upon those who organize social movements in order to enact the kind of progressive social policies that truly value both work and welfare.

REFERENCES

Amenta, Edwin (1998). *Bold Relief: Institutional Politics and the Origins of Modern American Social Policy.* Princeton, NJ: Princeton University Press.

Blau, Joel (1999). *Illusions of Prosperity: American Workers in an Age of Economic Insecurity.* New York: Oxford University Press.

Blau, Joel with Mimi Abramovitz (2004). *The Dynamics of Social Welfare Policy.* New York: Oxford University Press.

Crouse, Joan (1981). Transiency in New York State: The Impact of the Depression. PhD Dissertation, State University at Buffalo.

House Ways and Means Committee (2000), 2000 Green Book, *Background Material and Data on the Programs Within the Jurisdiction of the Committee on Ways and Means.* Washington, DC: U.S. Government Printing Office.

Katz, Michael B. (1986). *In the Shadow of the Poorhouse.* New York: Basic Books.

Katz, Michael B. (2001). *The Price of Citizenship: Redefining the American Welfare State.* New York: Henry Holt and Company.

Mohl, Raymond (1971). *Poverty in New York: 1783-1825.* New York: Oxford University Press.

Schneider, David M. (1938). *The History of Public Welfare in New York State, 1609-1866,* Volume I. Chicago: University of Chicago Press.

Schneider, David M. (1941). *The History of Public Welfare in New York State, 1867-1940,* Volume II. Chicago: University of Chicago Press.

Chapter 5

Lessons from Vermont

Margaret K. Nelson

When a harsh restructuring of welfare was proposed in Vermont over a decade ago (and before then-President Clinton had promised to "end welfare as we know it") Sally Conrad, a Vermont state senator, staged a struggle. She held the bill in committee to prevent its coming to a vote, and at the same time sent out an urgent call to women across the state to resist the mandatory work provision that the governor promised would be reintroduced in the next legislative session (McCrate & Smith, 1998). The coalition subsequently formed under Conrad's leadership, which became known as the "Women's Union," was unable to stem the tide of change: time limits and work requirements became the norm in Vermont, as they soon did throughout the nation. The coalition did, however, have a significant impact, within Vermont, on the extent and implications of that change. Two modifications of the proposed reforms are noteworthy. First, the sanctions applied to welfare recipients who did not find employment were less severe than the immediate termination of the welfare benefit proposed by Governor Howard Dean. Second, Vermont assumed a legal obligation to provide a variety of services (including quality child care and transportation) to those required to transition off welfare, and to defer the work requirement if such services were not forthcoming.

Flush with this modest, but significant, success, the Women's Union remained an active and effective watchdog for another decade: its meeting agendas, announced in a monthly newsletter, included a wide range of issues relevant to the lives of welfare recipients and low-income women; the group's members wrote letters to their local and national representatives, advising them of ongoing concerns; and its leaders leaned on delegates from the Department of Social Welfare

doi:10.1300/5608_06

to attend meetings and to account for and explain new policies. In 2002, however, the Women's Union disbanded. Although the newsletter did not offer a full explanation, it was clear that the group had few funds and fewer members to carry on its work. The final newsletter urged those interested in the issues it had embraced to seek action under the purview of the Burlington, Vermont-based Peace and Justice Center which defines its role as working for "economic justice and a livable wage," among other causes (Peace and Justice Center, 2004).

In what follows, I use this story of engagement followed by dissolution to explain why I believe that we can no longer expect those most affected by changes in the provision of welfare—namely low-income single mothers—to protect themselves. I also turn from the specifics of the Vermont situation to offer a set of modest proposals for social change with an eye toward what I believe is possible within the current political climate. I conclude with a call for scholars to become active participants in ensuring that change.

THE DISAPPEARANCE OF GRASSROOTS RESISTANCE

The 1960s and 1970s history of welfare rights organizations provides clear evidence that welfare recipients can organize into a vibrant coalition of resistance (Funiciello, 1998); this capability was demonstrated again in Vermont when urgent need and leadership came together in a fortuitous and meaningful way in the form of the Women's Union (McCrate & Smith, 1998). Today, however, that capability of resistance appears to have disappeared. I could start with an obvious reason: as a result of caseload declines across the country, there are now fewer welfare recipients altogether (Administration for Children and Families, 2004). This fact combines with a second, equally obvious one: because of time limits, the pool of welfare recipients changes far more rapidly than it did in the past, thus leaving a less stable base from which to recruit. Perhaps even more significant as a reason for declining resistance is the altered situation of individual welfare recipients themselves. Welfare no longer offers a long-term, stable (albeit miserly) income; time limits require that welfare recipients always keep an eye on a ticking clock, and work requirements may well preclude individuals from having either the time or the energy to participate in activities that resist welfare "reform."

A Vermont woman described the security of welfare reliance under the old regime:[1]

> It's like a lousy, meager, paltry handout. But there's a mentality that is incredibly strong, that at least you know it's there. You know it's coming. . . . You can always plan on that. There's, you know, birth, death, taxes, and welfare payments.

She also described how this secure impoverishment allowed her the time to bring her young daughter to a "family room" provided by the Visiting Nurse's Association, which is where she learned about the Women's Union, and even to follow up on her interest and to attend a meeting:

> I went down [to the family room] and I met some women. And there was a little political undertone there, you know, like talking about our benefits and the government. And so I'm listening, and putting in some two cents here and there, and thinking about it . . . And then I heard something about this "Women's Union." . . . So, I called and went to a meeting.

Once subjected to work requirements, this woman described her life in very different terms. She no longer had the security of knowing how much income she would have:

> But when you go to work, suddenly you're in a state of panic all the time. Because you're never quite sure, are they going to do the right paper, is the check going to come at the right time, are they going to lose the paperwork? Did I earn too much this month in my job and now next month I'm going to get less in my welfare? My food stamps are up, then they're down, then they're over here. And for someone that's just anxiety they can't cope with.

The new work requirement also precluded having any "extra" time in her life:

> And you know, it's like the guy on . . . whatever TV it was when I was a kid, that had about five or six different plates spinning on sticks. And he's going through and giving each one a little whirl

and then running back to the first one. That's what life is when you're poor and working. It's just this series of pie plates.

And she now worries that word of her political activities will reach her employer and thus jeopardize her job: "There's also a fear factor. There's an extremely high degree of anxiety that the person can have when they are faced with doing something that might, say, make their employer angry."

The loss of modest economic stability and time, and the emergence of fear, combine with other changes wrought by the new welfare regime. Welfare-reliant women no longer have access to a discourse that grants mothers the *right* to stay home and care for their own children. Another active member of the Women's Union reported that she became reliant on welfare because she wanted to raise her own child and to be the "major influence" in her daughter's life. Her opposition to the proposed changes was prompted by learning that she would no longer be able to exercise what she perceived to be her right to care: "They were going to tell me that I had to go to work, and I had to leave my daughter. And it's like, 'uh, uh, uh.' It's like, 'it's not your choice, that's *my* choice.'"

By way of contrast, women "educated" within the new welfare regime do not learn a language of rights. A young woman subjected to Vermont's experimental version of TANF spoke of herself as being an "investment opportunity" for the state; she did not root her understanding of the legitimacy of welfare reliance in her activities of care but rather in her progress toward that mythical state of self-sufficiency: "I'm using this to better myself, so that makes it okay."[2]

The most recent generation of welfare recipients does not pull this new rhetoric out of thin air. They have plenty of guides. In *Flat Broke with Children: Women in the Age of Welfare Reform*, Sharon Hays (2003) argues that the enactment of welfare often takes place within the context of highly personalized relationships with caseworkers who operate on the basis of both "caring maternalism" and a high degree of "caseworker discretion." Hays argues that while this new regime has positive aspects (because welfare workers can act on the basis of concern for clients and make needed adjustments for individuals), it also has intrinsic difficulties (because recipients are left relying on "judgments of middle class caseworkers" and are treated as "childlike dependents") (Hays, 2003, p. 90). The latter drawbacks are significant. In order to get the benefits of welfare today—the care of maternalism and the flexibility of caseworker discretion—recipients have to learn to present themselves as both special and compliant. Thus the welfare regime can fail to engender a collective politics and instead might encourage "sibling rivalry" as women compete for scarce resources and for what they perceive to be equally scarce approval.

In short, even (and perhaps especially) in the relatively benign state of Vermont, welfare recipients may no longer be in the position to engage in the hard work of fighting for reform themselves: the pool of potential political actors is smaller and more rapidly changing; individual struggles to prepare for and enact "self-sufficiency" are fraught with anxiety; the language of rights has largely disappeared; and relationships with welfare administrators may well engender complicity and a sense of oneself as being different from other recipients rather than a unified resistance and an awareness of common interests. Indeed, it hardly seems to be indulging in conspiracy theory to believe the consequences of these new forces marshaled against political opposition may well have been an *intended* side effect of welfare "reform."

To be sure, the deliberations around TANF reauthorization did evoke some new resistance nationwide (Bricker-Jenkins & Brookland, 2002; Sen, 1999); when these issues are debated again in the new Congressional term, that resistance might be reinvigorated. But, whether that happens or not, the future does not appear to hold the makings of effective opposition. The experience of the Women's Union in Vermont demonstrated that, in all probability, the most that can be hoped for will be pushing around the edges. The major provisions of the PRWORA (including block grants, time limits, and work requirements) appear to be here to stay. In November 2004, even the more liberal presidential candidate proudly stated that he voted for "welfare reform" (Commission on Presidential Debates, 2004); the winner of the election had already clearly indicated his priorities with respect to this issue.

MODEST SOCIAL CHANGE

A colleague and I used to have an admittedly not very funny, running joke about my scholarship. I would show him a draft of a paper complete except for the conclusion. He would make editorial comments, and then say, "Now, I assume, you'll round up the usual suspects," thus teasing me about the fact that every paper I wrote ended with the same call for broad social change. That call let me off the hook: if broad social change was not forthcoming, that was not my concern; I knew it was needed, I knew what it was, and I was an academic with more articles to write.

That stance seems even more irresponsible today than it was in the past. At least in the foreseeable future—and especially for the next four years—we cannot expect "broad social change" to improve the lives of our country's most vulnerable citizens; nor, as I have suggested, can we fairly expect those individuals to carry on the fight themselves. Hence, in what follows, I do not round up the (idealistic and unlikely) usual suspects, but instead I propose the practical and feasible. In doing so, I am guided by the step taken by the Women's Union when it suggested that its members find common ground with an organization promoting "economic justice and a livable wage" rather than one dedicated to welfare reform. In the era of work requirements and time limits, welfare recipients quickly become—and are likely to remain—low-wage workers.[3]

Although I am guided by the movement of the Women's Union toward the Peace and Justice Center's mission, I do not mean to say that we should cease to struggle against increased work requirements, against the presumption that marriage and responsible fatherhood will solve the problems of poor, single mothers, or, for that matter, against any cutbacks in services (especially child care) that may result from TANF reauthorization. At the same time, those with an interest in "welfare"—such as the scholars writing the essays in this collection, and the audience reading them—must recognize that in an era when welfare reliance so rapidly transmutes into life *without* welfare, we should focus on securing economic stability, benefits, and the right to care for dependants for those who make that transition from state support to "personal responsibility." The modest proposals that follow focus largely on existing state policies (in Vermont and elsewhere) that could be adopted more broadly and that could serve as national models if the federal government were to become more congenial to reform.

Economic Security and Benefits

Above all, we need to find ways to put money into the pockets of low-wage workers. Directly we can fight for a higher minimum wage; Vermont and five other states have raised the minimum wage to at least $7.00 an hour (U.S. Department of Labor, 2004). We can also lend our voices and energies to "living wage" campaigns in our states, cities, towns, and workplaces.

The tax system can also be used to provide another, albeit less direct, way to secure a more stable income for low-wage workers. The federal Earned Income Tax Credit is evidence of the tax system's potential, as it has proven to be an effective measure for lifting people out of poverty. Sixteen states (Vermont included) offer an earned income tax credit based on the federal credit, and twelve states (Vermont again included) make this credit refundable (National Center for Children in Poverty, 2004). This model could be adopted elsewhere.

The Child Tax Credit is not without flaws, but it, too, shows the tax system's potential. During the 2004 debates, President George W. Bush boasted about having increased the Child Tax Credit: "If you have a child, you got a $1,000 child credit. That's money in your pocket" (Commission on Presidential Debates, 2004). Clearly this is a goal he supports. Bush failed to mention, however, that because the arrangements he authorized do not accelerate the increase in the credit's refundability percentage, a single head of household with two children and an income level between $10,500 and $19,325 will not receive any benefit from the increase (Lee & Greenstein, 2003). There is no reason why this could not be rectified to benefit parents burdened with the lowest incomes and greatest need.

The often debilitating expenses of child care and transportation could also be reduced through refundable credits, thus relieving families of the burden of supporting their own employment. Twenty-seven states offer a Child and Dependent Care Tax Credit; thirteen make that credit refundable for varying amounts and at varying income levels. Other states could be urged to do the same so that families with no income tax liability also benefit through a kind of "negative" income tax (Maag, 2003). Similarly, we could recommend a tax credit for the expenses of transportation that enables employment. This is especially vital in rural areas where the costs of transportation can run to as much as 22 percent of a "real" self-sufficiency budget (Vermont State Legislature, 1999).

An associated line of struggle involves securing needed benefits. Vermont's model here is not perfect, but Vermont *is* among those states that provide extensions to Medicaid both to adults (up to 150 percent of the federal poverty level) and to pregnant women and to children under eighteen (up to 300 percent of the federal poverty level). As a result, in Vermont a smaller percentage of adults and children are left uninsured than is the case for the country as a whole (Henry Kaiser Family Foundation, 2004).

The Right to Care

Putting money into the hands of low-income families and protecting their benefits does not, however, respond to the care needs that were assured by earlier state and federal welfare policies. Securing the rights of family members to care for their young children by themselves may well be the hardest uphill battle, especially now that the vast majority of all mothers are employed outside the home and many (including many feminists) believe that steady employment is vital for the protection of women's long-term interests (Bergmann, 2004). In this context, we might consider excluding from the work requirements of TANF those with the greatest caregiving needs, such as the parents of disabled children (Litt, 2004) and the mothers of infants. With respect to the latter, it might be possible to make the twelve weeks ensured by the 1993 Family and Medical Leave Act an exclusion from the sixty-month lifetime TANF limits. This would protect welfare-reliant women from having to sacrifice that period of care for their future economic security, Alternatively, California's paid parental leave could by adopted by other states (Milkman & Appelbaum, 2004).

A MORE ACTIVE ENGAGEMENT

Activist scholars can become involved in the political fight for these kinds of policies at the state and local level. But we cannot simply stop with their creation. The "take-up" rate for most existing programs is very modest.[4] Although almost 90 percent of eligible taxpayers claim the EITC, many of those pay a portion of their refunds to commercial tax preparers. Even more problematic is the fact that considerably smaller proportions of those eligible take advantage of *other* means-tested programs, such as the State Children's Health Insurance Program (between 8 and 14 percent of those newly eligible), Food Stamps (between 54 and 66 percent of those eligible), the Women, Infants and Children Program (57 percent of those eligible), and Child Care Subsidies (40 percent of those eligible) (Currie, 2003). In California, a large survey found that less than a quarter of respondents were aware of the state's recently legislated program for paid family and medical leave, and that the "lowest level of awareness was found among precisely those groups who are least likely to have access to employer-provided paid leave" (Milkman & Appelbaum, 2004). Academics could use their already-developed skills to draw up and distribute easy-to-understand information sheets and to provide direct assistance to those needing help gain access to existing programs (e.g., free information sessions at local day care centers and public schools).

In addition, we could transform our own ongoing activities into occasions of incremental change. We could refuse to participate in community events (including parent-teacher conferences and "back-to-school" nights) that don't provide child care and transportation—or we could organize the provision of those services ourselves. When we raise money for nonprofit organizations working in the interests of low-income women or families, we could ensure that the fundraising mechanism itself does "good" at the same time. Instead of gathering sponsors for a 5K race, ask to be sponsored on a work team that would contribute time and skills to make minor home repairs for a family in need, to change the oil in the car of a single mother, or to plant and maintain a row of vegetables in a community garden.

At the very least we can clean up our rhetoric. We could refuse to call the PRWORA welfare "reform" and instead reserve that appellation for modifications that definitively and significantly improve the lives of our most vulnerable citizens. We could also reject the federal poverty level as a standard of need, and instead make a more realistic absolute standard (e.g., a self-sufficiency budget) or an appropriate relative standard (e.g., half the median after-tax income) the one we use in our research (Rainwater & Smeeding, 2003). In that way we would identify the vulnerable population more broadly, inclusively, and accurately.

None of the ideas suggested here would bring about the broad social change that many of us expected in the past, nor would they bring back the "paltry" security of the erstwhile AFDC program. But until more significant change is forthcoming, we can remain in our ivory towers and bemoan the past (and the most recent election), or we can work for modest change where it is likely to matter the most. The choice is ours.

NOTES

1. All quotes are from interviews conducted by the author. For a fuller description of research methods see Nelson (2002a).

2. For a description of how Vermont's welfare restructuring was introduced, see Nelson (2002b).

3. In this respect, Vermont is no different from the rest of the country. The Manpower Demonstration Research Corporation reported that the majority of the single mothers making the transition to employment worked in jobs which paid hourly wages of less than $7.50/hour and in jobs which rarely carried significant benefits of sick leave, vacations, and health insurance (Scrivener et al., 2002) at a time when the Vermont legislature estimated that at a minimum a single mother of two children (without health insurance) would need to earn more than three times that amount ($23.67) to make ends meet in an "urban area" of Vermont (Vermont State Legislature, 1999).

4. For an argument that the low take-up rates are intended in order to keep government costs low, see Danziger (2003).

REFERENCES

Administration for Children and Families. (2004). *ACF News: Statistics: Change in TANF Caseloads.* Retrieved December 31, 2004, from U.S. Department of Health and Human Services: <http://www.acf.dhhs.gov/news/stats/caseload.htm>.

Bergmann, B. R. (2004, July). What Policies Toward Lone Mothers Should We Aim For? *Feminist Economics, 10*(2), 240-245.

Bricker-Jenkins, M., & Brookland, B. (2002, September-October). Activists Take on Welfare Reform: Two Views. *Dollars & Sense,* 16-23.

Commission on Presidential Debates. (2004). Debate Transcript: The Second Bush-Kerry Presidential Debate. Retrieved from <http://www.debates.org/pages/trans2004c.html>.

Currie, J. (2003, December 12-13). The Take Up of Social Benefits. Berkeley Program on Housing and Urban Policy, University of California, Berkeley: Berkeley Symposium on Poverty, The Distribution of Income, and Public Policy. Accessed December 17, 2004, from <http://urbanpolicy.berkeley.edu/pdf/Ch3Currie0604.pdf>.

Danziger, S. (2003, December 12-13). Commentary on Janet Currie, The Take-Up of Social Benefits. Berkeley Program on Housing and Urban Policy, University of California, Berkeley: Berkeley Symposium on Poverty, The Distribution of Income, and Public Policy. Accessed December 17, 2004, from <http://urbanpolicy.berkeley.edu/pdf/Ch3CommDanzingeronCurrie.pdf>.

Funiciello, T. (1998). National Welfare Rights Organizations. In *The Reader's Companion to U.S. Women's History.* Retrieved December 18, 2004, from Houghton Mifflin: <http://colege.hmco.com/history/readerscomp/women/html/wh_026000_nationalwelf.htm>.

Hays, S. (2003). *Flat Broke with Children: Women in the Age of Welfare Reform.* Oxford: Oxford University Press.

Henry Kaiser Family Foundation. (2004). *Vermont: Health Coverage & Uninsured.* Retrieved November 11, 2004, from Henry Kaiser Family Foundation: <http://www.statehealthfacts.kff.org>.

Lee, A., & Greenstein, R. (2003, May 29). *How the New Tax Law Alters the Child Tax Credit and How Low-Income Families Are Affected.* Retrieved December 22, 2004, from <www.cbpp.org/5-28-03tax3.htm>.

Litt, J. (2004, October). Women's Carework in Low-Income Households: The Special Case of Children with Attention Deficit Hyperactivity Disorder. *Gender & Society, 18*(5), 625-644.

Maag, E. (2003, October 27). Recent Expansions to the Child and Dependant Care Tax Credit. In *Tax Notes.* Retrieved December 22, 2004, from http://<www.taxpolicycenter.org/taxfacts>.

McCrate, E., & Smith, J. (1998, February). When Work Doesn't Work: The Failure of Current Welfare Reform. *Gender and Society, 12*(1), 61-80.

Milkman, R., & Appelbaum, E. (2004). Paid Family Leave in California: New Research Findings. *The State of California Labor 2004* (1), 45-67.

National Center for Children in Poverty. (2004). *State Earned Income Tax Credit (EITC).* Retrieved December 28, 2004, from NCCP: <http://nccp.org/policy_index_8.html>.

Nelson, M. K. (2002a). The Commitment to Self Sufficiency: Rural Single Mothers Talk about Their Reliance on Welfare. *Journal of Contemporary Ethnography, 31*(5), 582-614.

Nelson, M. K. (2002b). Declaring Welfare "Reform" A Success: The Role of Applied Social Science. *Journal of Poverty, 63*(3), 1-27.

Peace and Justice Center. (2004). Retrieved December 10, 2004, from <http://www.pjcvt.org/center.htm>.

Rainwater, L., & Smeeding, T. M. (2003). *Poor Kids in a Rich Country: America's Children in Comparative Perspective.* New York: Russell Sage Foundation.

Scrivener, S., Hendra, R., Redcross, C., Bloom, D., Michalopoulos, C., & Walter, J. (2002, September). *WRP: Final Report on Vermont's Welfare Restructuring Project* (Manpower Demonstration Research Corporation). New York: Manpower Demonstration Research Corporation.

Sen, R. (1999). Grassroots Forces Gather for Impending Welfare Battle. *Colorlines: Race, Action, Culture, 1*, 22-23.

U.S. Department of Labor. (2004). *Minimum Wage Laws in the States.* Retrieved December 13, 2004, from <http://www.dol.gov/esa/minwage/america.htm>.

Vermont State Legislature, Livable Income Study Committee. (1999). *Act 21 Research and Analysis in Support of the Livable Income Study Committee,* by Kavet, T., Brighton, D., Hoffer, D., & McCrate, E. Montpelier, VT.

Chapter 6

Welfare Reform and the Transformation of the U.S. Welfare State

Michael Reisch

INTRODUCTION: THE ROOTS OF CONTEMPORARY WELFARE REFORM

For most of the nineteenth and twentieth centuries, public policy-making in the United States rested on several assumptions about the relationship between the state and social welfare. First, for the foreseeable future, industrialization and its consequences would lead to a gradual expansion of government's role in the economy and society in order to address what Titmuss (1969) called the "diswelfare" it produced. Second, that the creation of publicly funded social welfare systems would reduce the excesses and ameliorate the negative effects of a market-oriented economy by collectivizing what Kapp (1971) referred to as the "social costs of private enterprise." Third, that the expansion of state-sponsored welfare would sustain the legitimacy of government at all levels and expand the rights of citizenship. Fourth, that social welfare systems would operate within national boundaries; that is, that both the problems they addressed and the policy solutions they proposed would be constrained by finite political and economic borders. Finally, that the evolution of the welfare state would enhance the role of professionals within it and, ideally, improve the relationships of these professionals with their clients (Axinn & Stern, 2005; Jansson, 2001; Patterson, 2001; Young, 1999).

Developments during the past thirty years, however, have produced a new political-economic reality and challenged many of these prevailing assumptions. The pressures of economic globalization within a world system in which market values are ascendant have transformed the underlying values, goals, and consequences of welfare provision.

doi:10.1300/5608_07

69

This is best illustrated by the impact of the 1996 Personal Responsibility and Work Opportunity Reconciliation Act (PRWORA), better known as welfare reform. This chapter will discuss (1) how globalization has revealed the anachronistic nature of twenty-first century political institutions in terms of their ability to ameliorate the effects of market economies; (2) that although contemporary welfare policies bear some resemblance to prior reform efforts, the 1996 legislation symbolized a dramatic shift in the role of government precisely because it emerged in the context of a globalizing world economy; and (3) that the changes produced by PRWORA have altered some of the fundamental characteristics of the U.S. welfare state, particularly the role of nonprofit organizations, with significant effects on their staff, clients, and interorganizational relations.

AMERICAN "EXCEPTIONALISM"

It is widely accepted that the U.S. welfare state evolved quite differently from those of other industrialized nations (Midgley, 1997; Karger & Stoesz, 2002; Chatterjee, 1996). Pragmatic, rather than ideological in origin, it relied less on the national government and more on the private sector than its European counterparts (Gilbert & Gilbert, 1989). Its goals were also far more limited and, consequently, in contrast to Western European nations, the United States never forged a national network of services or a fully integrated income maintenance (i.e., welfare) system. In fact, welfare in the United States became a primary vehicle for maintaining racial, gender, and class hierarchies and divisions, and, in recent decades, often served as an effective proxy for less politically acceptable labels (Reisch, 2005; Quadagno, 1996; Schram, Soss, & Fording, 2003).

Throughout U.S. history, social welfare policies have focused primarily on the problem of poverty, rather than inequality. One consequence of this narrow focus was that, even after the modest reforms of the New Deal and the War on Poverty, the United States lagged considerably behind other Western nations in its degree of social provision. This so-called American exceptionalism has been explained in several ways: ideologically, as a consequence of the nation's Calvinist roots and resultant emphasis on individualism; politically, as a result of the absence of working-class, left-wing political parties to advocate for social democratic or socialist alternatives; demographically, as a means of stigmatizing certain populations, particularly people of color and, thereby, rationalizing institutional racism and sexism and their effects; and, culturally, as a way to reinforce hegemonic values and prevailing hierarchies (Rank, 2004; Abramovitz, 1998; Lieberman, 1998).

Another consequence of this approach to social welfare is that since low-income groups lack power in U.S. society, they have always borne the brunt of the social costs of growth and change. Yet, the normative structure of the U.S. welfare state has exacerbated the problems these groups experienced through its emphasis on work over income maintenance, its preference for marketplace solutions, and its distrust of an activist state. Rationales for these approaches have appeared in both moral and pseudoscientific forms since the eighteenth century (Schram, 1995; Gordon, 1994; Jansson, 2001).

During the past quarter century, several macrolevel developments have reinforced and intensified these tendencies. These include a marked increase in income and asset inequality; the strengthening of capital's power over labor; the growing insecurity of employment among all classes; the declining social character of work; the destabilization of communities; and the decline in the public's faith in government's ability to address these issues. The nation's policy responses to these developments, particularly the contraction of social welfare benefits and the spread of regressive modes of taxation, have further undermined public confidence in the state's potential to develop and implement ameliorative policy solutions.

RACE AND WELFARE REFORM

For many years, race has played a significant role in the development of welfare policies in the United States (Schram, Soss, & Fording, 2003; Brown, 1999; Lieberman, 1998; Thompson, 1998; Quadagno, 1996; Gordon, 1994). Even during periods of social reform, such as the 1930s and 1960s, persons of color faced discrimination in the application of eligibility standards and the distribution of social benefits; they also suffered the effects of white backlash against the modest gains they received (Quadagno, 1996; Axinn & Stern, 2005). Over the past forty years, significant changes in welfare policies—including the introduction of work requirements in the late 1960s and early 1970s and the contraction or elimination of a broad range of supportive services—have had dramatic consequences for persons of color (Schiele, 1998; Abramovitz, 1998). The perpetuation of racial stereotypes in the mass media and the use of racial codes for partisan political purposes further reduced public support for welfare programs as a whole. In the period leading up to the passage of PRWORA, social welfare came to be equated with handouts for racial minorities (DeParle, 2004; Edsall & Edsall, 1991; Clawson & Trice, 2000). As a result, racial stereotyping played a major role in shaping public opinion about the purposes and goals of welfare reform (Schram, Soss, & Fording, 2003; Reisch, 2003).

ANTIWELFARE IDEOLOGY

For decades, the goal of redefining the social contract at the heart of welfare reform was abetted by a resurgent antiwelfare ideology as reflected in the debates that preceded the passage of PRWORA in 1996. Proponents of welfare reform inflated the costs of welfare programs and focused on a minority of AFDC recipients—African-American adolescent mothers—to promote the myth of welfare failure (Schiele, 1998; Zucchino, 1997; Quadagno, 1996). In creating a wedge issue based on symbolic appeals to racial and gender bias, antiwelfare propagandists deliberately undermined the foundations of the U.S. welfare system itself. Many of the myths disseminated as analysis at the height of the welfare reform debate not only distorted data on welfare participation and benefit levels but also deliberately misled the public about the nature of dependency in modern industrial society (Patterson, 2001). From an ideological standpoint, therefore, welfare reform can best be understood as the spearhead of a broader campaign to reduce government's role in addressing the problems generated or overlooked by economic globalization (Deacon, 1999; Prigoff, 2001). In sum, the rhetoric underlying welfare reform contradicts the realities of modern life (Gil, 1998).

THE IMPACT OF WELFARE REFORM

Most research on the impact of PRWORA has focused on the extent to which Temporary Assistance for Needy Families (TANF) recipients have made a successful transition from welfare to work (DeParle, 2004).

Measured solely in these terms, welfare reform has been a considerable success. The nation's welfare caseload has dropped over 50 percent and, in some states such as Michigan, caseloads have decreased nearly 70 percent (U.S. Department of Health and Human Services, 2004). Yet, these indicators of success mask two other consequences of PRWORA: the increasing concentration of TANF recipients in urban areas and the conversion of longstanding racial stereotypes about welfare recipients into contemporary statistical reality.

In addition, amid the proclamations about the success of welfare reform, relatively little attention has been paid to its impact on the living standards of low-income households, the quality of life in low-income neighborhoods, or the availability of support services to these communities (Rank, 2004; DeParle, 2004). Yet, ample evidence demonstrates that welfare reform has intensified the economic and social problems confronting low-income neighborhoods, with particularly deleterious effects on populations who are most dependent on the services small, nonprofit, community-based organizations provide (Reisch & Bischoff, 2001; Abramovitz, 2002; Withorn, 1999). The reduction in caseloads appears to represent, therefore, a shift in emphasis and responsibility for needed social supports from the public to the nonprofit and private, for-profit sectors. Recent studies have also found that the dramatic decline in welfare caseloads does not provide an adequate measure of the consequences of welfare reform, particularly when they are placed in the context of the overall effect of the legislation on the availability of essential services and the capacity of community-based organizations to deliver them (Reisch & Sommerfeld, 2001; Abramovitz, 2002).

THE U.S. WORKFARE REGIME

Political-economic theorists such as Jessop (2002) have described the emergence of the neoliberal workfare regime as the successor to the Keynesian-style welfare state that first appeared in the 1930s. So-called post-Fordist theorists focus on the role played by welfare provision in balancing patterns of production and social demand. In other words, in a globalizing world economy the classic pattern of accumulation and growth in industrial societies results from both social and economic regulation.

This has produced significant alterations in the institutional fabric of welfare states to prepare recipients for "the pursuit of a competitive edge in a global economy" (Jessop, 1999, p. 353). Once conceived as a component of the rights of citizenship, the receipt of welfare has been reshaped into a means to enhance corporate rather than individual well-being (McDonald, Harris, & Winterstein, 2003).

In this light, it is clear that PRWORA significantly changed the structure and substance of the U.S. welfare state. It completed a generation-long process of devolving responsibility for public assistance to the states, eliminated the half-century old concept of entitlement for low-income children and families, and brought to fruition the long-standing preference of U.S. policymakers for work as the primary means of income support for the poor. By expanding, even mandating the role of the private sector and, most notably, religious organizations in policy implementation and service provision, it made their role critical to the legislation's definition of "success." Researchers in numerous U.S. cities have determined, however, that the underlying assumptions of PRWORA have not been validated by events since its passage. Although welfare reform—combined with a period of relative economic prosperity in the late 1990s—dramatically reduced caseloads (the official benchmark of success), it also produced substantial changes in the client populations served by community-based organizations and the character and mission of the agencies upon which low-income people were increasingly dependent (Abramovitz, 2002; Alexander, Nank, & Stivers, 1999; Reisch & Bischoff, 2001; Carnochan & Austin, 1999; DiPadova, 2000; Fink & Widom, 2001; Withorn, 1999).

As a result, since the 1990s, the intersectoral relationships in the U.S. welfare state most closely conform to what Young (1999) termed the "supplementary perspective"—i.e., private organizations have become the "support of last resort," providing goods and services that the state has eliminated or significantly reduced. This development raises two critical questions for policymakers, service providers, and scholars: To what extent can the private sector, particularly small, community-based nonprofit organizations, replace the state in terms of financing or service provision? And, what would be the consequences of this shift in the locus of social welfare responsibility for low-income families, those who assist them, and the private sector as a whole (Reisch & Sommerfeld, 2003)?

To date, researchers have answered these questions largely in pessimistic terms. Welfare reform has encouraged the spread of market mechanisms in the nonprofit sector with deleterious effects on agencies' mission, culture, values, and norms of employment. The combination of privatization and devolution has forced these agencies to take on responsibilities that they lack the resources and, in many cases, the capacity to bear. The transformation of the U.S. welfare state has also heightened intra- and interorganizational conflicts and produced recurring ethical dilemmas around such issues as confidentiality, informed consent, client self-determination, and divided professional loyalties (Alexander, 1999; Abramovitz, 2002; Reisch, 2003).

The implementation of PRWORA and its potential expansion in the near future represents a significant and complex challenge to the limited U.S. social safety net, one which jeopardizes the historically delicate framework of complementary, supplementary, and adversarial relationships between the public and nonprofit sectors (Young, 1999). Particularly since the 1960s, this relationship has shaped the size and direction of government funding, the distribution of sectoral responsibilities, and the balance of power around social welfare issues. Research by the author and other scholars found that welfare reform has increased the emphasis on the supplemental function of nonprofit organizations in ways that are both undesirable and potentially harmful (Reisch & Sommerfeld, 2003; Abramovitz, 2002; DeParle, 2004; Withorn, 1999).

WELFARE REFORM AND ECONOMIC GLOBALIZATION

The relationship between welfare reform and the transformation of the global economy began in the early 1970s and is linked to such phenomena as deindustrialization, technological innovations, class and racially based gaps in education, foreign competition and trade imbalances, and the decline of unions (Reisch & Gorin, 2000). It is also connected to the reorganization of work, particularly what Head (1996) termed "lean production," with the dual goals of expanding productivity and reducing labor costs. In this context, welfare reform served several interrelated purposes.

First, it helps to drive down the wage scale by increasing competition for unskilled jobs. Second, it strengthens the drive for greater workforce discipline and compliance, particularly in the service sector of the economy. Third, it promotes a general reduction in the role of government which has significant implications beyond the social welfare arena, in such areas as trade, banking, and environmental regulations. Finally, by calling into question the legitimacy of welfare entitlements and government's effectiveness in administering social programs, it created an enormous opportunity for the private sector to acquire new and vast resources of capital—the Social Security Trust Funds—as the recent political offensive by the Bush Administration to privatize Social Security demonstrates.

WELFARE STATE TRANSFORMATION AND THE NATURE OF SOCIAL WORK

The forces that are transforming the U.S. welfare state have also influenced the nature of the professions within it, particularly the character and purpose of social work. In the United States, social workers in both public and nonprofit organizations have wrestled with the contradictions between their self-proclaimed ethical imperative to work for social justice and their need for elite support. To some extent, U.S. social workers are reaping the consequences of a problem they helped create. Many of their long-standing criticisms of the nation's welfare system were appropriated by conservatives to justify welfare reform. During the past decade, their failure to proffer a viable alternative to PRWORA or its antecedents put the social work profession in the ironic position of defending the policies and programs it had fiercely criticized for nearly half a century. This contributed substantially to the marginalization of social workers from the major policy debates of the 1990s, a condition that persists today (McDonald, Reisch, & Chenoweth, 2004).

CONCLUSION: THE WORKFARE REGIME AND POWER

The ideological basis of PRWORA created a peculiar contradiction between its emphasis on individualism and self-sufficiency and the chronic dependency of TANF recipients and those who purport to assist them on external political factors largely beyond their control.

Ironically, in the new regime, independence is defined as acquiescence to the values and goals of neoliberal institutional forces, whose center of power has shifted from the state to the corporate sector. One consequence is the increasing depersonalization of the relationships between individuals and institutions. This reflects both the growing power imbalance in all sectors of U.S. society and the increasing privatization of social life. Another consequence appears in the changing functions of social work interventions: from personal maintenance to behavior modification; from long-term stability to short-term outcomes; and from voluntary to compulsory participation in the welfare system's rules.

Several factors contribute to the powerlessness of clients and workers in the transformed welfare state. First, critical resources are increasingly controlled by forces outside the reach of their organizations. These forces, which possess a monopoly of strategic resources, are guided by fundamentally different premises about the purpose and nature of welfare systems. Second, the principal actors within the welfare system, including many policymakers, have scant influence over decisions regarding environmental uncertainties. Finally, these actors often cannot even anticipate what these decisions will be. This produces an interesting paradox in which change can occur only through structural challenges to the hegemonic regime, yet those who promote change must operate from a situation of resource, power, and information deficiency. How this paradox will be resolved will have profound implications for our entire society, not merely for those who rely for their survival on its begrudging compassion.

REFERENCES

Abramovitz, M. (1998). *Regulating the lives of women: Social welfare policy from colonial times to the present* (2nd ed.). Boston: South End Press.

Abramovitz, M. (2002). *In jeopardy: The impact of welfare reform on nonprofit human service agencies in New York City.* New York: United Way of America.

Alexander, J. (1999). The impact of devolution on nonprofits: A multiphase study of social service organizations. *Nonprofit Management and Leadership 10*(1), 57-70.

Alexander, J., Nank, R., & Stivers, C. (1999). Implications of welfare reform: Do nonprofit survival strategies threaten civil society? *Nonprofit and Voluntary Sector Quarterly 26*(4), 452-475.

Axinn, J., & Stern, M. (2005). *Social welfare: A history of the American response to need* (6th ed.). Boston: Allyn and Bacon.

Brown, M. (1999). *Race, money, and the American welfare state.* Ithaca, NY: Cornell University Press.

Carnochan, S., and Austin, M. (1999). *Implementing welfare reform and guiding organizational change.* Berkeley, CA: Bay Area Social Services Consortium.

Chatterjee, P. K. (1996). *Approaches to the welfare state.* Washington, DC: NASW Press.

Clawson, R., & Trice, R. (2000). Poverty as we know it: Media portrayals of the poor. *Public Opinion Quarterly 64*(4), 53-64.

Deacon, B. (1999, January). *Towards a socially responsible globalization: International actors and discourses.* GASPP Occasional Papers, Helsinki, Finland.

DeParle, J. (2004). *American dream: Three women, ten kids, and a nation's drive to end welfare.* New York: Viking Press.

DiPadova, L. (2000). *Utah's charitable organizations face welfare reform: Concerns of charitable leaders.* Salt Lake City, UT: Center for Public Policy and Administration.

Edsall, T., & Edsall, M. (1991). *Chain reaction: The impact of race, rights, and taxes on American politics.* New York: Norton.

Fink, B., & Widom, R. (2001). *Social service organizations and welfare reform.* New York: Manpower Demonstration Research Organization.

Gil, D. (1998). *Confronting injustice and oppression: Concepts and strategies for social workers.* New York: Columbia University Press.

Gilbert, N., & Gilbert, B. (1989). *The enabling state: Modern welfare capitalism in America.* New York: Oxford University Press.

Gordon, L. (1994). *Pitied but not entitled: Single mothers and the history of welfare, 1890-1935.* New York: Free Press.

Head, S. (1996, February 29). The new ruthless economy. *The New York Review of Books 43*, 47-52.

Jansson, B. (2001). *The reluctant welfare state* (4th ed.). Pacific Grove, CA: Brooks/Cole.

Jessop, B. (1999). The change governance of welfare: Recent trends in its primary functions, scale, and modes of coordination. *Social Policy & Administration 33*, 348-359.

Jessop, B. (2002). *The future of the capitalist state.* Cambridge, UK: Polity Press.

Kapp, K.W. (1971). *The social costs of private enterprise.* New York: Schocken.

Karger, H. J., & Stoesz, D. (2002). *American social welfare policy: A pluralist approach* (4th ed.). Boston: Allyn & Bacon.

Lieberman, R. (1998). *Shifting the color line: Race and the American welfare state.* Cambridge, MA: Harvard University Press.

McDonald, C., Harris, J., & Winterstein, R. (2003). Contingent on context? Social work in Australia, Britain, and the USA. *British Journal of Social Work 33*, 191-208.

McDonald, C., Reisch, M., & Chenoweth, L. (2004, October). Social work in the workfare regime: Australia and the USA. Paper presented at the Global Social Work 2004 Conference, Adelaide, Australia.

Midgley, J. (1997). *Social welfare in global context*. Thousand Oaks, CA: Sage Publications.

Patterson, J. (2001). *America's struggle against poverty in the 20th century*. Cambridge, MA: Harvard University Press.

Prigoff, A. (2001). *Economics for social workers: Social outcomes of economic globalization with strategies for community action*. Belmont, CA: Brooks/Cole.

Quadagno, J. (1996). Race and American social policy. *National Forum 76*(3), 35-59.

Rank, M.R. (2004). *One nation underprivileged: Why American poverty affects us all*. New York: Oxford University Press.

Reisch, M. (2003). Welfare reform, globalization, and the transformation of the welfare state. In M.R. Gonzalez (ed.), *Community organization and social policy: A compendium* (2nd ed.). San Juan, PR: Editorial Edil.

Reisch, M. (2005). American exceptionalism and critical social work: A retrospective and prospective analysis. In I. Ferguson, M. Lavalette, & E. Whitmore (eds.), *Globalisation, global justice and social work* (pp. 157-172). London: Routledge.

Reisch, M., & Bischoff, U. (2001). Welfare reform strategies and community-based organizations: The impact on family well-being in an urban neighborhood. In F.F. Piven, J. Acker, M. Hallock, & S. Morgen (eds.), *Welfare, work, and politics* (pp. 333-346). Eugene: University of Oregon Press.

Reisch, M., & Gorin, S. (2000). The nature of work and the future of the social work profession. *Social Work 46*(1), 9-19.

Reisch, M., & Sommerfeld, D. (2003, fall). Welfare reform and the future of nonprofit organizations. *Nonprofit Management and Leadership 14*(1), 19-46.

Schiele, J. (1998). The personal responsibility act of 1996: The bitter and the sweet for African American families. *Families in Society 79*(4), 424-432.

Schram, S.F. (1995). *Words of welfare: The poverty of social science and the social science of poverty*. Minneapolis: University of Minnesota Press.

Schram, S.F., Soss, J., & Fording, R.C. (eds.) (2003). *Race and the politics of welfare reform*. Ann Arbor: University of Michigan Press.

Thompson, P.J.I. (1998). Universalism and deconcentration: Why race still matters in poverty and economic development. *Politics and Society 26*(2), 181-219.

Titmuss, R. (ed.) (1969). *Essays on the welfare state*. Boston: Beacon Press.

U.S. Department of Health and Human Services (2004). *Change in TANF caseloads*. Washington, DC: Administration for Children and Families.

Withorn, A. (1999). *Worrying about welfare reform: Community-based agencies respond*. Boston: Boston Area Academics Working Group on Poverty.

Young, D. (1999). Complementary, supplementary, or adversarial? A theoretical and historical examination of nonprofit-government relations in the United States. In E. Boris & E. Steuerle (eds.), *Nonprofits and government: Collaboration and conflict* (pp. 31-67). Washington, DC: Urban Institute Press.

Zucchino, D. (1997). *The myth of the welfare queen.* New York: Scribners.

Chapter 7

Living Economic Restructuring at the Bottom: Welfare Restructuring and Low-Wage Work

Sandra Morgen
Joan Acker
Jill Weigt
Lisa Gonzales

While policymakers were busy celebrating the so-called success of welfare restructuring in the late 1990s, low-income families across the country were struggling to make ends meet, even when they were employed. Although there has been considerable recent political and media attention to, and concern about, the "jobless recovery" as an indicator of the changing U.S. economy, there has been remarkably little attention to what this means for the millions of poor families affected by welfare-to-work policies. The basic goal of welfare "reform" in the United States during the 1990s was to decrease TANF caseloads by promoting employment and self-sufficiency. The implication was that employment would enable families to escape from poverty.

The combination of a very strong economy in the mid-to-late 1990s and changes such as time-limited/work-first welfare programs, tax credits for low-income families, and an increase in the minimum wage *did* result in declining TANF caseloads and a growing proportion of poor and near-poor families who relied on wages for the bulk of a family's income. The consequences of changing welfare policies were tracked closely in the five years immediately following the policy changes. National- and state-level studies repeatedly found increased employment among low-income poor women; significant economic hardship and insecurity; persistent difficulties meeting the

© 2006 by The Haworth Press, Inc. All rights reserved.
doi:10.1300/5608_08

competing demands of employment and families; and significant need for supplements to earned income, including the Earned Income Tax Credit, food stamps, Medicaid and SCHIP, housing subsidies, and other public and private programs.

A very significant proportion of people who left welfare after 1996 remained poor, whether employed or not. Those who found full-time jobs had lower poverty rates than those who left or were forced off welfare due to time limits or other rules before finding jobs. But even families with incomes above the poverty line faced considerable economic hardship. At the heart of the problem facing the vast majority of ex-welfare recipients who found jobs is a simple fact: most found only low-wage jobs. Many people believe that individual attributes (lack of skill, limited education or job experience, poor work attitudes) of particular workers explains their consignment to low-wage jobs. Although this may sometimes be true, the main reason most ex-welfare recipients landed low-wage jobs was these were the available jobs. The low-wage service sector is the fastest growing sector of the labor market today (Mishel, Bernstein, & Boushey, 2003, p. 178).

Low-wage jobs promote poverty and economic insecurity for employees and families dependent on this work because they pay much less than a living wage and, typically, don't provide health coverage or pensions to employees. As Beth Shulman (2003) argues in a recent book, what makes a low-wage job a bad job is not *just* the content of the work but the poor pay and lack of employer-provided benefits. But when policymakers wonder why so many hard-working families can't make ends meet, or why rates of food insecurity have soared, or why an illness can lead to spiraling debt, they rarely point their finger at the obvious culprits—employers who pay low wages. While poor women endure scrutiny from welfare caseworkers, politicians, and the media, employers are rarely subjected to similar public attention or derision. Here we turn *our* attention to the jobs the poor are obliged to take both in boom and weak labor markets.

We argue that welfare-to-work restructuring has not and cannot succeed in eliminating poverty or assuring self-sufficiency as long as the vast majority of available jobs are "bad" jobs. We first look at the extent of the "bad jobs" problem, discussing different approaches to estimating its size, including the official poverty measure, the alternative family budget approaches, and estimates of the proportions of good jobs and bad jobs in the economy. Next, using data from our study of welfare leavers in Oregon (Acker and Morgen, 2001), we take a closer look at the experience of ex-welfare clients who had such jobs during the mid-to-late 1990s in the wake of welfare "reform." We then examine what has happened since the 2001 recession and the ensueing "jobless recovery." Finally, we conclude with some policy suggestions.

WHAT IS A GOOD JOB?
MEASURING POVERTY AND GOOD JOBS/BAD JOBS

To assess the likelihood that a work-first welfare reform policy will meet antipoverty goals, it is important to examine whether the available jobs pay enough to lift a family out of poverty and provide sufficient benefits to promote a modicum of economic security. We suggest that the key measures currently used to quantify economic well-being, which can be used as a proxy indicator of the availability of good jobs, especially the official poverty level, are inadequate. These measures fail to adequately inform policymakers and the public of the extent of economic hardship facing millions of women, men, and children in this country today. The official poverty measure, formulated in the 1960s, has been adjusted for inflation over the years but has never been revised to reflect the changing expenditure patterns of families.[1] A number of researchers have been working for some time on alternative measures of poverty that more accurately reflect family needs today (for example, Pearce, 2003; Northwest Policy Center, 2001; Bernstein, Brocht, & Spade-Aguilar, 2000). They have put together low-cost but adequate family budgets for different states and localities that include, among other expenses, local housing costs, costs of day care, medical insurance, and small savings for emergencies. These studies show reasonable family budgets that are about twice the official poverty measure. Increasingly researchers are using the "twice poverty rate" (those with incomes below 200 percent of the poverty line) as a measure of "low income."[2] Using this measure, more than 9.2 million families in the United States were low income in 2002, 27.4 percent of all working families, and a shocking 40 percent of working families of color (Waldron, Roberts, & Reamer, 2004). In comparison, using the official measure, the poverty rate was 12.2 percent in 2002 for prime-age (household head age 25 to 54) families with children (Mishel, Bernstein, & Allegretto, 2005). Over one-third of these prime-age families had incomes under twice the poverty line (Mishel, Bernstein, & Allegretto, 2005). This was not due to lack of work effort. Almost three-fourths of these families nationally had at least one employed member, and the average annual "work effort" was 2,500 hours, equaling 1.2 full-time jobs (Waldron, Roberts, & Reamer, 2004).

In addition to low wages, low-wage jobs typically fail to provide basic employee benefits, the kind of benefits that middle- and high-income workers more often can count on. Sociologists Arne Kalleberg, Barbara Reskin, and Ken Hudson (2000) define a "bad job" as one that pays low wages and provides neither health insurance nor a retirement plan. They estimate that in 1995 14 percent of jobs had *all three* characteristics of bad jobs. If the proportion of jobs that are bad jobs today remained constant, that would mean that in the 2003 labor force of around 130 million, 18 million of these jobs are bad jobs.[3] Certain types of jobs, temporary, part-time, on-call, and temporary agency jobs, as well as self-employment, tend to be bad jobs. Even in the late 1990s, when the economy was booming, over 30 percent of U.S. workers were in these "contingent" or "nonstandard" jobs.[4] Researchers applying different criteria find varying percentages of "bad jobs" as a proportion of all jobs, but there is no doubt that a very significant number of jobs in today's labor market pay very low wages and provide no or minimal benefits. Poor women, especially those with young children, women of color, women with less than a college education, women in rural areas—all are more likely than others to hold these jobs. They, along with many others, have little chance of working their way out of poverty, even with full-time jobs.

JOBS, POVERTY, AND WELFARE REFORM IN OREGON

Data from our study of welfare restructuring in Oregon in the late 1990s allow a closer look at the specific jobs available to former welfare clients.[5] Oregon is in many ways a poster child for what welfare restructuring in a weak economy looks like and means for the families affected by it. The state has several dubious distinctions: having one of the highest TANF caseload declines in the country; the highest or second highest unemployment rate in the country most months of the past several years; and one of the highest rates of food insecurity among all states during the past several years. An analysis of our statewide random sample survey of families who left or were diverted from TANF and food stamps in 1998 (and followed for two years) documents the kinds of jobs that those who were employed had (type of job, wages, benefits, job tenure over two years, and the like).[6] Most were "bad jobs" based on the criteria of level of pay and levels and types of benefits offered, and this was at the height of the strongest economy Oregon had seen in a decade. These data enable us to make a strong argument about the limits of low-wage work as an antipoverty strategy and as a means of achieving self-sufficiency for individual families.

Respondents and their families, whom we studied from 1998 to 2000, struggled with very low incomes. How low is low? The "average" family in our study consisted of a single parent (most were women) and two children. The poverty threshold in 1999 for a family of three was a monthly income of $1,157. Sixty-five percent of our respondents had household earnings that were at or below the poverty line. However, as we have already suggested, the poverty line is artificially low, a fact that policymakers recognize given that many federal programs for the poor set eligibility at 150 percent, or even 185 percent, of the poverty line. Indeed, 86 percent of the families were at or below 150 percent of the poverty line and 94 percent of families were at or below 200 percent of the poverty line. If we compare the income data we gathered with the income that the Northwest Policy Center (2001) study has calculated to be a living wage (taking into account the amount a family would need to earn to meet their basic needs in Oregon), the picture looks worse still. A living wage calculated on the cost of living in Oregon in 1999 for a single parent with two children was $2,835 a month; 98 percent of our respondents' families fell at or below that amount.[7] And remember, this was during the economic boom and when Oregon had one of the highest minimum wage rates in the country.[8]

Where were respondents finding employment in Oregon? At the time of our second survey, the most frequent jobs reported by respondents included medical or health care aide, general office clerk, child care worker, general laborer, food service worker, and retail worker. Women more often reported employment in health or personal care work, general office work, child care, retail, and food service. Men more frequently reported employment in general labor, janitorial services, agricultural work, automobile repair, and heavy equipment operation. The jobs clients in our study were able to get were all in categories in which the median wage was below the living wage, as calculated in the North-west Policy Center (2001) study. How are these jobs contributing to the picture of economic insecurity illuminated by our study?

To answer that question, we devised a measure of "good jobs" based on these criteria: the job was full-time, paid a wage that can sustain a family, and provides workers with key benefits. More pre-cisely, we defined a good job as one that was at least thirty-five hours per week, had take-home earnings of $1,200 a month (about the pov-erty level for an adult and two children), had predictable shifts and sick leave, and offered some paid vacation and health insurance. Very few respondents' jobs met these minimal criteria, even two years after leaving or being diverted from public assistance: 13.8 percent of those who had been on and then left TANF had "good" jobs, 11.8 per-cent of individuals who had left the food stamp program had "good" jobs, and 4.3 percent of families who had applied for, but been diverted from, TANF had "good" jobs. Forty-eight percent of employed re-spondents had no health insurance, 59 percent had no paid sick leave, and 41 percent had no paid vacation. Hispanic respondents were the least likely to hold good jobs, and men were more likely than women to be in a good job.[9] Those very few respondents with an associate's or bachelor's degree (and even those with some college experience) were much more likely to hold good jobs.

In addition to the statewide random sample we surveyed over two years, our study included two in-depth face-to-face interviews with a subsample of 75 families. These interviews enable us to illustrate the rather bloodless discussions of poverty measures and criteria of bad jobs with the stories of some very live people who confront poverty and bad jobs in their daily lives. Our qualitative data demonstrate that the jobs that are available to most of the women leaving welfare have a tendency to ag-gravate and perpetuate poverty. Their shoddy remuneration, limited bene-fits, few opportunities for mobility, and constrained flexibility create con-ditions that wear away at women's chances for stability and opportunities over time. It was not unusual for these mothers to carry substantial debt, due to their low wages, the absence of comprehensive benefits, low benefit eligibility levels, and the expense of child care. Debt, in turn, constrained mothers in many additional ways. We found evidence of mothers who were unable or unwilling to take advantage of job opportunities because they could not afford or locate appropriate child care. They traded away better wages or benefits for the meager flexibility some employers offered. Given the structure of their jobs and responsibility for children, women frequently were unable to take advantage of educational opportunities. These situations frequently wrought conditions that fostered extreme stress and had very negative effects on mothers as well as their children.

Many of the women we interviewed provided evidence that low-wage jobs enabled neither self-sufficiency nor an escape from the grueling conditions of poverty. Even those with *above-poverty wages* faced considerable hardship for themselves and their families, as Teresa Pena's (a pseudonym) situation demonstrates. Pena was a certified nursing assistant (CNA) who earned $10.50 an hour which, when combined with her partner's part-time earnings, put her a few thousand dollars above the annual poverty line for a family of four. She worked 35.5 hours each week to support her two children and seriously ill partner but struggled to make ends meet. To save on child care costs, be available for her children during the day, and enable her partner to bring in additional money from odd jobs during the day, she worked a graveyard shift from 10 p.m. to 6 a.m. The family struggled financially over the four-year period in which we had contact with them.[10] Pena dealt frequently with collection agencies, being unable to pay rent, lacking money for food, and forgoing medical insurance because she made too much to qualify for the Oregon Health Plan and because she couldn't afford the premium for her employer-provided insurance. Consequently, the family became mired in medical debt. Four years after leaving welfare Pena's eldest child lost her monthly SSI check of $500. To compensate for this needed income, Pena had to work on an "on-call" basis, in addition to her usual hours, sometimes working double shifts. Her schedule fluctuated, leaving her with little time for her family and a drastically reduced sleep schedule. The family often turned to the local food bank and was considering applying for food stamps again. She characterized her financial picture as much worse than the year before, though they now purchased medical insurance and had curbed their medical debt.

Michelle Moran (also a pseudonym) is another example of a woman struggling to get by with low-wage work. She worked full-time at a factory in a job which, by the end of the study, increased in pay from $9 to $11 an hour. Her job offered medical benefits, paid leaves, and a schedule which allowed her to be available for her child when school let out. Despite earning more than most of the women we followed, she had trouble paying her bills (which included student loans from an abandoned attempt to combine college, parenting, and full-time work), was harassed by bill collectors, and had no resources for "extras" or savings. She felt unsafe in her apartment complex. Once her wages began to rise, she lost food stamps and the child care subsidies, undermining her economic security. "I think they are cutting people off too quick. . . . It seems like the minute you are on your feet you are slammed with all this stuff which just knocks you back." She lived alone with her eleven-year-old daughter in subsidized housing, until a miscalculation resulted in the loss of her subsidy. To make ends meet, Moran cut the only wiggle room in her budget—her daughter's before- and after-school care program. She had to leave her daughter alone in the mornings for a few hours, and she had to get herself to a neighbor's before school. In the afternoons, the neighbor kept an eye on the daughter while the daughter cared for the neighbor's small children. Moran worried about this arrangement and believed her daughter was missing out on the important activities the after-school program had offered.

For poor families such as these (and these two families had incomes *above* the official poverty line), employment did not mean poverty alleviation. Because the poverty line is so low, so unrealistic a measure of economic well-being or security, the stories we heard from many families above and below the official poverty line were very similar. The promotion of paid work as the route to self-sufficiency ignores the poverty-promoting qualities of low-wage work. The realities of low-wage work have only the most tenuous relationship to self-sufficiency, if by self-sufficiency we are referring to even a minimal level of economic security.

JOBS AND POVERTY IN THE ERA
OF GLOBALIZATION AND THE "JOBLESS RECOVERY"

In advance of the anticipated Congressional reauthorization of TANF five years after its enactment, most in-depth research on the program's effects on low-income families, including our own, was timed to produce documentation by 2000-2001. Most studies did not then extend through the 2001 recession and the ensuing "jobless recovery," the longest on record. But available data show that the supply of jobs began to grow only slightly in 2004, with almost all of the growth in service sector jobs (Economic Policy Institute, 2005). In addition, real wages declined for those in nonsupervisory positions (Economic Policy Institute, 2005). These realities of the labor market have had deleterious effects on job seekers, including many affected by welfare restructuring, and poverty and hardship have grown. Between 2000 and 2002 the official poverty rate rose .8 points and the twice-poverty rate rose 1.2 points, setting back important gains made from 1995-2000. In 2002 the official poverty rate was 12.1 percent and the twice-poverty rate was 30.5 percent (Mishel, Bernstein, & Allegretto, 2005). The poverty rate continued to rise in 2003 up to 12.5 percent (Center on Budget and Policy Priorities, 2004). By 2004, unemployment was still much higher than at the end of the 1990s. Despite the clear increase in need, the number of people who received TANF dropped almost 9 percent nationally between 2000 and 2003 (Center on Budget and Policy Priorities, 2004).

In Oregon in 2002 almost three of ten (29.5 percent) working families had incomes less than 200 percent of the poverty line (Waldron, Roberts, & Reamer, 2004) in a state with an official poverty rate that year of 11.7 percent. Not only did wages fall and unemployment rise for Oregonians, but the proportion of workers with employer-provided health insurance declined sharply, falling from 63 percent in the late 1990s to 60 percent by early 2002 (Leachman, 2004). Fewer than half of employees in low-wage firms were eligible for employer-provided health coverage in 2002, and because of rising premiums that have to be paid by the employee (the annual cost of which nearly doubled over the previous decade) some low-wage workers were forced to decline coverage even when it was offered as a benefit (Leachman, 2004). Far fewer families than before welfare restructuring received needed relief during the recession and jobless recovery. In 1991 the number of welfare recipients averaged 43 percent of the total number of unemployed in Oregon; in 2003 it was 12 percent of the number of unemployed (Leachman, 2004).

Low-income single mothers nationally have fared poorly in this difficult economic period, suffering extensive job losses, falling wages, rising economic hardship, and limited safety net assistance. According to the Economic Policy Institute (EPI) the real income of low-income single mothers fell 1.0 percent from 2000-2002 (Mishel, Bernstein, & Allegretto, 2005). A study of the private-sector industries where former welfare recipients were most highly concentrated, for example, found that since 2001 three of these eight industries experienced larger job losses than the private sector more generally (Boushey and Rosnick, 2004). Some groups of women have much higher unemployment than others, especially women of color and female heads of households. A report from the Institute for Women's Policy Research found that female heads of household saw their unemployment rate, which was 8.2 percent in September 2004, increase by almost half (44 percent) since their boom-time low of 5.7 percent (Hartman, Lovell, and Werschkul, 2004). Unemployment among black women and Latinos was significantly higher than for white women.

For those with jobs, wage growth has been slower than average for workers in the retail trade, food services and drinking places, temporary help, nursing and residential care, and child day care services than other private-sector industries; these are the industries where former welfare recipients are concentrated (Boushey and Rosnick, 2004). Moreover, the supply of good jobs has shrunk. As we mentioned earlier, data from the Census Bureau and Department of Labor show that in 2002, more than one in four working families earned incomes below 200 percent of the poverty line (Waldron, Roberts, & Reamer, 2004). Waldron, Roberts, and Reamer relate this directly to the pool of available jobs. They calculated the percentage of jobs paying below the poverty threshold for a family of four ($18,392/year, or $8.84/hour). One of five jobs in the United States fell below this line, ranging from a low of 7 percent in Alaska to a high of 36.3 percent in Arkansas; 14.8 percent of jobs in Oregon fell below this line (Waldron, Roberts, & Reamer, 2004).

In *The Miner's Canary,* Guinier and Torres (2002) argue that the racially marginalized in the United States today are like the canaries miners used to tell when the air in the mine was too toxic. They suggest that what is happening to the racially marginalized today "is the first sign of a danger that threatens us all" (p. 11). The same can be said for poor women in low-wage jobs. Their experiences reveal the poverty-producing effects of a labor market that offers a decreasing supply of good jobs and employees who, faced with shrinking alternatives for economic support other than these bad jobs, struggle mightily. Given the changes that global economic restructuring has had on the United States labor market and on workers, especially low-wage workers, it is critical that we refocus our attention on policies that both improve the stock of good jobs in the United States and ensure a stronger safety net for those who lose jobs, cannot find jobs, or toil in the low-wage labor market.

POLICY DIRECTIONS IN THE CONTEXT OF NEOLIBERALISM AND GLOBALIZATION

The restructuring of the economy poses historically specific challenges for public policy and civic-minded businesses. There *are* policy solutions that can raise the standard of living of the many, decrease economic inequality and polarization, boost the economic vitality of communities, and restore the promise of a decent quality of life to working people. We have tools to meet these objectives if our elected officials and captains of industry have the will, or if the people decide that *these* traditional values about work, family, and community should motivate public policy. We must begin by changing the way we measure poverty. Using the twice poverty level or the proportion of families with incomes below what has been determined to be a living wage in different localities give us a much more accurate picture of how many families are struggling to make ends meet. Given that about one in four working families in this country is low income based on the more realistic measure of the "twice-poverty rate," we need a stronger safety net that can catch families across the economic spectrum in times of need.

Ideally, economic, labor, and tax policies should work together to promote real economic development with incentives for employers to pay decent wages and provide retirement, health, and other critical benefits for the families of their employees. However, we have seen that incentives may be insufficient to foster the necessary changes. We can develop tax and regulatory mechanisms that oblige companies that fail to provide affordable health insurance to contribute to public retirement and health care programs. The experiences of other countries, especially in Europe, suggest that it might make better sense from the point of view of both economics and fairness to move away from the strategy of employer-provided health and retirement benefits entirely and develop or strengthen universal programs of health care and retirement coverage. Unfortunately, this is the reverse of current policy. When Bush pushes to privatize Social Security and enacts tax cuts that require huge cuts in vital health and other human services, he is not only putting the most disadvantaged families in great peril, but also weakening the very programs that promise the greatest degree of economic security to even moderate-income families.

In 1996 policymakers focused their regulatory powers on poor families, mandating that they comply with stringent work requirements, time-limiting welfare receipt, and, in some states, practicing social engineering by using incentives and punishments to modify the behavior of poor women. What if we applied similar strategies to low-wage employers? What if we set time limits on how long employers could pay low or even stagnant wages to employees without sanctions? What if low-wage employers had to attend workshops about, and then change practices and policies that undermine the well-being of their employees' families? What if low-wage employers were taxed above and beyond their current tax rates for every employee to whom they did *not* provide decent health care coverage or contribute toward a pension? What if employers were accountable to a fair social contract between employers and employees to share the rewards of economic productivity more equitably among workers, managers, and owners?

We need policies that promote living wages *and* those that strengthen the safety net for families and individuals in need. Policies such as increasing the minimum wage, with increases not dependent on which party controls Congress, but instead with automatic cost of living adjustments to keep wages more in line with rising costs of living. Beyond this it will be important to develop stronger, smarter local and state campaigns to promote the concept of living wages and policies to reward businesses that pay them. In recent years the unemployment insurance program has covered a diminishing proportion of workers; that needs to be reversed so that more, and then all, workers are covered. The history of social welfare in the United States and in Europe has shown that universal programs such as Social Security and Medicare have a much stronger political base than means-tested programs. Strengthening, not privatizing, Social Security and creating universal health coverage (building on the accomplishments of Medicare) would go a long way toward promoting enhanced economic security. None of this is on the agenda of the Bush administration; quite the contrary. But that is no reason to retreat from a vision of economic justice that is not only possible, even in the age of global capital, but that could resonate broadly with working people across the economic spectrum.

NOTES

1. See Mishel, Bernstein, & Boushey, 2003, pp. 319-329, for a discussion of issues in the statistical definition of poverty.

2. For example, the Economic Policy Institute's (Bernstein, Brocht, & Spade-Aguilar, 2000) research rigorously examining family budgets shows that the twice-poverty rate is a much more realistic measure of a family's ability to meet its basic needs, and many others now report data using this measure.

3. Indeed, the likelihood is that the proportion of bad jobs has increased due to rising health care costs, higher unemployment, and intensifying economic restructuring.

4. Admittedly, some of these are well-paid consulting or other good jobs. It is important not to equate job quality with type of employment arrangement, but rather to investigate in greater detail the actual wages and benefits provided.

5. It is necessary to look at particular states to understand the complexities of the jobs situation because each state has a somewhat different economic situation and every state implemented the reform in somewhat different ways.

6. We conducted a statewide random sample of TANF leavers, food stamp leavers, and diverted TANF applicants in Oregon who had left those programs in the first three months of 1998. Of this sample, 970 respondents completed the first telephone survey twelve to fifteen months later. Seven hundred fifty-six of this group completed a second telephone survey eighteen to twenty-one months after their program exit or diversion.

7. In order to calculate an average monthly household income, we used administrative data from the Oregon Department of Employment. Earnings for each respondent and other earners in the household were reported quarterly. We had data from all four quarters of 1998 and three quarters of 1999. First we calculated a household's earnings for 1998 and 1999 and then we took the sum of both years and divided by twenty-one months (the duration of our study) to arrive at a monthly average. This does not include any "other" income a family may have garnered, but it is a variable representing the systematic tracking of family earnings over time.

8. Oregon voters approved an increase in the minimum wage to $6.00 an hour effective January 1998.

9. The majority of respondents were women, making up 86 percent of the study sample. Given the small sample of men, there were still observable differences in employment and wages. Women in our study typically earned 70 percent of what men earned.

10. Jill Weigt interviewed a subsample of the low-income mothers in the original study over an additional two years as part of her doctoral research.

REFERENCES

Acker, Joan and Sandra Morgen. 2001. "Oregon Families Who Left Temporary Assistance to Needy Families (TANF) or Food Stamps: A Study of Economic and Family Well-Being from 1998 to 2000." Eugene, OR: Center for the Study of Women in Society, University of Oregon.

Bernstein, Jared, Chauna Brocht, and Maggie Spade-Aguilar. 2000. *How Much is Enough? Basic Family Budgets for Working Families.* Washington, DC: Economic Policy Institute.

Boushey, Heather and David Rosnick. 2004. "For Welfare Reform to Work, Jobs Must be Available." Center for Economic and Policy Research. Available at <http://www.cepr.net/labor_markets/welfarejobshit-2004april01.htm>.

Center on Budget and Policy Priorities. 2004. "Census Data Show Poverty Increased, Income Stagnated and the Number of Uninsured Rose to a Record Level in 2003." August 27. Available at <http://www.cbpp.org/8-26-04pov.htm>.

Economic Policy Institute. 2005. "Jobs Picture, Feb. 4, 2005." Available at <www.epinet.org>.

Guinier, Lani and Gerald Torres. 2002. *The Miner's Canary: Enlisting Race, Resisting Power, Transforming Democracy.* Cambridge, MA, and London: Harvard University Press.

Hartmann, Heidi, Vicki Lovell, and Misha Werschkul. 2004. "Women and the Economy: Recent Trends in Job Loss, Labor Force Participation, and Wages." Institute for Women's Policy Research Briefing Paper #B245. Available at <http://www.iwpr.org/pdf/B245.pdf>.

Kalleberg, Arne L., Barbara F. Reskin, and Ken Hudson. 2000. Bad Jobs in America: Standard and Nonstandard Employment Relations and Job Quality in the United States. *American Sociological Review,* 65, 2:256-278.

Leachman, Michael. 2004. *In the Shadows of Recovery: The State of Working Oregon 2004.* Silverton, OR: Oregon Center for Public Policy.

Mishel, Lawrence, Jared Bernstein, and Sylvia Allegretto. 2005. *The State of Working America 2004-2005.* Ithaca, NY, and London: Cornell University Press.

Mishel, Lawrence, Jared Bernstein, and Heather Boushey. 2003. *The State of Working America 2002/2003.* Ithaca, NY, and London: Cornell University Press.

Northwest Policy Center. 2001. *Northwest Job Gap Study: Searching for Work That Pays.* Seattle: University of Washington, Evans School of Public Affairs. Available at <http://www.depts.washington.edu/npc/npdpdfs/NWJobGapOR.pdf>.

Pearce, Diana. 2003. *Setting the Standard for American Working Families.* Washington, DC: Wider Opportunities for Women.

Shulman, Beth. (2003). *The Betrayal of Work: How Low-Wage Jobs Fail 30 Million Americans and Their Families.* New York: New Press.

Waldron, Tom, Brandon Roberts, and Andrew Reamer. 2004. "Working Hard, Falling Short: America's Working Families and the Pursuit of Economic Security." Working Poor Families Project. Available at <http://www.aecf.org/publications/data/working_hard_new.pdf>.

PART II:
POVERTY AND WELFARE REFORM

Chapter 8

Welfare Reform and the American Dream

Laura R. Peck
Sarah Allen Gershon

A central ideology pervasive in United States history is that of the American Dream (White, 2003). For years authors and leaders have referred to this concept as the promise of success in exchange for hard work and honesty (Hochschild, 1995). As President Bill Clinton once put it, "The American dream that we were all raised on is a simple but powerful one—if you work hard and play by the rules you should be given a chance to go as far as your God-given ability will take you" (Hochschild, 1995, p. 18). Clearly the American Dream does not promise predetermined success for all Americans, but it implies unlimited possibility of success for those who wish to work for it.

This Dream, whether real or simply a very powerful myth, permeates American society, shaping public attitudes toward the poor and government aid to the poor (Kinder & Mendelberg, 2000). Recently, a flurry of discussion has centered on the American Dream, specifically as it applies to welfare recipients. For example, journalist Jason DeParle's (2004) new book—*American Dream: Three Women, Ten Kids, and a Nation's Drive to End Welfare*—has earned wide attention in popular and academic venues. Despite telling compelling stories of a family's experience with welfare and work in the 1990s, DeParle's book addresses its title only implicitly. Nowhere does it describe what the Dream is and whether the research subjects are any closer to it since welfare reform than they were before. That vagueness is characteristic of much of the popular work that deals with the American Dream, but academic literature is only marginally better at defining the American Dream. In pop culture, the American Dream generally promises upward mobility, perhaps symbolized by home

doi:10.1300/5608_09

ownership or by combining entrepreneurial spirit with hard work to achieve some rags-to-riches story.

This chapter offers an operational definition of the American Dream and assesses how welfare reform has influenced welfare recipients' and low-income populations' ability to reach that Dream. As he signed the Personal Responsibility and Work Opportunity Reconciliation Act (PRWORA) of 1996 into law, President Clinton said, "This legislation provides an historic opportunity to end welfare as we know it and transform our broken welfare system by promoting the fundamental values of work, responsibility, and family" (On the Issues, 2000). The notion of achieving the American Dream is intertwined with the goals of PRWORA, and with reauthorization of PRWORA imminent, the time has come to assess whether PRWORA's rhetoric promoting the fundamental values associated with the American Dream has, in the nine years since its passage, become a reality.

WHAT IS THE AMERICAN DREAM?

Historian James Truslow Adams—who reportedly coined the term "American Dream" in the 1930s—wrote that President John Quincy Adams believed that America represented opportunity, "the chance to grow into something bigger and finer" (White, 2003, p. 55). Americans continue to believe in a hopeful, more prosperous future, and our leaders continue to rely on the Dream's rhetoric. President Ronald Reagan's hope (in 1983) for the United States was that "this remains a country where someone can always get rich" (White House, 1983), and, as stated previously, President Clinton referred to the Dream in reforming welfare and in his vision for the country. Current President George W. Bush's advocacy of an "ownership" society is closely related.

Much of the academic literature on the American Dream deals with immigrants and ethnic and racial minorities. In particular, scholars have focused on coming from one of these disadvantaged backgrounds to achieve the American Dream. As such, it is difficult to disentangle the issues of immigrant status, race, and ethnicity from the ability to achieve the American Dream in part because the Dream suggests that no matter one's background, "the land of the free and the home of the brave" will offer abundant opportunities for success.

Hochschild and Scovronick (2003) describe the American Dream as an ideology that many Americans subscribe to, summarized as "I am an American, so I have the freedom and opportunity to make whatever I want of my life. I can succeed by working hard and using my talents; if I fail, it will be my own fault" (p. 1). This definition, as is common in the literature, incorporates several similar values—hard work, individual responsibility for failure, and unlimited possibility for success (Hochschild, 1995; Ownby, 1999). Similarly, White (2003) defines the American Dream as a combination of three concepts: freedom, individualism, and equal opportunity. Bostrom (2001) describes the American Dream as requiring hard work in the context of opportunity: "Fundamentally we believe that anyone can grow up to be Bill Gates with enough initiative and hard work, because we see opportunity as unlimited in the U.S." (p. 6). After hard work comes "the ability of a good education to help one succeed in life" (Bostrom, 2001, p. 6).

More specifically still, the National League of Cities' (NLC) (2004) recent report defines the Dream as follows: "Fairness. Opportunity. A quality education. An affordable home. Living in freedom. Having a family. This is the 'American Dream' in 2004" (p. 1). Unlike other definitions, the NLC's includes home and family. As applied research, the NLC survey and analysis is somewhat different from the academic literature; it highlights that the home-ownership aspect of defining the American Dream is part of the popular discourse on the Dream despite its relative absence from the academic literature.

Bostrom (2001) explores the locus of responsibility for three key elements of the Dream: working hard, generating that unlimited opportunity, and providing a good education. Not surprisingly, public opinion polls conclude that hard work is an individual's responsibility, but overwhelmingly the public believes that government holds responsibility for the other two legs of the tripod, opportunity and education. Although Hochschild and Scovronick's (2003) data suggest that the public still strongly believes in their ability to achieve the Dream, the NLC (2004) finds that the public believes that it has become more difficult to attain the Dream in recent years, and that government is partly responsible for the shift.

Since immigrants are believed to have a shot at the Dream, then certainly welfare recipients should have a shot as well, especially given the vision for welfare reform as a hand up. Here we apply the notion of the American Dream to low-income families and welfare recipients in particular. The American Dream embodies, for most of us, the underlying assumptions that America is the land of opportunity, that success is therefore available to everyone, and that all Americans should have a reasonable expectation of achieving it. Coupled with the belief in opportunity is respect for the value of hard work. The core element of the American Dream that is *measurable* is financial stability—having a job that sets food on the table, provides access to health insurance, earns sufficient income to save for a home and establish savings to deal with emergencies, and leads to upward mobility. Financial stability is facilitated by having sufficient education or at least access to quality education or training.

Of course, the level of success required for realization of the Dream is difficult to specify. As one subject of Studs Terkel's (1980) research on *American Dreams, Lost and Found* puts it, "The American Dream is to be better off than you are. How much is 'enough money'? 'Enough money' is always a little bit more than you have" (p. 38). Although the definition of financial success is certainly relative, financial success involves building financial assets sufficient for self-reliance, including the ability to manage minor to moderate emergencies. As one scholar notes, "Most people who leave poverty . . . do so because they save and invest in themselves, in their children, in property, in securities, or in enterprises to improve their circumstances" (Sherraden, 2000, p. 162). Individuals must be able to create their own financial safety net to realize the American Dream. Financial self-reliance is the first step toward the economic success promised by the American Dream and must therefore be considered when assessing PRWORA's success in assisting welfare recipients. Financial stability includes securing adequate housing and moving toward home ownership, a central indicator of achieving the American Dream.

Secondary indicators of financial stability include having enough food, adequate health care, and transportation for oneself and family. If, for example, a family consistently runs short of food, lacks dependable transportation, or cannot seek medical treatment when necessary, then that family has not achieved the stability that defines the Dream. Another important indicator is upward mobility, which refers primarily to lifetime economic mobility, the extent to which people can move upward financially over time. Those who start at the bottom must be able to rise beyond their current economic class. The same factors that facilitate basic economic security—gainful employment and sufficient education—facilitate upward mobility and are essential to one's ability to achieve the American Dream.

HOW HAS WELFARE REFORM INFLUENCED THE AMERICAN DREAM?

The 1996 PRWORA is riddled with conflicting messages about the goals of welfare and of welfare reform. Though the longer-term "self-sufficiency" of program participants is a goal in theory, few real practices or policy prescriptions support reaching that goal. Instead, the shorter-term goals of cutting program costs and reducing the number of people receiving welfare assistance prevail. The legislation couples these goals with behavioral transformation goals such as increasing work levels and marriage levels while reducing nonmarital childbearing, particularly among teenagers. Some of these goals are linked to the stated goal of promoting self-sufficiency, revealing that a web of interrelated goals exists.

At least two problems with these goals for welfare policy and programs are evident. First, goals related to self-sufficiency exist only in relation to welfare programs, but the labor market—particularly the low-wage labor market—is an important target for reform if welfare recipients are to be able to achieve independence from cash assistance. The self-sufficiency goal operates through welfare policy in the form of established work-level requirements including the numbers of hours per week that one must participate in work or related activities (and the percent of a state's caseload that must meet this hours threshold). The underlying assumption has been that "work first" is a more effective way of moving people off welfare, presumably into jobs; however, evidence has shown that the labor market is not hospitable to these low-skill workers, and their lack of increasing education and skills limits their ability to advance, even from entry-level jobs. Unless welfare reform is coupled with labor market reform, the goal of self-sufficiency will not be met.

Second, behavioral reforms are far secondary to economic needs, and they deflect political energy from what might really matter for welfare recipients and other low-income or low-skill workers. Little evidence supports the idea that getting married will transform a couple's life in such a way that they will be on a new trajectory toward achieving the

American Dream. Granted, evidence suggests that two-parent families may provide a better environment for children such that children's future outcomes might be better compared to the outcomes of children from single-parent families. But other factors and not the finite act of marriage itself is likely to cause this difference. Although some definitions of the American Dream include morality (e.g., Hochschild, 1995, pp. 16-23), PRWORA overemphasizes moral behaviors relative to the more concrete benefits of financial stability. Outcomes related to financial stability are clearly more important than behavioral outcomes in achieving the American Dream.

Why does this matter in the context of the current discussion of the American Dream? One's ability to advance in American society depends on enjoying at least a basic level of income stability, let alone self-sufficiency. Both current and former welfare recipients, now and in the ten years since PRWORA passed, have faced increasing barriers to their progress toward the Dream *because* of the nature of welfare reform. Although PRWORA appears to emphasize hard work as key to financial success, moving recipients into low-paying jobs without sufficient education or ongoing job training almost ensures that they will not move out of poverty. Instead, "these new workers . . . have swelled the ranks of the working poor—those with low wage jobs, minimal health benefits, and not enough money to pay the bills" (Miller-Adams, 2002, p. 15). A synthesis of studies about people leaving welfare reports that 60 percent of "leavers" were employed one year after leaving welfare, and their earnings were about $7.00 per hour (Jarchow, 2002). Wide state variation means that in only one of thirteen states studied were families able to reach the poverty level through employment (Jarchow, 2002). In brief, despite work, few families have been able to escape poverty and achieve the financial stability needed to become self-sufficient, to make progress toward the Dream a reality. In addition to unjustified faith in the labor market to lift poor families, assistance programs' income eligibility requirements inhibit wage growth. Medicaid eligibility thresholds, for example, result either in people losing their health assistance or in people having stagnant incomes (since working more hours or a second job disqualifies them from assistance).

Schattschneider's (1960) classic view of issue division is perhaps no more evident than in the arena of welfare reform. He writes that issues defined one way cannot, by default, be defined some other way. Here we observe that focus on marriage precludes focus on jobs;

focus on fathers precludes focus on mothers; focus on becoming self-sufficient through workfare precludes focus on the low-wage labor market; and focus on caseload reduction and cost savings precludes focus on real poverty reduction. The lip service that surrounded PRWORA's passage—that it would "transform our broken welfare system by promoting the fundamental values" that lead to self-sufficiency—offered a vision of what we might have wanted for our changing world, but the reality of the act, its implementation, and its results, have been markedly different.

Recent research with cash assistance and working poor families has shown that added costs of simply being poor are an additional barrier to economic advance (Peck & Segal, 2006). That is, having low and limited income can impose greater costs of day-to-day activities than financially comfortable families might face. For example, without enough to maintain a minimum balance at a conventional bank, poor families pay monthly fees to hold a bank account, if they can even get one, and more often pay large fees to check cashing services in order to gain access to their own money. This is only one of very many examples of how it actually *costs more* to be poor. And this observation—borne out in empirical research—demonstrates an important problem for low-income families' ability to move up.

Edin and Lein (1997) meticulously document the cash inflows and outflows among welfare-reliant and working-poor single mothers to find that saving for a home or future investment in business or education is not even remotely an option. But the ability to save is *prerequisite* to starting on the path toward the American Dream. Although human resources—including motivation, organization, and so on—are important, financial resources, even modest, are essential.

Policy analysts far and wide have been working diligently to document and explain the implications of the 1996 reform. The preponderance of evidence suggests some key findings. People leaving welfare for work were generally better off than they were before leaving welfare, particularly during the economic expansion, but they overwhelmingly remained poor and offered few examples of true self-sufficiency. Since the recession that began in 2001, evidence is even less favorable. After several years of enormous caseload declines between 1994 and 2000 (14.2 to 5.8 million recipients over those years), the recession brought returns to welfare, a clear sign that the labor market, as expected, rejected those at the bottom first in times of distress.

Although a reduction in caseload may be a political success, it is no measure of an individual's success. Of course the potential dignity that comes from putting in a hard day's work is important, but so too is the real dignity of being rewarded sufficiently for that work. Workfare provides an opportunity for welfare recipients to exchange work for assistance, in the spirit of paternalism and meeting social obligations (Mead, 1986). But exchange for that work is a less-than-minimum wage task that some have argued displaces positions that offer better pay and living benefits (Feder, 2003).

If evidence from research were not enough, public opinion corroborates the view that it has become harder to achieve the American Dream and that government's ability to help has declined in recent years. Whereas 54 percent of NLC survey respondents in 2001 believed that the government was helping families to achieve the American Dream, 41 percent of those surveyed in 2004 believed that the government was helping. Furthermore, only 31 percent of those who are not living the American Dream believe that the federal government "cares" about helping people like them. In contrast, 20 percentage points more (a small majority, 51 percent) of those living the Dream assert that government cares (NCL, 2004, pp. 20-21). That government is a hindrance to people's ability to achieve the American Dream is evidence—not only overall as these findings show but also among population members who are least well-off—that welfare reform's promises of self-sufficiency have not been realized.

DISCUSSION AND CONCLUSION

For PRWORA reauthorization, outside-the-box thinking is ideal but politically unlikely. That innovative thinking might involve truly ending welfare as we know it in lieu of a national family allowance that would support all parents. Within the narrower confines of the cash welfare program, PRWORA might be reauthorized specifically to refocus on education (and perhaps training). Focusing on education—and then actually delivering it—would poise people to be able to achieve self-sufficiency (and not languish in low-paying, dead-end jobs), the financial stability that is the precursor to achieving the American Dream.

Related welfare programs—including the food stamp program, Medicaid, and subsidized child care, for instance—are as important to reauthorization as the cash assistance program itself. The broader social safety net must provide a minimum level of assistance, and food stamps have generally been thought to fill that role through support for what is perhaps most fundamental, food. Medicaid, on the other hand, might be reconceptualized as part of a broader health care reform package that insists on assisting all Americans, working and not, young and old. People should not have to choose between medication and food or other necessities; the promise of America suggests that we have the ability to have it all.

The policy actions that are more likely to propel poor Americans toward the American Dream fall outside the current purview of cash welfare (and related) assistance alone. Wage and work supports are imperative in order to improve the amenability of the low-wage labor market to provide economic security. For example, increasing the minimum wage (or establishing a living wage) and increasing the Earned Income Tax Credit (and state counterpart EITCs) increase the value of work and the ability of those at the bottom of the labor market to care for their families. Widespread child care for all family types and suitable to all kinds of work schedules does so as well. Outside the labor market, this chapter's findings suggest that increasing the quality of education and the equitable distribution of quality education is important for future generations to continue striving for the Dream.

The goal—to achieve the American Dream—is the same for everyone, and the myth is that the race is the same as well; the reality is that the race differs such that most low-income Americans, and welfare recipients in particular, cannot reach the goal. When did the American Dream become restricted? When did it become available only to those who have a better shot—by virtue of chance and the family they were born into—and not available to all? If one value underpins American society, it is that of equal opportunity; it is not clear that there is indeed equal opportunity for welfare recipients to strive for—and therefore achieve—the American Dream.

The rhetoric of welfare reform dangled the myth of the American Dream in front of welfare recipients (and low-income people, and state and local welfare administrators, for that matter) in a misguided effort to do something draconian: cut welfare rolls and force work.

Although forcing work is not necessarily bad in and of itself, it becomes draconian when the low-wage labor market into which people are forced is inhospitable not only to their growth but also to their advancement toward our American Dream.

REFERENCES

Bostrom, M. (2001). *Achieving the American Dream: A Meta-Analysis of Public Opinion Concerning Poverty, Upward Mobility, and Related Issues.* New York: Ford Foundation.

DeParle, J. (2004). *American Dream: Three Women, Ten Kids, and a Nation's Drive to End Welfare.* New York: Viking.

Edin, K., & Lein, L. (1997). *Making Ends Meet: How Single Mothers Survive Welfare and Low-Wage Work.* New York: Russell Sage Foundation.

Feder, D. (2003). "'Work First'—Where Are the Wages?" In A. Gluckman, A. Offner, A. Reuss, T. Williamson, & the Dollars and Sense Collective (Eds.), *Current Economic Issues: Progressive Perspectives from Dollars and Sense* (8th ed., pp. 75-77). Cambridge, MA: The Economic Affairs Bureau, Inc.

Hochschild, J.L. (1995). *Facing Up to the American Dream: Race, Class and the Soul of the Nation.* Princeton, NJ: Princeton University Press.

Hochschild, J.L., & Scovronick, N. (2003). *The American Dream and the Public Schools.* Oxford, UK: Oxford University Press.

Jarchow, C. (2002). *Employment Experiences of Former TANF Recipients.* Washington, DC: National Conference of State Legislatures.

Kinder, D.R., & Mendelberg, T. (2000). "Individualism Reconsidered: Principles and Prejudice in Contemporary American Opinion." In D.O. Sears, J. Sidanius, & L. Bobo (Eds.), *Racialized Politics: The Debate About Racism in America.* Chicago, IL: University of Chicago Press.

Mead, L.M. (1986). *Beyond Entitlement: The Social Obligations of Citizenship.* New York: Free Press.

Miller-Adams, M. (2002). *Owning Up: Poverty, Assets, and the American Dream.* Washington, DC: Brookings Institution Press.

National League of Cities. (2004). *The American Dream in 2004: A Survey of the American People.* Washington, DC: National League of Cities.

On the Issues. (2000, December 6). Bill Clinton on welfare & poverty. Retrieved December 14, 2004, from <http://www.issues2002.org/Celeb/Bill_Clinton_Welfare_+_Poverty.htm>.

Ownby, T. (1999). *American Dream in Mississippi: Consumers, Poverty and Culture.* Chapel Hill: The University of North Carolina Press.

Peck, L.R., & Segal, E.A. (2006). The Latent and Sequential Costs of Being Poor: Explorations of a Potential Paradigm Shift. *Journal of Poverty,* 10(1): 1-24.

Schattschneider, E.E. (1960). *The Semisoverign People: A Realist's View of Democracy in America.* New York: Holt, Rinehart and Winston.

Sherraden, M. (2000). From Research to Policy: Lessons from Individual Development Accounts: The Colston Warne Lecture. *Journal of Consumer Affairs, 34*(2): 159-181.

Terkel, S. (1980). *American Dreams, Lost and Found.* New York: Pantheon Books.

White House. (1983). The President's News Conference, June 28, 1983.

White, J.K. (2003). *The Values Divide: American Politics and Culture in Transition.* London, UK: Chatham House Publishers/Seven Bridges Press.

Chapter 9

Welfare Reform: What's Poverty Got to Do With It?

Keith M. Kilty

Poverty puts the lives of hundreds of millions of people in peril each and every day. In the so-called developing world alone, the World Bank estimates that about 1.2 billion people live in "absolute poverty," struggling to survive on less than one dollar a day (Bright, 2003). Although industrialized societies are not as desperate, poverty exists there as well. Even in the United States, one of the richest societies that has ever existed, millions are mired deep in poverty.

The fact that poverty exists in America seems to come as a surprise to many—especially to those at the top. We as a society seem reluctant to acknowledge its existence, much less to do anything about it. From time to time, conditions get bad enough that we pay it some attention, but, for the most part, poverty and inequality are absent from public awareness and discussion. How often on television news programs do we see a focus on the affluent and their concerns about the rise and fall of the stock market, compared to a focus on the daily struggle faced by the poor to pay the rent or to feed their families? In 2003, the mean household income of the bottom quintile of the income distribution was $9,996, while it was $147,078 for the top quintile (DeNavas-Walt, Proctor, & Mills, 2004). That fact should shock everyone in America: it means that the bottom 20 percent of all households in this country lived on an average of $28.40 a day (in gross income)—or $11.05 per individual. But that "reality" is virtually invisible—especially in the mass media.

A good way to think about poverty is in terms of its visibility versus invisibility. On September 3, 2003, I participated in a symposium on poverty in the United States and Japan, held at Hokkaido University in

doi:10.1300/5608_10

Sapporo, Japan. The title for this symposium was "Poverty, Inequality, and Social Justice: Making Invisible Poverty Visible." I feel deeply indebted to the principal organizer, Professor Osamu Aoki, who put into words a feeling that I have had for a long time about poverty here as well as in other affluent societies. I have used the phrase "historical amnesia" to describe how I believe that America has long dealt with poverty, but I think that "invisible poverty" is a better way to characterize the issue. We in this country certainly do our best to forget about poverty and inequality, but we actually take a more active role in eradicating it from our consciousness than simply "forgetting" about it. We deliberately make it invisible. The "welfare reform" legislation of 1996 (the Personal Responsibility and Work Opportunity Reconciliation Act) is just the latest way that we as a society have tried to make poverty go away—to make it invisible. That is why "welfare reform" has had virtually nothing to do with poverty or its reduction—much less its eradication.

POVERTY: OUT OF SIGHT, OUT OF MIND

Making poverty invisible does not mean that we have no awareness of it at all. Rather, it means that we push it out of sight as much as possible. On some level, most of us probably realize that poverty really is there, but it certainly is easier to deal with when we don't actually have to see it. The poor are everywhere, but that doesn't mean that we have to set eyes on them. When we walk down a city street, or shop in a mall, or sit in a coffee shop, any of the people around us could be poor. But we don't have to know that. If the people we see look just like us, then they can't really be poor. Or if they don't quite look like us, if they are dressed in their Starbucks or janitor's uniform, then they are working and therefore not destitute. When they do become visible, particularly as some of the homeless did during the 1980s and 1990s, then we can restrict their presence and activities in public places. Out of sight, out of mind.

Unfortunately, there are times when reducing the visibility of poverty is not so easy—a circumstance that has been true throughout our history. From the beginning of European conquest of the Americas, a life of scarcity was the lot of most people—especially those who eventually came to be defined as nonwhite. In seventeenth-century colonial America, the mass of black and white laborers struggled to live through their time of indenturement, but becoming "free" did not mean that life would be easy: quite the opposite. Life in the colonies was harsh, and a closed circle of wealthy and powerful men—appointed by the king of England—controlled the lives of the masses. These men—the Washingtons, the Jeffersons, the Mathers, the Madisons—all expected their "servants"—white and black alike—to work hard for their subsistence, while they themselves enjoyed a life of affluence and comfort. Ultimately, these men of wealth would realize that they could amass even more riches by separating "black" from "white" through an ideology of white supremacy that justified forcing black laborers into the degradation of chattel slavery—even though most so-called free whites would live lives of paucity as well (Bennett, 1975). From its inception, the United States was built on a vast gap between rich and poor—on the exploitation of the poor, on a vast disparity of wealth between top and bottom.

Hiding poverty was difficult during the colonial era and the early days of the United States. Not only was life severe, but calamities could befall individuals and families at any moment, compounding ordinary circumstances. Ways to deal with poverty were modeled after the Elizabethan Poor Laws, and the poor came to be characterized in terms of being "deserving" or "undeserving" of aid (Katz, 1989)—a conception of the poor that continues to plague us three centuries later. In those days, the poor were put out of sight by being "farmed out" to other families in the community if they were deserving or dumped into poorhouses if they were undeserving. But, at least to some extent, their visibility could be reduced—particularly among the white population. Out of sight, out of mind.

Those who were seen as nonwhite—the indigenous North American population and the unwilling immigrants from Africa—fared much worse. They were clearly undeserving, and that sentiment was justified by the emerging ideology of racism, which appropriated biological ideas to validate their inferior treatment because of the color of their skin (Kilty & Segal, 1996). Slavery became the fate of blacks, while Native Americans were exterminated or driven from their lands, the survivors forced to relocate faraway on often desolate reservations. Out of sight, out of mind.

Race and ethnicity have always been intertwined with poverty in the United States, and our racial and ethnic categories have changed as needed to incorporate new groups. The "Hispanics" were living in the northern half of Mexico when it was appropriated by the United States following the Mexican-American War of 1846-1848. U.S. imperialist expansion into the Caribbean and the Pacific through the Spanish-American War of 1898 brought more nonwhite peoples into the United States (Kilty & Vidal, 2000). Many of these new "citizens" found themselves relegated to a life of peonage and invisibility (American Social History Project, 1992), much like the sharecropping experience of the post-Reconstruction South. Out of sight, out of mind.

After the Civil War, labor shortages in the American West led to the importation of contract laborers from a number of Asian countries, beginning with the Chinese. It was actually the English who pioneered this new version of indentured labor, as a way of replacing slaves lost to emancipation in British colonies during the 1830s (Northrup, 1995). The practice became common in the United States as well. The countries of origin of these Asian immigrants varied over the next several decades, as racist sentiments led to restrictions on entry of particular nationalities during periods of economic downturns and labor surpluses where whites directly competed with Asians for jobs (Kilty, 2002). Most of these immigrants experienced a new kind of invisibility when denied the opportunity to become citizens, under the Naturalization Act of 1790 which allowed only whites to become naturalized citizens or even to own the land on which they lived and worked (Kilty, 2003). They were here but not of here. Out of sight, out of mind.

It was not only in the West where labor shortages periodically happened during this time. By the late 1800s, the industrial revolution was in full swing on the East Coast, and new bodies were needed to toil in the factories and sweatshops in the growing urban centers of New York, Boston, Philadelphia, and Baltimore. The Irish had already been coming for years, but their numbers increased now, along with new white ethnic groups, including Italians and other southern Europeans (Feagin & Feagin, 2003) as well as eastern European Jews (Takaki, 1993). These new migrants found themselves unwelcome in their new homeland. The people who now called themselves "native-born Americans" expressed their fears in the form of Social Darwinism and eugenics, arguing that the newcomers were naturally inferior (Kilty & Segal, 1996). Even though more or less "white," it was clear that these immigrants were undeserving of aid because of their innate deficiencies. Racist and nativist sentiments about Asian immigrants in the West and southern and eastern European immigrants in the East ultimately brought about the National Origins Quota Law of 1924, the most restrictive immigration legislation in American history. They also helped to divert attention away from concerns about poverty, since the poor were held to be responsible for their condition. Once again, out of sight, out of mind.

WHEN POVERTY BECOMES TOO VISIBLE

The Great Depression represents the most profound economic crisis in the history of the United States. Recessions and depressions have occurred at regular intervals throughout our history, but the depth of misery during the Depression of the 1930s was stunning, and poverty could not be pushed out of sight quite so easily as before. The twentieth century saw not only a rapidly growing population but also one concentrated in urban areas. In earlier times, people could manage at least a subsistence living off their land. That was no longer an option for the millions of people living in cities. In fact, after World War I, a vast migration from the country to the city took place. So in addition to foreign immigration to the United States that was concentrated in urban areas, an internal immigration from rural to urban changed the American demographic landscape.

When a quarter of all workers are out of work, desolation will be visible. But not just the working class was affected. The middle class was also hit hard. Bank closings stole the savings and other assets of the middle class, who suddenly found themselves with nothing. Factory workers and middle-class shopkeepers and professionals alike lost their livelihoods, their homes, and their possessions. The crisis just worsened year after year, with no end in sight.

Franklin D. Roosevelt's New Deal programs were built around "relief, recovery, and reform." The New Deal, though, was not a coherent program; it reflected the reality of the American social, economic, and political context (Blau, 2004). Never was "relief" intended to be forever or a replacement for work; it was meant to be temporary. Most of the New Deal programs, however limited they may have been in reality, revolved around putting men back to work. Only the old age pensions authorized under the Social Security Act of

1935 were intended to be permanent, but those pensions were meant to reduce the number of people trying to get jobs by getting older workers out of the labor force. Of top of that, not all workers were deserving of old age pensions. Race played a major role in determining which jobs were included for eligibility for old age pensions, with farm and domestic workers (largely the occupations of black laborers) being left out to satisfy southern Democrats. Other relief programs remained limited in scope, with Aid to Dependent Children providing public assistance benefits only to children until 1950. But poverty had become quite visible and did not begin to fade into invisibility again until the post-World War II era, when the Depression itself started to disappear and good times were apparently once more had by all.

The 1962 publication of Michael Harrington's *The Other America* is often credited with helping to shock a complacent America into removing its rose-tinted glasses and recognizing that poverty was still a serious problem in the midst of the postwar affluence. According to Robert Clark (2002, p. 24), President John F. Kennedy "had been particularly impressed by Michael Harrington's book or at least by an elegantly written review of it by Dwight McDonald in *The New Yorker.*" During 1963, Kennedy began to devote considerable attention to the issue of poverty, and following his assassination President Lyndon B. Johnson picked up the task by declaring a "War on Poverty." As inspiring as that story may be, it is probably a myth (Katz, 1989). Other forces were at work at the time as well, particularly the civil rights movement and urban insurrections throughout the country. A cold war was being waged against the Soviet Union, and the United States also had to at least make an appearance of being an open, egalitarian, and antiracist society in response to revolutionary struggles against capitalism and imperialism throughout the so-called third world. The programs that comprised Johnson's War on Poverty were limited expansions of public assistance to those at the bottom of American society and were short-lived. The 1960s came to an abrupt end with the 1968 election of Richard M. Nixon, whose administration led a renewed attack on the idea that government should—much less could—help lift the oppressed out of poverty.

WELFARE REFORM AND POVERTY

The poor have long been seen as responsible for their circumstances. How exactly they are responsible has been stated a little differently from one era to another, but that is the underlying morality play. When contemporary notions of welfare reform began to emerge during the Nixon era, the message was the same as always: If we allow people to go on the dole, then they will become dependent and lazy. Only by making them pull themselves up by their very own bootstraps will they shake off the bonds of poverty. Only by learning proper work attitudes and skills will be they able to emerge from their dependency into a state of self-sufficiency. Welfare reform was necessary, since only a "tough love" approach would ultimately help the poor by forcing them to take responsibility for themselves. Ronald Reagan and the first Bush extolled that philosophy throughout the 1980s, and Bill Clinton took up the banner by promising "to end welfare as we know it" in 1992. He fulfilled his promise by signing legislation in 1996 that culminated thirty years of rhetoric by incorporating the phrase "personal responsibility" in its very title.

Women, in particular, need to learn that lesson. Rather than staying home with their children—which was the purpose of the original Aid to Dependent Children (ADC) program and its successor, the Aid for Families with Dependent Children (AFDC) program—mothers must work—the underlying purpose of welfare reform: the Temporary Assistance for Needy Families (TANF) program. According to the Administration for Children and Families Office of Public Affairs fact sheet (ACF, 2004), "TANF is a block grant program to help move recipients into work and turn welfare into a program of temporary assistance." According to this fact sheet, TANF has four major goals:

1. assisting needy families so that children can be cared for in their own homes
2. reducing the dependency of needy parents by promoting job preparation, work and marriage
3. preventing out-of-wedlock pregnancies
4. encouraging the formation and maintenance of two-parent families (AFC, 2004)

Is poverty a concern? Where is it even mentioned? In fact, misconceptions abound in this mission statement, including the idea that welfare leads to dependency or that marriage is a viable way for women and their children to get out of poverty (Segal & Kilty, 2003). So what does poverty have to do with welfare reform?

Does welfare reform have anything to do with poverty? Since the advent of the TANF program in 1997, welfare caseloads have declined dramatically, and many states now find themselves with surplus public assistance funds. The state of Ohio, for example, currently has $431 million laying around unused. According to Joan Lawrence, director of the Ohio Department of Aging, "Welfare [reform] has been overwhelmingly successful and that's why we have all these funds" (Pyle, 2004). Apparently, she defines "success" simply on the basis of welfare caseload reduction. Who cares what happens to the former recipients themselves?

Table 9.1 presents a summary of the number of recipients and caseloads/families receiving AFDC for the decade prior to TANF and the numbers of recipients and caseloads/families receiving TANF during its first four years—which is as much data on TANF as is currently available through the Administration for Children and Families Web site. There is no question that caseloads have become much lower since the advent of TANF. Just comparing the last year of AFDC with the most recent TANF data shows a decline of 2,310,463 cases (50.8 percent) and 6,731,265 recipients (53.2 percent), yet the poverty rate was down by only 2.4 points (a 17.5 percent decline). Welfare reform has reduced the public assistance rolls, but poverty persists. In fact, the official poverty rate (which is widely known to underestimate actual poverty) has increased during the past three years (DeNavas-Walt et al., 2004). If the intent of welfare reform was at all to reduce poverty, then—contrary to the statements of many public officials—it has been a dismal failure. If the goal of welfare reform has been to lift families out of poverty through work, then it has been nothing short of a disastrous failure.

The truth is that most poor families have always worked. At the height of the AFDC program, only about 5 percent of the United States population ever received public assistance, and that is now down to 1.7 percent. To survive, the poor—contrary to popular images—have always worked—and worked hard. Yet, according to columnist Bob Herbert (2004, p. A9), "9.2 million working families in the United States—one out of every four—earn wages that are so low they are barely able to survive financially."

TABLE 9.1. Monthly Average Total Recipients and Numbers of Families/Caseloads for AFDC (1987-1996) and TANF (1997-2000)

Year	Recipients	Families/Caseloads	Poverty Rate
1987	11,065,027	3,784,014	13.4
1988	10,919,695	3,747,949	13.0
1989	10,933,695	3,770,959	12.8
1990	11,460,379	3,974,321	13.5
1991	12,592,268	4,373,881	14.2
1992	13,625,342	4,768,495	14.8
1993	14,142,710	4,981,248	15.1
1994	14,225,651	5,046,326	14.5
1995	13,665,503	4,880,519	13.8
1996	12,644,076	4,551,731	13.7
1997	8,605,031	3,127,406	13.3
1998	8,786,226	3,194,273	12.7
1999	7,187,658	2,673,610	11.9
2000[a]	5,912,811	2,241,268	11.3

Source: AFDC and TANF recipients and caseloads data from the Administration for Children & Families, Department of Health and Human Services. Poverty rates taken from Table B-1 in DeNavas-Walt et al. (2004).

[a]For 2000, data available only through September.

Just how mean-spirited as a nation have we become when it comes to the poor? It is almost as if we must vilify and demonize them in order to salve our consciences. We continue to believe that the poor are responsible for their poverty. Social Darwinist ideas still dominate public discussions of poverty and assistance, as George Will illustrates in a column published in the *Columbus Dispatch* on December 31, 2004, titled "Bonds of Poverty Stronger Than Thought" (Will, 2004). These stereotypes about the poor and why they are poor are as old as America itself. Coontz (1992) shows how the rhetoric of contemporary politicians is not much different from the rhetoric of public officials at the end of the nineteenth century.

This mean-spiritedness emanates from the top of our society, but some at the bottom internalize it as well (Fitzgerald, 2004). Considering how common images of the poor as "welfare cheats" and "lazy" and "bad mothers" are, it should be no surprise that even some of the poor have come to believe that many of the poor are taking advantage of the system—though not themselves (Butler & Nevin, 1997). Is it any wonder, though, that there is so little sympathy for the predicament of the poor and the lack of recognition of poverty in our society when those at the top—the most privileged—are among the most uncaring and irresponsible and extravagant? Just look at George W. Bush's plans to spend some $40 million on his second inauguration (Silva, 2004).

As we become more stingy in providing aid for the poor, we become more punitive in how we treat them—perhaps to explain to ourselves why we are being so stingy. Some use religion to justify their sentiments about the poor, and self-avowed people of faith say that it is a decline in supposed moral values—particularly sexual promiscuity, children born outside of marriage, homosexuality—that underlie why the poor are poor. These sanctimonious platitudes have become a constant part of the political landscape and figured prominently in the elections of 2004 just as they have in past ones. This is blatant hypocrisy, just as are complaints about how the poor take advantage of public assistance.

If any group in American society takes advantage of public welfare, it is the affluent. Just look at the major form of housing subsidy in the United States: the tax deduction that middle- and upper-income individuals who itemize their income taxes can take advantage of. That will cost the U.S. government over $68 billion in 2004, and about 60 percent of that will go into the pockets of people with incomes over $100,000. According to Zepezauer (2004, p. 20), "One study found that in 1997, the total amount of tax subsidies to homeowners was more than *seven times* what the Department of Housing and Urban Development (HUD) spent on its housing programs for the poor" (italics in original). So who is taking advantage of what? Perhaps we should ask our political leaders to trade places for a year with a TANF mother and her children. Let her collect that senator's or representative's salary of $158,100 for a year and see how she manages her life with that—a personal salary that puts all 535 members of Congress in the top 5 percent of the U.S. household income distribution.

It is time now for progressives to challenge these prevailing ideas about poverty and the poor. We must make poverty visible again. We must bring back a sense of community and caring among people in this country, and the way to do that is to put human faces on the poor. We need to show the faces of people who are working but who cannot afford health insurance for their children. We need to show the faces of people who are working but cannot afford after-school programs for their children. We need to show the faces of the poor who mingle with the nonpoor every day—in stores, restaurants, schools, theaters, shopping malls—but who have become invisible to the nonpoor. We must separate the words "compassionate" and "conservative" since conservative values can never allow compassion for the victims of greed and wealth. We need to advocate humane social policies; we must no longer tolerate policies that are punitive and degrading. There is no moral justification for the continued existence of poverty in a nation with so much wealth.

REFERENCES

ACF. (2004). Office of Public Affairs: Fact Sheet—Office of Family Assistance (TANF). Available at <http://www.acf.hhs.gov/opa/fact_sheets/tanf_factsheet.html>.

American Social History Project. (1992). Who built America? *Working people and the nation's economy, politics, culture & society.* Volume Two, *From the gilded age to the present.* New York: Pantheon.

Bennett, L., Jr. (1975). *The shaping of Black America.* New York: Penguin.

Blau, J. (2004). *The dynamics of social welfare policy.* New York: Oxford University Press.

Bright, C. (2003). A history of our future. In Worldwatch Institute (eds.), *State of the world 2003* (pp. 3-13). New York: Norton.

Butler, S. S., & Nevin, M. K. (1997). Welfare mothers speak: One state's efforts to bring recipient voices to the welfare debate. *Journal of Poverty 1*(2), 25-61.

Clark, R. F. (2002). *The war on poverty.* Lanham, MD: University Press of America.

Coontz, S. (1992). *The way we never were.* New York: Basic Books.

DeNavas-Walt, C., Proctor, B. D., & Mills, R. J. (2004). *Income, poverty, and health insurance coverage in the United States: 2003.* (U.S. Census Bureau, Current Population Reports, pp. 60-226). Washington, DC: U.S. Government Printing Office.

Feagin, J. R., & Feagin, C. B. (2003). *Racial and ethnic relations* (7th ed.). Upper Saddle River, NJ: Prentice Hall.

Fitzgerald, J. (2004). The disciplinary apparatus of welfare reform. *Monthly Review, 56*(6), *53-62.*

Harrington, M. (1962). *The other America.* New York: Macmillan.

Herbert, B. (2004). Plight of America's working families draws little attention as it worsens. *Columbus Dispatch,* October 11, A9.

Katz, M. B. (1989). *The undeserving poor: From the war on poverty to the war on welfare.* New York: Pantheon.

Kilty, K. M. (2002). Race, immigration, and public policy: The case of Asian Americans. *Journal of Poverty, 6*(4), *23-41.*

Kilty, K. M. (2003). Poverty, exclusion, and racial and ethnic minorities in the United States. Presented at the Japan—U.S. Symposium: Poverty Inequality, and Social Justice: Making Invisible Poverty Visible, Sapporo, Japan (September 3).

Kilty, K. M., & Segal, E. A. (1996). Genetics and biological determinism: Scientific breakthrough or blaming the victim revisited? *Humanity & Society, 20,* 90-110.

Kilty, K. M., & Vidal de Haymes, M. (2000). Racism, nativism, and exclusion: Public policy, immigration, and the Latino experience in the United States. *Journal of Poverty, 4*(1/2), 1-25.

Northrup, D. (1995). *Indentured labor in the age of imperialism, 1834-1922.* New York: Cambridge University Press.

Pyle, E. (2004). Proposal would give cash to caregivers of relatives. *Columbus Dispatch,* October 14, C3.

Segal, E. A., & Kilty, K. M. (2003). Political promises for welfare reform. *Journal of Poverty, 7*(1/2), 51-67.

Silva, M. (2004). Big donors ante up for three days of inaugural events. *Columbus Dispatch,* December 29, A8.

Takaki, R. (1993). *A different mirror: A history of multicultural America.* Boston: Little, Brown.

Will, G. F. (2004). Bonds of poverty stronger than thought. *Columbus Dispatch,* December 31, A13.

Zepezauer, M. (2004). *Take the rich off welfare* (rev. ed.). Boston: South End Press.

Chapter 10

Microenterprise Development, Welfare Reform, and the Contradictions of New Privatization

Nancy C. Jurik

During his first term as U.S. president, Bill Clinton promised to end welfare as we knew it. In 1996, Congress passed the Personal Responsibility and Work Opportunity Reconciliation Act (PRWORA), which replaced a fifty-year system of federally controlled benefits with state-controlled community development block grants. The grants, referred to as Temporary Assistance for Needy Families (TANF), included more restricted time limits and more rigid work requirements than did previous legislation. In 2003, at the request of President George W. Bush, the U.S. House voted to renew the 1996 welfare law and impose even stricter work requirements on people who receive cash assistance from the federal government (Pear 2003). The Senate did not take such action, so the PRWORA was continued for another year as it stood.

Systematic research on the effects of welfare reform has been difficult because Congress refuses to require tracking of individuals who leave welfare rolls (Piven 2002). However, preliminary evaluations suggest that former welfare recipients who find jobs do so in low-wage and highly unstable employment sectors (Finder 1998; Eitzen and Zinn 2000; Vartanian and McNamara 2000). Moreover, early reports of success in reducing TANF rolls have been attributed to a creaming process: better-off welfare recipients were those most likely to gain quick employment and better wages (Eitzen and Zinn 2000; Albelda 2002). In addition, the economic recession that began in late 1999 has significantly reduced the number of jobs available to most U.S. workers and, in particular, to present and former welfare recipients whose education

doi:10.1300/5608_11

and job training credentials may locate them at the lower end of the employment spectrum. Despite ongoing reports of such problems, both media and politicians have characterized welfare reform as a huge success (Pear 2003). Given these real material issues, how can we explain the popularity of welfare reform?

In this chapter, I will argue that a key to understanding the appeal of welfare reform lies in examining new privatization trends—the discursive and material restructuring of public sector organizations so that they mimic characteristics associated with private business (Jurik 2004). Along with the new privatization of state and nonprofit services comes an increasing individualization of collective responsibility for social well-being (Blau 1999). In the following pages, I will briefly describe these trends and then elaborate one example of a group of nonprofit organizations that has been posed as a market-oriented alternative to traditional welfare—microenterprise development programs (MDPs). MDPs offer training and lending to individuals who wish to begin their own very small businesses (or "microenterprises"), and many programs purport to target marginalized entrepreneurs, including poor women and men, many of whom are people of color. MDPs illustrate both the appeal and the limitations of new privatization agendas that view free market principles as offering the best avenue for solving today's most pressing social problems.

THE PRIVATIZATION OF COLLECTIVE WELFARE

Although work, self-sufficiency, and personal responsibility have always been heralded as solutions for poverty and disadvantage in the United States, welfare reform dramatically extended these principles (Sidel 2000; Naples 1997). Both ideologically and materially, welfare reform is one important part of a much larger agenda to privatize and individualize social responsibility.

In her presidential address to the American Sociological Association, Jill Quadagno (1999, p. 3) describes welfare reform as one aspect of the United States' shift toward what she calls a "capital investment welfare state" that focuses on market-based and private investment solutions to social welfare. Welfare reform concentrates on spending for the poor (which comprises less than 1 percent of the federal budget) and leaves more costly universal social programs such as social security and Medicare intact. However, proposals to alter the amount and form of support for these other programs are in the works. Quadagno identifies three ways in which the capital investment welfare state is apparent:

> [F]irst in efforts to restructure public benefits to coincide with trends in the private sector, second, in efforts to reduce collective responsibility for social welfare needs and increase individual responsibility, and third, in proposals to transform public welfare programs from cash benefits and direct services into incentives for personal savings and investing. (Quadagno 1999, p. 3)

The capital investment welfare state has been greatly advanced by moves to directly privatize many government services. This kind of privatization has been going on for years but was greatly accelerated during the Reagan administration; it directly involves business in the provision of government services (Dantico and Jurik 1986; Sclar 2000). Direct privatization of government services is consistent with neoliberalism—a policy orientation linked to the revitalization of laissez-faire capitalism (Friedman 1977, 1981). Neoliberal policies stress an unfettered market as the key to national and global economic success (McMichael 2000). According to this logic, nations should cut spending by reducing social investment, welfare, and entitlement expenditures, and free corporations from taxation and regulation. Indeed, the state's only legitimate role is to keep markets open. Global competition, growths in entitlement spending, and state fiscal crises provide fertile ground for neoliberalism. Within this context, privatization is advocated as the logical avenue for saving money and increasing the flexibility and efficiency of services. Over the past three decades, there has been significant growth in contracting for security, education, prisons, and the military (Sclar 2000). Welfare reform has also ushered in the increased involvement of for-profit corporations in the administration of welfare-related services such as food stamps and TANF payments (Finder 1998).

In response to criticism of increased government contracting to business, some have pointed to the nonprofit sector as a "third way" or alternative method for social service delivery that is more flexible, innovative, and cost-effective than government on the one hand, and more humane and responsive than for-profit businesses on the other hand (Giddens 1998). Increasing numbers of research studies are exploring the role of nonprofit organizations in promoting civic participation and citizen well-being (Putnam 2000).

Other researchers have challenged claims that nonprofits are clearly distinct from government and for-profit firms (Smith and Lipsky 1993; Hammack and Young 1993). Further still, new privatization trends move beyond government contracting to the restructuring of government and nonprofit organizations so that they operate more like businesses (see Jurik 2004). New privatization agendas call for increased competitiveness in nonprofits and government. Competitiveness can be enhanced through either private-sector bidding alternatives or competitions created within government and nonprofit organizations themselves (unit competition or competition with past records of cost savings). Organizational success is judged according to standardized and measurable outcomes, and unit or individual continuation is tied to the production of successful measures. Cost-effectiveness is typically one of the strongest points of emphasis. These objectives are accompanied by a discourse of empowerment that calls on even the lowest level of staff persons and clients to take responsibility for service quality and cost-effectiveness.

MICROENTERPRISE DEVELOPMENT PROGRAMS

MDPs are compatible with privatization agendas in many respects. By encouraging individual investments in self-employment in lieu of reliance on government safety nets, they are consistent with principles of the capital investment welfare state. By promising to target the poor, many of whom are women, persons of color, and former welfare recipients, they present the case that even the most economically marginalized individuals can be integrated into the new economy. In Congressional hearings on a variety of issues, ranging from hunger legislation to job training, microenterprise development has been heralded as an alternative to welfare as an avenue for assisting the poor (Jurik 2005). MDPs also hold out the hope that with hard work and entrepreneurship, women can successfully combine parenting and income-generating activities by operating small businesses based in or out of their homes. MDPs promote individual independence and responsibility for social welfare, and thus reinforce the individualization of responsibility for social welfare (Howells 2000). MDPs also reinforce beliefs about the merits of direct privatization when they promise to provide an alternative to costly government welfare service provision through smaller, localized, private, nonprofit-sector organizations. Finally, MDPs are highly consistent with new privatization trends because they promise to provide services in a cost-effective and business-like manner.

Although it has become very popular over the past two and a half decades, microenterprise development is by no means entirely new. Poverty alleviation through the provision of subsidized loans was a key component of international development strategies beginning in the 1950s (Adams and Von Pishke 1992). Most of these experiments ended with poor loan repayment rates and the diversion of credit to well-off rather than poor entrepreneurs (Morduch 2000).

Microenterprise development was rediscovered and revamped in the late 1970s when Mohammed Yunus founded the Grameen, a non-profit bank, to provide credit for poor, landless men and women in Bangladesh. Since then, MDPs have exploded in numbers and popularity (Otero and Rhyne 1994). The Grameen Bank now serves over 2.4 million borrowers, operates in over 40,000 villages, and serves as a model for microenterprise development worldwide (Grameen Bank n.d.). Other well-known MDPs include ACCION International and FINCA, which were developed in Latin America, and SEWA, which was begun in India as a women's trade union and later incorporated lending and savings components.

This new generation of MDPs promises not only to target truly poor entrepreneurs but also to operate in a more cost-effective manner. For example, a 1997 Summit of microlending practitioners and advocates set a goal of getting credit to the "world's poorest families" (Microcredit Summit 1997). Furthermore, some of the larger networks of southern hemisphere MDPs (e.g., ACCION) have adopted goals of program self-sufficiency and aim to move toward the commercialization of their operations (Christen and Drake 2002).

Although U.S. programs are often described as an outgrowth of innovations spreading from southern hemisphere ("developing") nations to northern hemisphere ("industrialized") countries, the pioneering southern hemisphere MDPs were financially supported and heavily influenced by international development organizations from northern nations (e.g., U.S. Aid for International Development [USAID], the World Bank, and the Ford Foundation). Some of these same organizations (e.g., Ford, Mott, Ms., and CalMeadow) also encouraged the diffusion of MDPs to northern hemisphere countries. During the 1980s, MDPs became popular in the United States, and now more than 300 programs offer training, lending, and other support to U.S. microentrepreneurs (Walker and Blair 2002).

U.S. programs aim to fill a void left by commercial establishments and government small business lending programs. They lend to borrowers in very small businesses with fewer than five employees and less than $20,000 in start-up capital, and make business loans of less than $10,000, much smaller than those offered by banks (Clark and Kays 1995). MDPs often waive collateral requirements and credit checks, and lend on the basis of business plans or client character alone, even to clients with poor credit histories. Their most notable innovation is the peer lending approach through which loans are made to groups of borrowers ("circles") instead of to individuals, and the entire group may be held accountable for a member's failure to repay. Some peer lending programs boast repayment rates of up to 98 percent (Auwal and Singhal 1992).

Despite many commonalities, MDPs also vary widely. For example, many southern hemisphere programs maintain strong participatory components, and some are client owned. A number of southern hemisphere programs also encourage borrowers' circles to become involved in local and regional networks that aim to strengthen community participation and build the local infrastructure and economy (Rose 1996; Counts 1996).

In contrast, U.S. MDPs tend to be more narrowly focused on self-employment training and lending to individuals (Coyle et al. 1994) rather than on group or community empowerment goals. Although U.S. programs offer more extensive self-employment training than southern hemisphere programs, they are less likely to focus on client problems that go beyond self-employment basics. Data suggest that few U.S. programs go beyond business training and banking components to offer other services such as child care (20 percent) and transportation (7 percent); only two programs directly attempted to link circles to community activism or empowerment activities (Jurik 2005, Chapter 3). Moreover, despite the widespread media publicity about peer lending programs like the Grameen in the United States, less than 20 percent of U.S. MDPs offer peer lending services (Walker and Blair 2002). Nevertheless, MDP peer lending opportunities have been praised as an avenue for promoting community development by creating networks of entrepreneurs whose voice in program affairs such as lending may provide a kind of training ground for increased involvement in community affairs.

MDPs IN ACTION: THE CONTRADICTIONS
OF NEW PRIVATIZATION

A growing body of research has documented not only successes but also contradictions in MDP promises to promote successful businesses among disadvantaged entrepreneurs in a cost-effective manner. Drawing on both a cross-sectional study of a national sample of U.S. MDPs and a longitudinal case study of one peer lending program, I have detailed several problem areas (see Jurik 2005; also see Carr and Tong 2002). It is my argument here, however, that the MDP experience also demonstrates the contradictions of new privatization agendas that seek to remodel government and nonprofit services in the market's image. MDP goals exemplify key components of the new privatization agenda—a focus on funding competitiveness, measurable outcomes, cost-effectiveness, and client empowerment/responsibility.

My data (Jurik 2005) suggest that U.S. MDPs struggled to compete for funding with other nonprofits and government groups. They endeavored to show successful outcomes in the form of high client loan repayments and businesses successes, and simultaneously to keep their operating costs low. Many programs sought to recoup some of their operating expenses by charging fees for program services. Banks and government were anxious to provide funding for loan dollars but were less willing to provide monies for operating and training expenses. This made it difficult for MDPs to offer as many services as needed by highly disadvantaged clients (e.g., poor mothers, the disabled). However, without additional services, such as transportation and child care, needy clients often had a difficult time completing program training and starting or maintaining their businesses. And without business successes, poor entrepreneurs experienced difficulty in repaying their loans. Programs quickly discovered that services to highly disadvantaged clients produced expensive operating costs, but without such expenditures, clients were more likely to fail and negatively affect program outcomes and funding competitiveness. Cost-effectiveness often came at the expense of success outcomes or reductions in services to highly disadvantaged clients. Accordingly, MDPs were pressured to scale up their target clientele to more moderate-income clients who would have the personal and social resources to develop successful businesses and repay loans with less costly service investments.

To sustain funding, MDP staff developed methods for recruiting clients who would be successful in their program. Staff developed guiding definitions of worthy and successful clients, and individuals who did not fit these definitions of worthiness were viewed negatively. With varying degrees of salience, these assessments were also class laden, gendered, and racialized. Over time, MDP staff increasingly distanced their program image and content from welfare and social service models in favor of a more businesslike image (Cowgill and Jurik 2005). Program training content typically emphasized traditional business models and failed to address the racial, ethnic, and gender disadvantages so often faced by women and minority entrepreneurs (Jurik 1998). Instead of promoting woman-oriented models of entrepreneurship, programs tended to rely on traditional models of business and to emphasize hard work and individual responsibility as the most effective avenues for success.

Peer-lending MDPs also discovered that operating effective borrowers' circles increased demands on staff time and further increased operating expenses. Without effective circles, loan repayment rates were again negatively affected. MDP staff also felt pressured to either eliminate peer lending programs or to assume increasing control over borrower circle decision-making processes. These changes in peer lending negated some of the widely praised collective empowerment functions of MDPs (Jurik 2005). Despite these service trends, national MDP advocates in need of funds continued to lobby for a greater share of support from government job training and TANF funds (Friedman 1998; Greenberg 1999).

CONCLUSION

Support for welfare reform is derived from many sectors of our society. State fiscal crises, structural unemployment, and globalization trends have increased public concern with social expenditures. However, it is my contention that the form of response to those concerns is shaped by new privatization agendas. New privatization discourse reinforces the individualization of responsibility for social welfare and the negation of state and nonprofits as alternatives to market-based logic. On the surface, these ideas are attractive because they are compatible with popular U.S. values of entrepreneurialism and individualism, but upon a closer look at one particular case—that of microenterprise development—the contradictions of this discourse become more readily apparent.

Although MDPs provide important services to more moderately resourced clients, their orientation tends to reinforce the extension of traditional business models and individualistic explanations of economic success to aid for the socially marginalized. New privatization cost-effectiveness and empowerment agendas discourage programs from systematically engaging structural sources of disadvantage. By offering only nominal financial support (i.e., small loans), emphasizing personal growth, and ignoring the structural disadvantages, MDPs actually reinforce economic and cultural marginalization (Howells 2000). Success in even the most micro of enterprises typically demands solid skills, related work experience, and access to sufficient resources to get the business going. Small loans and a little bit of training are rarely sufficient to overcome the many barriers confronting former welfare recipients who want to start microenterprises. Based upon their study of microenterprise success, Timothy Bates and Lisa Servon (1996) argue that successful microentrepreneurs typically have safety nets that include education, family and friendship support networks, and relevant business experience. They find that MDP participants "do not fit the underclass stereotype that attracts the lion's share of the attention in the media and in Washington" (Bates and Servon 1996, p. 27). Accordingly, Bates and Servon (1996) conclude that microenterprise loan programs are not a solution to the problem of urban poverty.

By claiming effectiveness for poor and former welfare recipients, MDPs set up a situation that reinforces demands for "welfare reform" and blames the poor for their economic failures, e.g., their businesses could succeed if only they were committed enough or worked hard enough (see Ehlers and Main 1998). Such MDP success discourse reinforces views that social problems can be solved by reliance on market ideologies and that true alternatives to market logic are no longer needed.

REFERENCES

Adams, Dale W., and J. D. Von Pishke. 1992. "Microenterprise Credit Programs: DejaVu." *World Development* 20:1463-1470.

Albelda, Randy. 2002. "What's Wrong with Welfare-to-Work." In *Work, Welfare and Politics: Confronting Poverty in the Wake of Welfare Reform* (pp. 73-80), edited by Frances Fox Piven, Joan Acker, Margaret Hallock, and Sandra Morgen. Eugene: University of Oregon Press.

Auwal, Mohammad A., and Arvind Singhal. 1992. "The Diffusion of the Grameen Bank in Bangladesh." *Knowledge* 14:7-28.

Bates, Timothy, and Lisa Servon. 1996. "Why Loans Won't Save the Poor." *Inc Magazine* 18 (April): 27.

Blau, Joel. 1999. *Illusions of Prosperity: America's Working Families in an Age of Economic Insecurity.* New York: Oxford University Press.

Carr, James H., and Zhong Yi Tong. 2002. "Introduction: Replicating Microfinance in the United States: An Overview." In *Replicating Microfinance in the United States* (pp. 1-18), edited by James H. Carr and Zhong Yi Tong. Washington, DC: Woodrow Wilson Center Press.

Christen, Robert P., with Deborah Drake. 2002. "Commercialization: The New Reality of Microfinance." In *The Commercialization of Microfinance* (pp. 2-21), edited by Deborah Drake and Elisabeth Rhyne. Bloomfield, CT: Kumarian Press, Inc.

Clark, Peggy, and Amy Kays. 1995. *Enabling Entrepreneurship: Microenterprise Development in the U.S.* Washington, DC: Aspen Institute.

Counts, Alex. 1996. *Give Us Credit: How Muhammad Yunus's Micro-lending Revolution is Empowering Women from Bangladesh to Chicago.* New York: Random House.

Cowgill, Julie, and Nancy Jurik. 2005. "The Construction of Client Identities in a Post-Welfare Social Service Program: The Double Bind of Microenterprise Development." In *Deserving and Entitled: Social Constructions and Public Policy* (pp. 173-196), edited by Anne L. Schneider and Helen M. Ingram. Albany: State University of New York Press.

Coyle, Mary, Mary Houghton, Connie Evans, and Julia Vindasius. 1994. *Going Forward: The Peer Group Lending Exchange November 2-4, 1993.* Toronto, Canada: CALMEADOW.

Dantico, Marilyn, and Nancy Jurik. 1986. "Where Have All the Good Jobs Gone: The Effect of Government Service Privatization on Women Workers." *Contemporary Crises* 10:421-439.

Ehlers, Tracy, and Karen Main. 1998. "Women and the False Promise of Microenterprise." Gender & Society 12:424-440.

Eitzen, D. Stanley, and Maxine Baca Zinn. 2000. "The Missing Safety Net and Families." *Journal of Sociology and Social Welfare* 27:53-72.

Finder, Alan. 1998. "Evidence Is Scant that Workfare Leads to Full-Time Jobs." *The New York Times,* April 12, pp. A-1, A-18.

Friedman, Jason. 1998. Testimony of Jason J. Friedman, before the U.S. House of Representatives, Banking and Financial Service Committee. (Washington, DC: House of Representatives, September 23 (cited February 10). Available at <http://www.house.gov/banking/92398fri.htm>.

Friedman, Milton. 1977. *From Galbraith to Economic Freedom.* London: Institute of Economic Affairs.

————. 1981. *The Invisible Hand in Economics and Politics.* Pasir Panjang, Singapore: Institute of Southeast Asian Studies.

Giddens, Anthony. 1998. *The Third Way: The Renewal of Social Democracy.* Cambridge: Polity Press.

Grameen Bank. n.d. "Grameen: Banking for the Poor." Washington, DC: Grameen Bank (cited February 10, 2004). Available at <http://www.grameen-info.org>.

Greenberg, Mark. 1999. *Developing Policies to Support Microenterprise in the TANF Structure: A Guide to the Law.* Washington, DC: The Aspen Institute.

Hammack, David, and Dennis Young (eds.). 1993. *Non-profit Organizations in a Market Economy: Understanding New Roles, Issues, and Trends.* San Francisco: Josey-Bass Publishers.

Howells, Louise. 2000. "The Dimensions of Microenterprise: A Critical Look at Microenterprise As a Tool to Alleviate Poverty." *Journal of Affordable Housing and Community Development* 9:161-182.

Jurik, Nancy. 1998. Getting Away and Getting By: The Experiences of Self-Employed Homeworkers. *Work and Occupations* 25:735.

————. 2004. "Imagining Justice: Challenging the Privatization of Public Life." *Social Problems* 51:1-15.

————. 2005. *Bootstrap Dreams: U.S. Microenterprise Development in an Era of Welfare Reform.* Ithaca, NY: Cornell University Press.

McMichael, Philip. 2000. *Development and Social Change: A Global Perspective,* Second Ed. Thousand Oaks, CA: Pine Forge.

Microcredit Summit. 1997. *Declaration and Plan of Action.* Washington, DC: Microcredit Summit (cited February 10, 2004). Available at <http://www.microcreditsummit.org/declaration.htm>.

Morduch, Jonathan. 2000. "The Microfinance Schism." *World Development* 28:617-629.

Naples, Nancy. 1997. "The 'New Consensus' on the Gendered 'Social Contract': The 1987-1988 U.S. Congressional Hearings on Welfare Reform." *Signs* 22:907-945.

Otero, Maria, and Elisabeth Rhyne. 1994. "Financial Services for Microenterprises: Principles and Institutions." In *The New World of Microenterprise Finance: Building Healthy Financial Institutions for the Poor* (pp. 11-26), edited by Maria Otero and Elisabeth Rhyne. West Hartford, CT.: Kumarian Press.

Pear, Robert. 2003. "House Endorses Stricter Work Rules for Poor." *The New York Times,* February 14, p. A, 25.

Piven, Frances Fox. 2002. "Welfare Policy and American Politics." In *Work, Welfare and Politics: Confronting Poverty in the Wake of Welfare Reform* (pp. 19-34), edited by Frances Fox Piven, Joan Acker, Margaret Hallock, and Sandra Morgen. Eugene: University of Oregon Press.

Putnam, Robert. 2000. *Bowling Alone: The Collapse and Revival of American Community.* New York: Simon & Schuster.

Quadagno, Jill. 1999. "Creating a Capital Investment Welfare State: The New American Exceptionalism." *American Sociological Review* 64:1-11.

Rose, Kalima. 1996. "SEWA: Women in Movement." In *The Women, Gender & Development Reader* (pp. 382-388), edited by Nalini Visvanathan, Lynn Duggan, Laurie Nisonoff, and Nan Wiegersma. London, England: ZED Press Ltd.

Sclar, Elliot D. 2000. *You Don't Always Get What You Pay For: The Economics of Privatization.* Ithaca, NY: Cornell University Press.

Sidel, Ruth. 2000. "The Enemy Within: The Demonization of Poor Women." *Journal of Sociology and Social Welfare* 27:73-84.

Smith, Steven R., and Michael Lipsky. 1993. *Nonprofits for Hire: The Welfare State in the Age of Contracting.* Cambridge, MA: Harvard University Press.

Vartanian, Thomas, and Justice McNamara. 2000. "Work and Economic Outcome After Welfare." *Journal of Sociology and Social Welfare* 27:41-77.

Walker, Britton A., and Amy Kays Blair. 2002. *The 2002 Directory of U.S. Microenterprise Programs.* Washington, DC: The Aspen Institute.

Chapter 11

Welfare Reform and Housing Retrenchment: What Happens When Two Policies Collide?

Jessica W. Pardee

To consider poverty in the absence of housing is to ignore the inextricable link between the two. Housing directly determines one's access to employment, education, credit, transportation, and even garbage collection (Massey and Denton, 1993; Oliver and Shapiro, 1995; Wilson, 1987, 1996; Edin and Lein, 1997; Yinger, 1995). Poverty determines access to housing, that housing reinforces poverty, and the dialectic relationship is complete. Unfortunately, the major federal policies addressing both welfare and housing do not account for such reciprocity. Moreover, they ignore the nearly 50 percent overlap among program participants in welfare and public housing programs (Newman, 1999, cited in Crump, 2003). Which begs the question: What happens when two policies collide?

UNDERSTANDING WELFARE POLICY

The first social assistance programs of the War on Poverty encouraged and supported education, community development, workforce participation, and the enhancement of job-related skills, not direct income transfers (Danziger et al., 1986). These programs were designed to increase human capital, making workers more competitive in the labor market. Coupled with human capital approaches, the War on Poverty considered problems of the nation's economy, such as high unemployment and low labor force participation of the poor, as

doi:10.1300/5608_12

macroeconomic problems (Danziger et al., 1986). Likewise, Aid for Families with Dependent Children (AFDC) was available for single-mother families, who were often widowed or abandoned. In its inception, welfare policy promoted labor market participation and the increase of individuals' skill levels. It did not, however, punish single-mother families for the structural realities well beyond their control.

During the 1970s, the country faced a massive restructuring of the economy. With the emergence of deindustrialization trends and the globalization of the production process, American laborers increasingly faced a splitting labor market (Bonacich, 1976), as the limited number of manufacturing jobs continued to erode. At the same time, cash and in-kind transfer programs such as AFDC and food stamps began to see large increases in benefits. These increases resulted from changes such as increased leniency by welfare administrators, expanded rights and entitlement, the raising of state benefit levels, and the reduced stigma of welfare (Danziger et al., 1986). With these spending increases also came an increase of criticisms about the cost and effectiveness of these same programs. Most notably, during the Reagan administration welfare programs took a severe financial blow, and by the early 1980s AFDC was criticized for rising costs, discouraging work, encouraging out-of-wedlock childbearing, and promoting laziness (Murray, 1984). This decline in support for AFDC continued into the 1990s, when Congress eliminated the program and replaced it with Temporary Assistance for Needy Families (TANF).

In 1996, Congress enacted the Personal Responsibility and Work Opportunity Reconciliation Act (PRWORA) as a blanket law to amend numerous acts and consolidate financial resources into large block grants for discretionary use by the states (CIS Legislative Histories, 1996). In addition to financial consolidation, the reform also redefined federal standards for assistance, transforming welfare from an entitlement program to one of limited assistance. Compared to its predecessor, TANF offers substantially less aid by limiting support to a total of five years over a lifetime, offering no increase for the birth of additional children, denying assistance to unwed women under age eighteen, altering criteria for food stamps, creating child care block grants for administration at the state level, and requiring workforce participation (U.S. Congress, 1996).

Key to the TANF legislation is a significant transfer of responsibility to the state and local levels. The block grant, in particular, allows individual states more discretion in how money is spent, as well as authority to design, implement, and administer programs (Robbins & Barcus, 2004). Potentially, devolution of administrative control from the federal level suggests that states have the ability to coordinate welfare with housing and other programs, yet few reports of such efforts have been documented in the literature to date. What research does suggest, however, is that the states are using welfare reform to reduce their caseloads. Lichter and Crowley (2004) report that, while there has been a 22 percent decline in poverty from 1996 to 2000, the caseload decline was 48 percent, suggesting that the welfare poor are being transformed into the working poor.

Second, individual participants have inherited a new level of accountability under TANF. With the lifetime eligibility limitations and work requirements, recipients face increased pressure to enter the workforce or lose assistance. One consequence of this new approach has been a decrease in the socioeconomic well-being of households. According to Robbins and Barcus (2004), despite a strong economy "more stringent welfare rules are related positively to success in employment and housing, but not to quality of life. . . . Those receiving public assistance remain economically and socially vulnerable despite welfare rules designed to enhance success and improve their status" (p. 453). Furthermore, maintaining those jobs has been difficult, with many women losing their employment within a year (Danzinger et al., 2000). In short, as TANF mothers work to keep their diminishing benefits, at the sacrifice of life quality, they are still vulnerable to economic trauma and homelessness.

Finally, it is important to acknowledge that TANF legislation makes a significant paradigmatic shift in the perception of poverty. Under TANF, poverty is inherent to the individual, not consequential of macrolevel structural shifts, such as deindustrialization and globalization (Wilson, 1987) or segregation and discrimination in housing (Massey & Denton, 1993; Oliver & Shapiro, 1995). The individualization of poverty views recipients as failing to work hard and participate in the American dream (Murray, 1984) and holds them accountable for that failure. Simultaneously, individualizing poverty removes the accountability government and society hold in promoting capitalism as the sole form of economic development, despite the fundamental contradictions capitalism entails, such as unemployment, underemployment, low-wage labor, and labor discrimination. Thus, adopting an individualized perspective of poverty allows government to blame the victim for failure to be a successful laborer, rather than acknowledge the structural barriers under capitalism that inhibit opportunities in employment and wealth generation.

UNDERSTANDING HOUSING POLICY

Concurrent with the implementation of TANF, the federal government is involved in a process of devolving their responsibility as providers of low-cost housing (Gotham and Wright, 1999). At this time, three major types of public housing are available. First, conventional housing projects shelter a large proportion of families. Originating in the late 1930s to offer housing in areas where private investment was absent, these units are large-scale developments, often high rise in form, housing thousands of individuals (Von Hoffman, 1998; Marcuse, 2001). As the majority of public housing, conventional housing is a supply-side approach by federal and local governments to address the need for affordable housing. Although many of the units now lay in disrepair, they originally housed working-class families and were opened to welfare recipients only in the late 1970s through the Brooke amendments (Gotham & Wright, 1999).

Since the 1970s, a second program, Section 8, emerged as a major source of housing. Composed of two types of subsidy, Section 8 includes both supply-side and demand-side approaches to subsidized housing. The original program subsidized private landlords to build small-scale multiunit sites, for twenty-five-year contracts, to rent to low-income families (Gotham & Wright, 1999). Currently, the contracts on many of these units are ending, leaving a hole in the affordable housing safety net (MacDonald, 2000). The second Section 8 subsidy type, the portable rental voucher, allows families to receive vouchers to seek units in the private sector. Increasingly, rental vouchers dominate housing policy and allow HUD to shift responsibility away from physical unit provision to merely subsidizing the private housing market (Marcuse, 2001; Goetz, 2000). Through vouchers, HUD relinquishes their obligation to provide and maintain units. Now, individual families bear the responsibility of locating housing, negotiating with landlords, arranging payment, and paying their own utility bills.

The third housing program is HOPE VI, a redevelopment grant allowing local housing authorities to tear down their traditional developments and replace them with mixed-income units (NHLP, 2002).

HOPE VI is a response to the recommendation of the Federal Commission on Severely Distressed Housing, which was formed in 1992 (Finkel et al., 2000). The commission found that several of the large-scale housing developments suffered from extreme decay and structural incapacitation (NHLP, 2002). With HOPE VI, local housing authorities received funding to raze their large-scale units and replace them with mixed-income alternatives. HOPE VI is also unique in that it encourages authorities to secure funding from multiple sources, including private investors (Howell and Leonard, 1999). Finally, HOPE VI grants require that social service programs such as job training, adult education, homemaking instruction, and others be incorporated to support the residents with the goal of ultimately projecting them out of public housing altogether (Finkel et al., 2000). With these changes, housing policy, similarly to welfare, is shifting toward greater resident involvement and accountability.

DISCUSSION

In considering welfare and housing policy, the inextricable link between the two must be examined critically. For the poor, housing and poverty reinforce each other in a dialectic way. For example, in their work on housing and poverty, Massey and Denton (1993) document the ways in which institutionalized housing segregation creates, intensifies, and maintains poverty within communities that were once racially diverse and socially healthy. In particular, segregation concentrates factors associated with poverty to create social environments where welfare dependency and single parenthood are normalized categories of social and economic behavior. Understanding this basic interconnectedness opens the door for critical examination of the interaction of housing and poverty policies, particularly as the legislation of each is largely ignorant of the other.

Currently, changes to federal poverty policy have resulted in an exodus of people from welfare programs into low-wage, low-skill labor. Although certainly a valid form of employment, low-wage labor is highly unstable, poorly paid, and offers few, if any, additional benefits, such as medical, dental, optical, or other types of insurance. In some states, other social service programs, such as Medicaid and food stamps, may be linked to welfare, meaning an individual's employment may cost them or their children access to benefits.

Simultaneously, the reduction in welfare entitlements coincides with a set of housing policies that encourage the massive reduction and demolition of thousands of public housing units. This housing stock reduction increases competition for subsidized housing and is accompanied by several one-strike policies, which allow for eviction in the incidence of children skipping school, arrest of any individual on the lease (even without conviction), or incidences of domestic violence. Through such strict rules, the public housing sector increasingly funnels the "best" needy families into subsidies, while other more troubled but equally needy families must seek options in a limited private sector (Popkin et al., 2000).

These changes in both policies reduce and redefine the role and responsibility of government while shifting policy emphasis to a framework of "self-sufficiency." By focusing on participants' qualities, the government can back away from support altogether with little political fallout. Yet, with nearly 50 percent overlap among program participants in welfare and public housing programs (Newman, 1999, cited in Crump, 2003), the failure to coordinate between programs indicates that the path to self-sufficiency is not institutionally supported. Under this new legislative reality, mothers move into the low-wage workforce while facing decreasing housing options, with little help or attention paid to the double challenge they now face on employment and housing fronts.

To date, only one program exists for the overlapping welfare-housing populations: the HUD-based welfare-to-work housing voucher program (WtW). WtW is structured to link a family's housing subsidy to their successful participation in the labor force. According to Crump, the program fails to promote self-sufficiency, instead indebting participants to their employers to keep their housing, and functioning, in a de facto way, to keep low-income families impoverished as a source of reserved labor (Crump, 2003). Furthermore, the program's structure is largely punitive, since loss of employment leads to immediate loss of housing, making its promotion of self-sufficiency a questionable goal at best.

Ultimately, with the number of subsidized housing units on the decline, achieving self-sufficiency through low-wage labor without subsidized housing may be unrealistic, and even with subsidized housing, difficult at best. Thus, when trends in both welfare reform and housing policy are considered in conjunction, the road to self-sufficiency has more potential to maintain poverty than to actually reduce it.

CONCLUSION

Starting in the Reagan years and continuing through the 1990s, U.S. policy in both welfare and housing made a drastic paradigm shift away from liberal, structure-based approaches toward privatized, individualized solutions. With this shift, previous policy intended to address inadequacies in employment and housing markets were replaced by policies narrowly focused on individual worthiness, accountability, training, and life-skills attainment. At the intersection of both public housing and welfare policy is a single population: the poor. Yet, neither housing policy nor welfare reform have been sufficiently examined in the context of the other. By individualizing the problem of poverty, the federal government has taken a blind eye to social structure, dissolving their responsibility in the process; for, if poverty is the fault of the individual, then what is the government supposed to do?

On the other hand, if one acknowledges that social structure still exists, and that economically, that structure takes the form of capitalism, then there is a different possibility. By understanding that capitalism is based on competition, with competition creating both economic winners and losers, then society does bear a responsibility. For, if we adopt capitalism as a society, with the understanding that it will create economic winners and losers, are we not therefore responsible for those losers, who emerge out of a system we willfully adopt?

Yes, we are responsible for all our citizens. Current welfare and housing policy leave families in precarious situations as they stand at the abyss of capitalism's failure to provide competitive-wage jobs for all potential workers, as well as affordable housing. The problems stem from the driving force of capitalism: profit. Low-cost housing fails at profitability, so it is not widely available. Even subsidized housing is limited, and it is increasingly reserved for the deserving poor, those who show steady, unfaltering progress toward self-sufficiency. Yet, neither welfare nor housing policy challenges the structural inequalities that re-create and maintain poverty. TANF does not require job creation as part of its policy initiatives. Housing policy is moving away from supplying low-cost units. Neither challenges the educational system. As it stands, today's poor face less affordable housing and less public assistance, in a world of low-wage employment prospects. Although we still don't know exactly what happens as these policies collide, the emerging evidence suggests the possibilities are not very optimistic.

REFERENCES

Bonacich, E. (1976). Advanced Capitalism and Black/White Race Relations in the United States: A Split Labor Market Interpretation. *American Sociological Review*, 41(1), 34-51.

Crump, J. R. (2003). The End of Public Housing As We Know It: Public Housing Policy, Labor Regulation, and the U.S. City. *International Journal of Urban and Regional Research*, 27(1), 179-187.

Danzinger, S., Corcoran, M., Danzinger, S., & Heflin, C. M. (2000). Work, Income, and Material Hardship After Welfare Reform. *Journal of Consumer Affairs*, 34(1), 6-30.

Danzinger, S. H., Haveman, R. H., & Plotnick, R. D. (1986). Antipoverty Policy: Effects on the Poor and the Nonpoor. In S. H. Danzinger & D. H. Weinberg (Eds.), *Fighting Poverty* (pp. 50-77). Cambridge, MA: Harvard.

Edin, K. & Lein, L. (1997). *Making Ends Meet: How Single Mothers Survive Welfare and Low-Wage Work*. New York: Russell Sage Foundation.

Finkel, A. E., Lennon, K. A., & Eisenstadt, E. R. (2000). Hope VI: A Promising Vintage? *Policy Studies Review*, 17(2/3), 104-119.

Goetz, E. G. (2000). The Politics of Poverty Deconcentration and Housing Demolition. *Journal of Urban Affairs*, 22(2), 157-173.

Gotham, K. F. & Wright, J. D. (1999). Housing Policy. In J. Midgley, M. Livermore, & M. B. Tracy (Eds.), *Handbook of Social Policy* (pp. 237-255). Thousand Oaks, CA: Sage.

Howell, J. T. & Leonard, M. W. (1999). Marketing Hope VI Housing: Getting It Right in Mixed-Income Communities. *Journal of Housing and Community Development*, 56(3), 25-32.

Lichter, D. T. & Crowley, M. L. (2004). Welfare Reform and Child Poverty: Effects of Maternal Employment, Marriage, and Cohabitation. *Social Science Research*, 33, 385-408.

MacDonald, H. I. (2000). Renegotiating the Public-Private Partnership: Efforts to Reform Section 8 Assisted Housing. *Journal of Urban Affairs*, 22(3), 279-299.

Marcuse, P. (2001). The Liberal/Conservative Divide in the History of Housing Policy in the United States. *Housing Studies*, 16(6), 717-736.

Massey, D. S. & Denton, N. A. (1993). *American Apartheid: Segregation and the Making of the Underclass.* Cambridge, MA: Harvard.

Murray, C. (1984). *Losing Ground.* New York: Basic Books.

National Housing Law Project (NHLP). (2002, June). *False HOPE: A Critical Assessment of the HOPE VI Public Housing Redevelopment Program.* Oakland, CA: Author.

Oliver, M. L. & Shapiro, T. M. (1995). *Black Wealth, White Wealth.* New York: Routledge.

Popkin, S. J., Buron, L. F., Levy, D. K., & Cunningham, M. K. (2000). The Gautreaux Legacy: What Might Mixed-Income and Dispersal Strategies Mean for the Poorest Public Housing Tenants? *Housing Policy Debate,* 11(4), 911-942.

Robbins, S. M. & Barcus, H. R. (2004). Welfare Reform and Economic and Housing Capacity for Low-Income Households, 1997-1999. *The Policy Studies Journal,* 32(3), 439-460.

U.S. Congress. (1996, August 21). Personal Responsibility and Work Opportunity Reconciliation Act of 1996. Public Law 104-193 [HR 3734].

Von Hoffman, A. (1998). The Curse of Durability: Why Housing for the Poor Was Built to Last. *Journal of Housing and Community Development,* 55(5), 34-38.

Wilson, W. J. (1987). *The Truly Disadvantaged.* Chicago: University of Chicago Press.

Wilson, W. J. (1996). *When Work Disappears.* New York: Vintage.

Yinger, J. (1995). *Closed Doors, Opportunities Lost: The Continuing Costs of Housing Discrimination.* Russell Sage Foundation: New York.

Chapter 12

Changing the Face of Homelessness: Welfare Reform's Impact on Homeless Families

Bart W. Miles
Patrick J. Fowler

If the Administration's discourse offends us, we have a moral
obligation to change public discourse.

George Lakoff

INTRODUCTION

The Personal Responsibility and Work Opportunity Reconciliation
Act (PRWORA) of 1996 has significantly impacted many families
throughout the United States. This chapter focuses on the consequences of welfare reform for the homeless population, and in particular, for homeless families. We discuss the relationship between welfare
reform and the changing demographics of the homeless in America,
the impact of welfare reform on homeless families, and suggestions for
changes to public assistance.

THE DISCURSIVE FRAME OF WELFARE REFORM

Welfare reform is a conservative frame that is an extension of the
strict father model (Lakoff, 2002, 2004). Attached to this strict father
model is the assumption that a man is the head of the household, and

doi:10.1300/5608_13

143

therefore financially responsible for the family's well-being. This construction presupposes an ideal family that consists of a present/dominant father, opposite-sex adult parenting, and marriage. In this scenario welfare is not necessary if the father is doing his duty. The rhetoric of welfare reform references the ideals of the Protestant work ethic (Weber, 2002), which assumes that in a free market economy if you work hard you will always have your needs met. Rather than welfare reform, this is welfare repeal (National Coalition for Homelessness, 1999b) which is the first step in the slippery slope toward removing all public assistance.

THE GOALS OF WELFARE REFORM, AND ITS IMPACT ON HOMELESS PEOPLE

The goals of this welfare reform frame are neither to create a standard of well-being among all citizens nor to provide support to the needy among us. Solving the problems of poverty is not the goal. The goal is to negate responsibility of the government for poverty and the people it affects.

The objectives of welfare reform are

- reducing government welfare rolls and financial responsibility through time limits, restrictions, and being cut off from assistance;
- encouraging and enforcing ideal family styles through incentives for reducing out-of-wedlock births, reducing teen pregnancy, and enforcing child support; and
- punishing weak moral character through work requirements to get assistance, reductions for violations, and punishing certain behaviors, such as having a child or a drug felony.

This conservative frame has many features that affect the homeless population. One way it does so is by cutting benefits and restricting who qualifies for assistance, which has coincided with major demographic changes within the homeless population in the United States (O'Toole et al., 2002). Furthermore, welfare reform has created barriers to transition out of homelessness for many families (NCH & NLCHP, 2004). Welfare reform will continue to propel the United

States toward a country plagued by chronic and cyclical homelessness among families.

CHANGE IN DEMOGRAPHICS
AMONG HOMELESS PEOPLE

On any given night, 800,000 people may be without a home in the United States, and 3.5 million Americans may experience homelessness each year (Burt, 1996; National Low Income Housing Coalition, 2003). Historically, the homeless have been thought of as single adult males who suffer from mental illness and/or substance abuse problems. However, families comprise 40 percent of the homeless population and represent its fastest growing segment (U.S. Mayors Conference, 2004; Freeman, 2002). The number of requests for emergency shelter from homeless families increased by 7 percent between the years 2003 and 2004, which follows double-digit increases in every report since 1998 (U.S. Mayors Conference, 2004). Furthermore, homeless families are more prevalent in rural areas compared to urban centers.

INCREASE IN THE NUMBER OF HOMELESS FAMILIES

One of the key contributing factors to this tremendous growth in the number of homeless families is the issue of welfare reform, particularly with regard to Temporary Assistance for Needy Families (TANF) restrictions. It is no coincidence that the double-digit percentage growth happened during the time in which welfare reform was implemented.

Research has found that current and former TANF recipients report being precariously housed or homeless. In a longitudinal study of 1,362 current and former TANF recipients in Illinois, 23 percent of families were unable to pay rent, and 21 percent of families who left TANF with full-time employment were unable to pay rent. Similarly, 23 percent of 1,621 TANF recipients surveyed in New Jersey reported having a housing crisis in the past year, which included utilities cut off, doubling up to save on housing costs, living in a homeless shelter, or being homeless (Du, Fogarty, Hopps, & Hu, 2000). A survey of 401 TANF recipients in Iowa found that 25 percent of families reported being unable to pay rent, and 27 percent reported doubling up to save on housing; 7 percent reported becoming homeless after leaving TANF. In a survey of 527 former TANF recipients in rural areas of Washington, 14 percent reported being homeless (Rangaran & Wood, 2000).

In addition, homeless families eligible for TANF have had their assistance cut. In a study of 602 homeless families in Los Angeles, 20 percent of families had their income reduced or cut, and of those families, more than half became homeless and 17 percent had to split up as a family (Rozell et al., 2001). Another study in Atlanta found that, of 370 women calling a homeless hotline, 46 percent had received benefits. Of those receiving benefits, 31 percent had benefits discontinued in the past year, 9 percent had their benefits cut, and 30 percent had sanctions and paperwork problems (National Coalition for Homeless, 1998). A study of 481 homeless families in Chicago found that 44 percent of families had their welfare benefits stopped or reduced (Chicago Coalition for the Homeless, 2000). Also, surveys of homeless families have found that only half received TANF benefits (Chicago Coalition for the Homeless, 2000; Nunez & Fox, 1999). Evidence suggests that cutting benefits intensifies the problems of poverty and often leads to homelessness.

IMPACT OF WELFARE REFORM
ON HOMELESS FAMILIES

Welfare reform restrictions that impact families before and after becoming homeless often relate to TANF. The elements of TANF that impact these families are the lifetime assistance limitations, work requirements, family cap provisions (which punish families for having children while receiving assistance), restrictions for teenage parents, restrictions for paternity/child support, restrictions on moving or living without children, restrictions on persons with felony offenses, restrictions on substance use, and penalties for noncompliance as deemed by the state. Other aspects of welfare reform that impact homeless families are the reductions in allotments of food stamps, restrictions for child nutritional programs, reductions in SSI benefits for families with disabled children, limited transitional child care, and lack of housing assistance (NCH & NLCHP, 2004). The priority goal of PRWORA is to reduce public assistance rolls of the states, and these restrictions are used to maximize this goal. States are given financial reinforcement for reductions in public assistance roles, including up to $100 million to the five states that decrease out-of-wedlock births the most.

In looking at TANF restrictions, the lifetime limitations of five years are particularly harsh on homeless mothers, given their lack of resources. Most homeless mothers are in their twenties or thirties, have a high school education, and have one to two children, five years old on average (Bassuk et al., 1996; Hicks-Coolick et al., 2003). The job opportunities available to someone with a high school education are often limited to the service industry. Service industry jobs are low paying, often have no benefits, and tend to be transitional or short-term jobs (Danzinger et al., 2000). Therefore, even if a homeless mother makes it out of homelessness, it is likely that she will experience the inability to pay rent or will spend time without a job, which increases the potential for homelessness or doubling up in the lifetime of her children (National Center on Family Homelessness, 2003).

States vary on what they count as work and how much time is given to find a job, but finding work is difficult to do when homeless. This difficulty is compounded if you also care for your children. If you find a job, keeping it can be difficult due to a myriad of factors: work hours often must coincide with shelter hours, finding or paying for child care can be difficult, and transportation is often prohibitively expensive, slow, or unavailable, causing difficulties particularly for parents with school-aged children (National Center on Family Homelessness, 2003).

Welfare reform restrictions are primarily a facade for eliminating public assistance for citizens who are most in need. For example, restrictions on teen parents require them to be in school or vocational training and in the supervision of an adult, unless they are married. This could impact homeless populations since teen pregnancy is an issue for homeless adolescents (Greene & Ringwalt, 1998). Often homeless teens are not "consistently" under the direct supervision of an adult and are often not in school. Other restrictions include provisions on paternity and child support which state that benefits can be stopped if women are not complying in establishing paternity or if they do not give the state authority to collect child support from the responsible party. Homeless families are often disconnected from their social and familial relationships while living on the streets or in shelters (NCH & NLCHP, 2004), so establishing paternity or identifying locations of the financially responsible party may be difficult. A homeless family member's limited information could be deemed refusal to assist the state and result in the termination of or reduction in welfare assistance. Furthermore, homeless families often have to split up due to the circumstance of homelessness, with the result that children spend periods of time with extended family or in the foster care system (Park et al., 2004). This could lead to termination of assistance as defined under either the absence of the child for a significant period, forty-five days, or the failure to inform the state within five days of the child's absence.

Felony offenses and substance use are significant issues for homeless families. The war on drugs (another conservative frame) has created a major growth in felony offenses (The Sentencing Project, 2001). Many homeless women with children are felons and might be in violation of parole or probation due to living situation, location, and transportation issues. Felons who are in violation of probation or parole have assistance terminated. Welfare reform suggests the use of drug testing for welfare recipients and requires sanctioning those who test positive. This further decreases the TANF rolls, but increases the economic strain on homeless families.

These restrictions and limitations of TANF not only increase the potential for homelessness through reductions in income assistance, precarious housing situations, and job opportunities with unlivable wages, but also decrease the opportunities for transitioning out of homelessness for homeless families. The poor prospect for transi- tioning out of homelessness is greatly exacerbated by the lack of housing opportunities, transportation, child care, and medical care available to homeless families (National Center on Family Homelessness, 2003). A recent study found that only five states use TANF funds to meet the special needs of homeless families (NCH & NLCHP, 2004).

CONCLUSION

Welfare reform has accomplished what its creators had intended: reducing government responsibility for the poor and homeless. However, it has created a new problem by increasing the number of homeless people, particularly among families. This increase in homeless families creates a crisis for current homeless service providers throughout the country, who already lack the capacity to address the special needs of homeless families (NCH & NLCHP, 2004). Historically, the size and demographics of the homeless population today are comparative to those of the homeless during the Great Depression, with a large percentage of families and substance-abusing single adults (Kusmer, 2002). Economic crisis created this change in the homeless population in the 1930s, while the current change was produced through a political ideology as reflected in welfare reform.

RECOMMENDATIONS

Welfare reform is a conservative discursive frame, and using the term "welfare reform" recalls the conservative agenda. So let us begin by reframing welfare with a progressive frame, by referring to it as *Well-Being Reinforcement: Creating a Structure of Support for All American People.* This makes welfare a practice that empowers people and maximizes people's potential. Welfare should be framed as an investment in the future of American families and citizens. This frame emphasizes that economic disparities in our society are structural and create economic injustices that require compensation for disparities. Welfare becomes the solution to poverty and homelessness through providing opportunity and resources to persons who are economically disenfranchised.

The Discursive Frame of Well-Being Reinforcement

The agenda now changes within this frame; the purpose is not welfare reform. It creates a desire for human enrichment and empowering the potential of Americans through public assistance. If you are poor or homeless, it is due to society's structural flaws. This is tied to the conceptions of the nurturing parent model of progressives, as noted by George Lakoff (2002, 2004). This nurturant parent model is gender neutral and assumes that children/citizens are naturally good and can be made better. When government has the role of the nurturant parent, then it emphasizes responsibility and empathy. Thus, poverty and homelessness are indicators of a gap in community responsibility. This is why well-being reinforcement should emphasize incentives for community, initiatives to end homelessness, incentives for reduction in the poverty rate, universal health care access, and drug treatment for all those struggling with addiction.

The Goals of Well-Being Reinforcement and Its Impact on Homelessness

The goals of this ideological frame are not to dissolve social programs. *Well-Being Reinforcement* is about creating a standard of well-being among all citizens. The goals of this frame are to solve the problems of poverty and homelessness by

- increasing mutual responsibility for poverty and homelessness through funding local projects to end homelessness, community task forces that address specific needs of that community, and federal programs that transition current chronic homeless off the streets;
- compensating for economic disparities through financial assistance for the poor and homeless, guaranteeing shelter for all people, and ensuring transitional living situations for those experiencing economic crises; and
- preventing homelessness and poverty through creation of a national research institute that funds major research projects that study causes of homelessness and poverty and promotes prevention and intervention strategies that address homelessness and poverty.

Let us take this new frame and challenge the conservative discourse of welfare reform. We should push to establish progressive values that highlight the structural factors behind homelessness and poverty in our society.

REFERENCES

Bassuk, E.L., Weinreb, L.F., Buckner, J.C., Browne, A., Salomon, A., & Bassuk, S.S. (1996). The characteristics and needs of sheltered homeless and low-income housed mothers. *Journal of the American Medical Association, 276,* 640-646.

Burt, M. (1996). Homelessness: Definitions and counts. In J. Baumohl (Ed.), *Homelessness in America* (pp. 15-23). Phoenix, AZ: Oryx Press.

Chicago Coalition for the Homeless (2000). *Families hardest hit: The impacts of welfare reform on homeless families.* Retrieved December 21, 2004, from Chicago Coalition for the Homeless Web site: <http://www.chicagohomeless.org/factsfigures/hardesthit.pdf>.

Danziger, S., Corcoran, M., Danziger, S., Heflin, C., Kalil, A., Levine, J., Rosen, D., Seefeldt, K., Siefert, L., & Tolman, L. (2000). *Barriers to the Employment of Welfare Recipients.* Ann Arbor: University of Michigan Poverty Center.

Du, J., Fogarty, D., Hopps, D., & Hu, J. (2000). A study of Washington state TANF leavers and TANF recipients: Findings from the April-June 1999 telephone survey. Available at <http://aspe.hhs.gov/hsp/leavers99/state-rpts/wa/Exit3Report.pdf>.

Freeman, L. (2002). America's affordable housing crisis: A contract unfulfilled. *American Journal of Public Health, 92,* 709-714.

Greene, J.M., & Ringwalt, C.L. (1998). Pregnancy among three national samples of runaway and homeless youth. *Journal of Adolescent Health, 23,* 370-377.

Hicks-Coolidge, A., Burnside-Eaton, P., & Peters, A. (2003). Homeless children: Needs and services. *Child and Youth Care Forum, 32*(4), 197-210.

Kusmer, Kenneth (2002). *Down and Out, on the Road: The Homeless in American History.* Oxford: Oxford University Press.

Lakoff, G. (2002). *Moral Reasoning: How Liberals and Conservatives Think* (2nd ed.). Chicago, IL: University of Chicago Press.

Lakoff, G. (2004). *Don't Think of an Elephant! Know Your Moral Values and Frame the Debate.* White River Junction, VT: Chelsea Green Publishing.

National Center on Family Homelessness (2003). *Social Supports for Homeless Mothers.* Newton Centre, MA: The National Center on Family Homelessness.

National Coalition for the Homeless (1996). Legislative wrap-up: The 104th's legacy on homelessness. *Safety Network:* October/November 1996. Washington, DC: National Coalition for the Homeless.

National Coalition for the Homeless (1998). The impact of welfare reform on homelessness. *Safety Network:* May/June 1998. Washington, DC: National Coalition for the Homeless.

National Coalition for the Homeless (1999a). National Coalition for Homeless Fact Sheet #1: *Why people are homeless.* Washington, DC: National Coalition for the Homeless.

National Coalition for the Homeless (1999b). *Welfare repeal: The impact of HR. 3734 on homelessness in America.* Retrieved December 21, 2004, from <http://www.nationalhomeless.org/publications/facts/How_Many.pdf>.

National Coalition for the Homeless (2002). National Coalition for Homeless Fact Sheet #2: *How many people experience homelessness?* Retrieved December 21, 2004, from <http://www.nationalhomeless.org/publications/facts/why.pdf>.

National Low Income Housing Coalition (NLIHC) (2003). *2002 Advocate's Guide to Housing and Community Development.* Retrieved December 21, 2004, from <http://www.nationalhomeless.org/numbershtml>.

NCH & NLCHP (2004). *State TANF Programs Targeted at People Experiencing Homelessness.* Washington, DC: National Coalition for the Homeless.

Nunez, R., & Fox, C. (1999). A snapshot of homeless across America. *Political Science Quarterly, 114,* 289-307.

O'Toole, T.P., Gibbon, J. L., Seltzer, D., Hanusa, B., & Fine, M. J. (2002). Urban homelessness and poverty during economic growth and welfare reform: Changes in self-reported comorbidities, insurance, and sources for usual care, 1995-1997. *Journals of Urban Health: Bulletin of the New York Academe of Medicine, 79,* 200-210.

Park, J. M., Metraux, M., Brodbar, G., & Culhane, D.P. (2004). Child welfare involvement among children in homeless families. *Child Welfare, 83,* 423-437.

Personal Responsibility and Work Opportunity Reconciliation Act, Pub. L. No. 104-193, 110 Stat. 2105-2355 (1996).

Rangaran, A., & Wood, R.J. (2000). Work First New Jersey Evaluation. Current and former Work First New Jersey clients: How are they faring 30 months later. *Mathematica Policy Research.* Available at <http://www.mathematica.org/ PDFs? wfnj.pdf>.

Robertson, M.J., & Toro, P.A. (1999). Homeless youth: Research, intervention, and policy. In L.B. Fosburg & D.L. Dennis (Eds.), *Practical Lessons: The 1998 National Symposium on Homelessness Research* (pp. 3-1–3-32). Washington, DC: U.S. Department of Housing and Urban Development.

Rozell, M., Harrington, S., Erlenbusch, B., Gleason, M.A., & Phillips, S.W. (2001). *Welfare to What? Part II.* Los Angeles, CA: National Coalition for the Homeless and the Los Angeles Coalition to End Hunger & Homelessness.

The Sentencing Project (2001). *Drug Policy and the Criminal Justice System.* Washington, DC: The Sentencing Project.

Sommer, H. (2001). *Homelessness in Urban America: A Review of the Literature.* Institute of Governmental Studies. Berkley: Institute of Governmental Studies Press.

U.S. Mayors Conference (2004). *A Status Report on Hunger and Homelessness in America's Cities: 2004.* Retrieved December 21, 2004, from U.S. Conference of Mayors Web site: <http://www.usmayors.org/uscm/hungersurvey/2004/ onlinereport/HungerandHomelessnessReport2004.pdf>.

Weber, M. (2002). *The Protestant Work Ethic and the Spirit of Capitalism and Other Writings.* (G. Wells & P. Baehr, trans.). London: Penguin Books.

PART III:
FAMILY CONSTRUCTION
AND DESTRUCTION:
MARRIAGE, FATHERHOOD,
AND DOMESTIC VIOLENCE

Chapter 13

Ending Single Motherhood

Gwendolyn Mink

In 1996, a new welfare law replaced the sixty-year-old Aid to Families with Dependent Children (AFDC) program with the Temporary Assistance for Needy Families program (TANF). The new welfare program emphasized the temporary nature of welfare assistance and directed poor families to attenuate their own poverty through work and child support. These changes in the welfare system appeared to promote mothers' economic independence and children's material well-being. Work requirements appeared to move poor mothers into the labor market where they could earn their own income, and child support enforcement requirements appeared to promote financial equity in biological families while augmenting the economic resources available to children.

The pillars of the new welfare system—work and child support—were not particularly new to welfare reform. Ever since the 1960s, welfare reformers had insisted that the welfare system should encourage mothers to seek alternatives to cash assistance—either in the labor market or from the biological fathers of their children. Yet the 1996 welfare law was heralded as "the end of welfare as we know it." What was new in the 1996 law—what promised welfare's end—was its commitment to ending single motherhood.

HOW THE 1996 WELFARE LAW UNDERMINES SINGLE MOTHERHOOD

This commitment was forecast in the "findings" that prefaced the 1996 law. The findings began with the assertion that "marriage is the

doi:10.1300/5608_14

foundation of a successful society." They then proceeded to blame numerous social ills on nonmarital childbearing and single mother-hood. One finding, for example, announced that "children born out-of-wedlock are more likely to experience low verbal cognitive attain-ment, as well as more child abuse, and neglect."[1] Another finding claimed: "Children from single-parent homes are almost four times more likely to be expelled or suspended from school."[2] The penulti-mate finding asserted that "areas with higher percentages of single-parent households have higher rates of violent crime."[3]

The unrelenting, twenty-point indictment of single motherhood detailed in the 1996 law's findings led ineluctably to the conclusion that the goal of the new TANF program must be to prevent out-of-wedlock pregnancy and reduce out-of-wedlock births.[4] To accom-plish this goal, the 1996 law announced new statutory purposes for welfare. These statutory purposes govern the TANF program as a whole, authorizing and guiding implementing agencies—primarily the Department of Health and Human Services (HHS). As spelled out in the 1996 law, three of the four purposes of TANF involve promot-ing marriage, preventing nonmarital childbearing, and fostering two-parent family formation.[5] In other words, three of the four purposes of TANF involve ending single motherhood.

Programmatic provisions in the 1996 law regarding teenage moth-ers, illegitimacy, sexuality education, mandatory work, and child sup-port put the TANF system to work meeting these statutory goals.

TANF provisions for teenagers require teenage mothers to live with an adult or in an adult-supervised setting as a condition of re-ceiving benefits—but only if they are unmarried. Although there's been much public hand-wringing by welfare reformers about "babies having babies," TANF is not concerned about teenage motherhood per se. The program does not place special hurdles in the way of mar-ried teens who choose to bear and raise children.[6] The program cre-ates obstacles only for teenagers who are single mothers.

TANF's illegitimacy provision offers bonus funding to states to en-list them in devising programs to discourage unmarried childbearing and to encourage marital family formation. To compete for an "ille-gitimacy reduction bonus" of up to $20 million in any given year, a state must accomplish a decline in the number of nonmarital births in comparison to the previous two-year period while also showing that the number of abortions dropped below 1995 levels.[7] Theoretically, at least, illegitimacy reduction bonus money gives states incentive to encourage unmarried pregnant women either to get married or to surrender the nonmarital child to adoption at birth.

The 1996 welfare law also addressed sexuality education, providing funds to states for abstinence-before-marriage sexuality education programs. Dedicating $50 million each year to fund local programs, the abstinence education provision requires states to target "those groups which are most likely to bear children out-of-wedlock" with "educational or motivational" initiatives that teach that sex outside of marriage is deviant, psychologically harmful, physically risky, and damaging to children conceived.[8] States also must teach "the importance of attaining self-sufficiency before engaging in sexual activity," or no sex for the poor.

In addition to the $50 million explicitly dedicated to abstinence-only education by the 1996 law, HHS has made federal TANF funds available to states to promote abstinence, as well. According to HHS, states may use their TANF block grants for activities that advance the TANF purpose of reducing out-of-wedlock pregnancies, including abstinence programs, and "may also fund a media campaign for the general population on abstinence or preventing out-of-wedlock childbearing."[9]

As a companion to programs to prevent single women from bearing children, the Department of Health and Human Services also gives states incentives to increase the number of children residing in marital families. A "high performance bonus" goes to states that best increase the proportion of marital families with children. In 2002, ten states received $10.2 million in such family formation bonuses.[10]

TANF work requirements include a mandatory work provision that directly impairs a single mother's ability to raise her child as she sees fit, including by working in the home as her family's caregiver. A single mother must work outside the home twenty or thirty hours a week, depending on the age of her child; a mother who does not will be sanctioned and will jeopardize her family's eligibility for cash assistance. In contrast, the work provision subjects only one parent in two-parent families to mandatory work outside the home. Two-parent families must meet a thirty-five-hour weekly work requirement, but one parent may remain in the home caring for children if the other parent is in a work activity full-time.[11]

Finally, TANF's child support provisions require mothers to assist in establishing children's paternity and in collecting child support from biological fathers. Mothers who cannot or choose not to meet these requirements stand to lose at least 25 percent of their family's grant.[12] As with other TANF provisions, child support enforcement rules do not actually end single motherhood, but they do pressure single mothers into marriage-like financial relationships with biological fathers. Related provisions encourage states to develop visitation programs for noncustodial parents—overwhelmingly fathers—to promote fathers' social relationships with children.[13] Together, TANF's child support and paternal access provisions form the entering wedge for recent, more aggressive policies to reinstate fathers in biological families through married fatherhood promotion.

The coup de grace in TANF's war on single motherhood is its collaboration with child removal programs. By statute, TANF requires states to maintain foster care and adoption assistance programs as a condition of receiving the TANF block grant.[14] Federal TANF guidelines about sanctions—punishments for violating a TANF rule—encourage states to monitor sanctioned families for signs of child neglect. The child welfare system treats poverty as a sign of neglect, with "neglectful" poor mothers more likely to lose custody of children than are nonpoor mothers.[15] TANF's sanctions, which vastly increase the risk of destitution for single-mother families, correspondingly compound the risk of child removal from such families. TANF rules and punishments thus facilitate the end of single motherhood by ending some single mothers' care and custody of children.

The Adoption and Safe Families Act of 1997 augmented TANF's assault on single motherhood. ASFA speeded termination of parental rights, permanently removing children from their mother's custody if they have been in foster care for fifteen out of twenty-two months. It also provided incentive bonuses to states of $4,000 for each adoption accomplished ($6,000 for a special needs child).[16] While adoption bonuses reward states for placements, they also discourage states from promoting reunification of a child's original family. Reunification after child removal often requires investing in services for destitute mothers—e.g., substance abuse, mental health, domestic violence, or employment services—but states do not receive federal funds to pay for those services. Instead, ASFA gives states money to assist adoptive families, thus making adoption more fiscally prudent than family reunification.

Restrictions on unmarried teenage mothers, illegitimacy and family formation bonuses, and abstinence-only education all aim to prevent single women from becoming mothers. Work and child support requirements punish mothers who are single, putting mothers who do not comply at risk of losing their children. Child removal measures provide a powerful, final weapon in the war on single motherhood. Each of these elements of the 1996 welfare reform regulates and disciplines single mothers' reproductive and caregiving decisions. However they do not actually reconfigure single mothers' families.

HOW THE DEPARTMENT OF HEALTH AND HUMAN SERVICES PROMOTES MARRIED FATHERHOOD

Charged with implementing TANF, the Department of Health and Human Services has worked administratively to augment TANF's family formation aspirations with substantive initiatives. Claiming programmatic authority based on TANF's statutory purposes, HHS has developed programs to promote *married fatherhood* as the alternative to single motherhood. The idea is to transform single-mother families into families headed by married biological fathers.

Toward this end, HHS allows states to spend TANF dollars on *any* "needy parent," including a noncustodial, nonresident, biological father who has no established social relationship with his children or their mother—as long as he's poor. HHS further maintains that TANF's call "to encourage the formation and maintenance of two-parent families" justifies helping noncustodial fathers through

> parenting skills training, premarital and marriage counseling, divorce mediation services; activities to promote parental access and visitation; job placement and training for noncustodial parents; initiatives to promote responsible fatherhood and increase the capacity of fathers to provide emotional and financial support for their children; and crisis or intervention services.[17]

In other words, according to HHS, TANF's original statutory purposes authorize the diversion of funds from income assistance for mothers and children to social services to enhance the role (and marriageability) of fathers.

Congressional initiatives since 1996 endorse the HHS emphasis on fathers. The TANF program acquired specific legislative authority to promote fatherhood in 1997, when the new Welfare-to-Work block grant explicitly authorized spending for noncustodial parents of children receiving TANF—overwhelmingly fathers.[18] The idea was that poor fathers need a helping hand if they are to become family breadwinners.

The 1997 action proved to be the opening salvo in a still-ongoing campaign for governmental promotion of fatherhood. Beginning with the first "Fathers Count" bill in 1999, various fatherhood promotion bills have proposed programs to improve the income potential of men whose biological children receive TANF and to encourage residential fatherhood. Although first touted by Republicans, fatherhood promotion legislation has not been the monopoly of any particular political camp. In the House of Representatives, for example, Democrats Jesse Jackson Jr. and Julia Carson have authored fatherhood promotion bills that closely resemble Republican proposals. Whether authored by conservatives or progressives, fatherhood promotion legislation uniformly has promoted marriage.

Although fatherhood legislation has not yet passed the Congress, the Department of Health and Human Services has continued to encourage states to develop marriage and fatherhood initiatives. Many of the initiatives are paid for with TANF funds, reducing funding for initiatives that might enhance single mothers' prospects for economic independence—such as education and training, or services to overcome domestic violence. In 2001, Michigan directed 1 million TANF dollars toward a fatherhood program and another $250,000 to support marital counseling. Oklahoma set aside $10 million from its TANF surplus in 2001 to establish a marriage initiative run by two "marriage ambassadors" who are each paid $250,000 per year. Utah earmarked $600,000 of its TANF funds in 2001 to support marriage education activities, divorce-avoidance counseling, and marriage mediation; it also set up a Marriage Commission.[19]

HHS has promoted marital family formation since the late 1990s, but marriage and fatherhood initiatives did not materialize full-bore until the Bush Administration came to power in 2001. Since 2002, the Administration for Children and Families (ACF), which runs TANF for HHS, has sponsored a Healthy Marriage Initiative, which includes the racially-targeted Hispanic Healthy Marriage Initiative and

African American Healthy Marriage Initiative. Under the initiative, various agencies fund local efforts to make healthy marriage a component of programs affecting children and families.

The Children's Bureau, for example, has awarded Florida $1.7 million over three years for marriage and marital family programs.[20] The Office of Child Support Enforcement has allocated about $9 million to several states to promote marriage and fatherhood—$9 million that would otherwise go to collecting child support awards for custodial mothers who are no longer in relationships with biological fathers.[21] The Office of Refugee Resettlement has provided the U.S. Conference of Catholic Bishops $1 million in support of efforts to integrate "marriage and family enrichment services" into refugee assistance programs in seventeen localities.[22]

Alongside the marriage initiative, ACF encourages fatherhood initiatives by its various agencies. Head Start, for example, instructs local centers to foster father involvement through a series of program changes and additions. In a recent Head Start Bulletin on father involvement, ACF chief Wade Horn called for "restor[ing] a culture that uplifts men in their role as fathers."[23] Casting fathers as victims of women's unreasonable expectations and prejudices, the manual instructs Head Start staff to create father-friendly environments. The first step is to retrain the predominantly female Head Start staff to be nice to men and to "help moms . . . understand how fathers can be positive influences on their children."[24] The next step—according to the manual — is to defeminize the Head Start workplace—to rid it of comments or consciousness about women's issues that might be offensive to men.

One instruction reads: "The initial reception area [should be] free of signs or posters that would be possibly intimidating for men, e.g., *posters that target men as batterers.*"[25] Another instruction tells Head Start centers to make sure that they employ male staff who are "listened to with open minds, their ideas . . . considered thoughtfully."[26] Yet another instruction urges staff to make sure as well that "there are no informal negative conversations about men to be overheard."[27]

The preferences and concerns of mothers appear nowhere in the Head Start manual. Instead, its sole concern is how to protect biological fathers from female staff and mothers so as to smooth their access to and involvement with children. The problem, here, is not the goal of father involvement. The problem is that custodial mothers have no say about a given father's involvement. The problem also is that mothers' legitimate concerns—domestic violence, men's behaviors—are demeaned as harmful to fathers.

The Head Start manual is a disturbing prototype for governmental promotion of fatherhood. It conditions successful father involvement on the censorship of mothers—on the erasure of their issues and perspectives. It illuminates the misogyny and patriarchalism that undergird the agenda for married fatherhood. It strongly warns that the end of single motherhood means the subordination of women in men's families.

CURRENT PROPOSALS TO MARRY SINGLE MOTHERS

The diversion of social services funding from Head Start, child support enforcement, and refugee resettlement to married fatherhood programs has not sated proponents of married fatherhood. So, as he has each year since taking office, President Bush in 2005 proposed dedicating more than $1 billion over five years for marriage and fatherhood initiatives through the TANF program. The proposed new statutory commitment to married fatherhood promotion is not merely a funding commitment. It also commits the federal government to enforcing married fatherhood promotion in all fifty states.

In announcing the marriage and fatherhood proposal, Bush congratulated the original TANF program for recognizing the importance of father-mother marital families. But he also concluded that states have done too little to advance TANF's married-family goals. That's in part because TANF currently does not actually require states to promote marriage or fatherhood; it simply supports them if they do. Only eleven states signed up to promote fatherhood in 2004. Only nine states have offered financial incentives to welfare recipients who marry. And although two states forgive child support arrearages for fathers and mothers who reunite, one state (Vermont) does not specifically mention marriage.[28]

So in addition to adding funds to pay for marriage and fatherhood promotion, the Bush proposal requires states to describe their efforts to promote marriage as a condition of receiving their TANF block grants. If the proposal becomes law, states will have to (1) report, annually, just what they are doing to promote marital family formation; (2) provide, annually, numerical performance goals for their marriage programs (by projecting improvements in marriage rates, for example); and (3) document, annually, progress toward those goals. Enlisting states in developing plans to promote marriage, these new requirements will proliferate heteromarital family formation activities across all fifty states.

The marriage promotion component of the Bush agenda has received considerably more attention than has the fatherhood component. It also is in line for considerably more funding. This does not mean that the Bush government is less interested in fatherhood than it is in marriage. Marriage and fatherhood are inextricably linked in the ultimate goal of married fatherhood. As Assistant Secretary for Children and Families Wade Horn has explained: "If the goal is to produce lifetime fathers for children, and not merely a temporary increase in father involvement, something else needs to be added to the mix. That something else is marriage."[29] Marriage promotion, then, is a means to secure married fatherhood, while fatherhood promotion is a means to prepare men to secure their role in the marital family.

The point of marriage promotion is not to help single mothers find a soul mate—it's not a dating service. Nor is it the point of fatherhood promotion to recruit helpmeets for single mothers. The point of marriage and fatherhood promotion is to instate biological fathers in single mothers' families. Marriage and fatherhood promoters have already decided *whom* single mothers should marry: the DNA father of the single mother's child. Hence marriage programs emphasize paternity establishment, while fatherhood programs focus on men with biological progeny.

The Bush administration leads the campaign for married fatherhood, but many Democrats have climbed on the bandwagon. Some Democrats have sponsored or co-sponsored Bush-like fatherhood bills that call for marriage promotion—Democrats as disparate as Evan Bayh in the Senate and Jesse Jackson Jr. in the House of Representatives. A few Democrats are wary of governmental meddling in the individual's marriage decision. But even those Democrats who have questioned marriage promotion by government do favor governmental support for two-parent family formation and "responsible fatherhood."[30]

ENDING INDEPENDENT MOTHERHOOD

Behind the consensus to promote two-parent families is the claim that children are better off if raised by married, biological parents. Espoused by groups as ideologically dissimilar as the Center for Law and Social Policy and the Heritage Foundation, the argument that married fatherhood should be part of an antipoverty strategy seems to hold considerable sway.

The Center for Law and Social Policy's marriage agenda is gentler than the agenda advocated by the Heritage Foundation, in that CLASP wants to "ensure that public policy helps all parents—whether never-married, cohabiting, separated, divorced, or married." But there is very little wiggle room between CLASP and Heritage about the bottom line principle that married biological parenthood is a desirable public policy goal—meaning that government should promote that goal. As CLASP stated in a recent report: "public policy should try to help more children be born into, and grow up with, two biological married parents, who have a reasonably healthy, cooperative relationship."[31]

Two kinds of arguments sustain the married fatherhood agenda, one instrumental and one ideological. The instrumental argument is largely economic, but also makes certain sociological claims, such as that children raised by married biological parents are better off than children raised in different family arrangements. The instrumental argument is best captured by posters that are mounted in most metro stations in Washington, DC—nine of them in the Capitol Hill metro station alone. One reads: "Kids of Married Parents Do Better in School. . . . Marriage Works!" Another reads: "Married People Make More Money. . . . Marriage Works!" The "marriage works" part of the message betrays instrumentalism—marriage works because it has desirable social effects.

This instrumentalism is not intrinsically patriarchalist, but in practice pushes hard in patriarchal directions. The instrumentalist argument for married fatherhood begins by noticing that two-parent families are better off than single-mother families—they have more money, are economically more stable, etc. Economic measurements of family status and stability are then correlated with child outcomes—such as bad behavior, crime, nonmarital pregnancy.

The number of single father families has risen exponentially since 1970 (from half a million to 2 million) just as has the number of single mother families (from 3 million to 10 million). But no one singles out *father*-only families to show the harms of one-parent childraising and the benefits of married parenthood. This is no doubt because the economic disparities between single father and two-parent families are less extreme than between single mother and two-parent families. Thirty-two percent of single-mother families have incomes below the poverty level, as compared to 16 percent of single-father families.[32] Moreover, of all female-headed families with children in poverty in 2002, 50 percent were never married.

Instrumentalist correlations among family finances, stability, and child outcomes produce support for marriage and fatherhood promotion, even among liberals. The instrumentalist argument begins by defining single motherhood as the problem and proceeds to make married fatherhood the solution. What's ignored in this rush to the altar is why single-mother families might be economically unstable and poor in the first place. What's ignored is how the labor market enforces single-mother poverty and how the welfare system robs single mothers of time to spend caring for their children. Instead, marriage and fatherhood are allowed to stand in for time and resources, as if the inequality that sustains single-mother poverty doesn't matter at all.

Instrumentalist proponents of married fatherhood don't ask why single-mother families are disproportionately poor. They syllogistically assert that since married, biological-father families are less poor, single mothers should get married. As the Heritage Foundation's Robert Rector told the House Ways and Means Committee in February 2005: "If poor single mothers were married to the fathers of their children, nearly 70 percent would be immediately lifted out of poverty."[33]

But what if single mothers had access to better-paid jobs, more secure welfare assistance, and affordable, high-quality child care? Would they then need to depend on a man and his wages to escape poverty?

The ideological argument for married fatherhood offers brazenly patriarchal responses to these questions. The ideological argument finds that women's independence is the cause of social problems and that the goal of women's equality is incompatible with the purpose of married biological parenthood. For pro-father ideologues, the purpose of married fatherhood promotion is to restore fathers as the leaders of their families and to return mothers to a domestic role.

The Republican TANF bill under consideration in the House of Representatives at this writing justifies fatherhood promotion programs this way: they will "improv[e] fathers' ability to effectively manage family business affairs by means such as education, counseling, and mentoring in matters including household management, budgeting, banking, and handling of financial transactions, time management, and home maintenance."[34] The goal is for *fathers* to "manage family business affairs." Sounds like patriarchy to me.

Some pro-father ideologues take the patriarchal mission a step further, arguing for married fatherhood programs because of the distinctive and inherent virtues of biological fathers. Father-present families are considered to be by definition good for children because it is the father who forms the moral center of the family. According to Wade Horn, "Children with involved, loving fathers do better in school, have healthy self-esteem, exhibit empathy and pro-social behavior, and avoid high risk behaviors such as drug use, truancy, and criminal activity compared to children who have uninvolved fathers."[35] According to another pro-father ideologue, David Popenoe:

> Fathers are more than just "second adults" in the home. Involved fathers—especially biological fathers—bring positive benefits to their children that no other person is as likely to bring. They have a parenting style different from that of a mother and that difference is important in healthy child development.[36]

From Jesse Jackson Jr. to Wade Horn, from the Center for Law and Social Policy to the Heritage Foundation—the claim that married fatherhood will end single-mother poverty resounds widely. Married fatherhood policies may well accomplish greater economic security for more children. A male wage is, after all, a higher wage. But this family arithmetic is premised on mothers' inequality and reinforces it. Pro-father/anti-mother marriage promotion by government will compel poor single mothers to choose between an impoverished independence that puts their custody of children at risk and dependent economic security in the core institution of women's inequality: the patriarchal family.

NOTES

1. PL 104-193, Title I, Sec. 101(8)(C).
2. Ibid., Title I, Sec. 101(9)(K).
3. Ibid., Title I, Sec. 101(9)(L).
4. Ibid., Title I, Sec. 101(10).
5. Ibid., Title I, Part A, Sec. 401(a)(2), 401(a)(3), 401(a)(4).
6. PL 104-193, Title I, Part A, Sec. 408(a)(4) and (5).
7. Ibid., Title I, Part A, Sec. 403(a)(2).
8. PL 104-193, Title IX, Sec. 912.
9. Department of Health and Human Services, Administration for Children and Families, Office of Family Assistance, *Helping Families Achieve Self-Sufficiency: A Guide on Funding Services for Children and Families Through the TANF Program.* "Use of Federal TANF Funds," (1)(c). Available at <http://www.acf.hhs.gov/programs/ofa/funds2.htm>.
10. Department of Health and Human Services, Administration for Children and Families, Office of Family Assistance, "High Performance Bonus Awards for Performance Year 2002," Table 7.
11. PL 104-193, Title I, Sec. 407(c).
12. Ibid., Title I, Sec. 408(a)(2).
13. PL 104-193, Title III, Subtitle I, Sec. 469B.
14. PL 104-193, Title I, Part A, Sec. 402(a)(3).
15. Jim Moye and Roberta Rinker, "It's a Hard Knock Life: Does the Adoption and Safe Families Act of 1997 Adequately Address Problems in the Child Welfare System?" *Harvard Journal on Legislation,* 39 (2002).
16. PL 105-89; 42 U.S.C. Sec. 673b(d)(1) (2003).
17. DHHS, *Helping Families Achieve Self-Sufficiency,* Available at <http://www.acf.hhs.gov/programs/ofa/funds2.htm>.
18. U.S. House of Representatives, Report 105-217, *The Balanced Budget Act of 1997,* pp. 347, 348.
19. Testimony of NOW Legal Defense and Education Fund on "Welfare Reform and Marriage Initiatives," submitted to the Human Resources Subcommittee, Ways and Means Committee, U.S. House of Representatives, May 22, 2001.
20. <http://www.acf.hhs.gov/healthymarriage/funding/childrens_bureau.html>.
21. <http://www.acf.hhs.gov/healthymarriage/funding/child_support.html>.
22. <http://www.acf.hhs.gov/healthymarriage/funding/orr_projects.html>.
23. *Head Start Bulletin,* "Father Involvement," (June 2004), p. 3.
24. Ibid., p. 17.
25. Ibid., p. 19. My italics.
26. Ibid., pp. 19-20.
27. Ibid.
28. Theodora Ooms, Stacey Bouchet, and Mary Parke, *Beyond Marriage Licenses: Efforts in States to Strengthen Marriage and Two-Parent Families* (Washington, DC: Center for Law and Social Policy), April 2004, pp. 14-16.
29. Wade Horn and Isabel Sawhill, "Fathers, Marriage, and Welfare Reform," in Rebecca Blank and Ron Haskins, eds., *The New World of Welfare* (Washington, DC: Brookings Institution, 2001) p. 427. See also, Wade Horn testimony, U.S. House of

Representatives, Committee on Ways and Means, Subcommittee on Human Resources, *Hearing on Fatherhood Legislation,* 106th Congress, 1st sess., October 5, 1999. Available at <http://waysandmeans.house.gov/legacy.asp?file=legacy/humres/106cong/10-5-99/10-5horn.htm>.

30. See, for example, HR 751, the Democratic TANF Reauthorization bill introduced in the House of Representatives by liberal Congressmember Jim McDermott in February 2005.

31. Paula Roberts and Mark Greenbert, "Marriage and the TANF Rules: A Discussion Paper," Center for Law and Social Policy (Washington, DC), p. 2.

32. U.S. Census Bureau, "America's Families and Living Arrangements: 2003" (Washington, DC), November 2004, pp. 8-9.

33. Robert Rector, "Welfare Reform and the Healthy Marriage Initiative," testimony before the U.S. House of Representatives, Committee on Ways and Means, Subcommittee on Human Resources (Washington, DC), February 10, 2005, p. 2.

34. U.S. House of Representatives, H.R. 240, 109th Congress, 1st sess.

35. Wade F. Horn and Tom Sylvester, *Father Facts,* National Fatherhood Initiative, 2002. Quoted in *Head Start Bulletin,* op. cit.

36. David Popenoe, *Life Without Father* (New York: The Free Press, 1996), p. 163. Quoted in *Head Start Bulletin,* op. cit.

Chapter 14

Wedlock, Worship, and Welfare:
The Influence of Right-Wing Think Tanks
and the Christian Right
on Welfare Reform

Ellen Reese

In the mid-1990s, right-wing think tanks and Christian right groups successfully promoted a coherent set of welfare policies to promote conservative family values and Christianity—or wedlock and worship—among the poor. Right-wing think tanks and Christian right groups made a powerful team. The Heritage Foundation, the American Enterprise Institute, the Hudson Institute, Empower America, and other right-wing think tanks financed the promotion of socially conservative policy ideas through lobbyists, the mainstream news media, and a barrage of books and articles. Meanwhile, Christian right organizations, such as the Christian Coalition and Eagle Forum, hired their own lobbyists and provided grassroots support for social conservatives' policy campaigns. This chapter explores the role of these two socially conservative groups in shaping the 1996 welfare reform act and their continuing influence on Congressional debates about its reauthorization.

This chapter draws on ideas and information discussed in more detail in my forthcoming book, *Backlash Against Welfare Mothers: Past and Present* (2005, Berkeley and Los Angeles, University of California Press). The author wishes to thank Shoon Lio for his research assistance. This research was supported by an academic senate grant from the University of California, Riverside.

doi:10.1300/5608_15

SOCIAL CONSERVATIVES' INFLUENCE IN THE 1990s

Social conservatives' political reach increased with the growth of right-wing think tanks. Beginning in the 1970s, wealthy families, bankers, oil barons, and other corporations increasingly invested in right-wing think tanks through direct donations and a tightly integrated network of conservative foundations.[1] As a result, by the late 1990s, budgets of leading conservative think tanks were about four times the size of the typical liberal think tank's budget. As right-wing think tanks grew in size, their directors gained prominence within policy planning networks, while their fellows were appointed to high-ranking government positions under Republican administrations (Callahan, 1999; Covington, 1997, p. 15; Domhoff, 2002, pp. 83-94; Himmelstein, 1990, pp. 130-151).

Right-wing think tanks promoted a highly conservative agenda based on free market principles, which included labor market deregulation, tax cuts for the wealthy, privatization, and reduced federal spending on and authority over welfare (Callahan, 1999). Many combined this agenda with policies and rhetoric that upheld socially conservative values, particularly conservative Christian and "family" values. Ideologues employed by these think tanks tirelessly promoted antiwelfare propaganda and welfare reform policy proposals, publishing a massive array of books, position papers, magazine articles, and newspaper editorials by "social scientific" experts (Coltrane, 2001; Domhoff, 2002, p. 70). They also organized seminars, conferences, and forums to build consensus on welfare issues among politicians, business leaders, philanthropists, and conservative scholars. Shared policy prescriptions resulted from these meetings as well as common funding sources, interlocking boards, and collaboration on joint projects (Domhoff, 2002, pp. 82-84; Weicher, 2001).

Right-wing think tanks did not simply lobby and monopolize public debates. They crafted a coherent welfare reform agenda and an emotionally powerful and culturally resonant rhetoric to justify it. Through their writings and appearances on television and radio, conservative "experts," such as Charles Murray and William Bennett, revived behavioral and "culture of poverty" arguments. Such arguments blamed poverty on the "bad behavior" and purported cultural deficiencies of low-income people, namely their lack of a strong work ethic, the absence of traditional "family values," and their inability to delay immediate gratification. Deflecting attention away from larger structural problems, such as inner-city job shortages or employer discrimination, they blamed poverty on poor people themselves (Hardisty & Williams, 2002; O'Connor, 2001, pp. 242-283; Stefancic & Delgado, 1996). They also blamed the welfare system for being overly permissive and encouraging the poor to be lazy and irresponsible, and to have children out-of-wedlock. Appealing to the "strict father" model of morality (Lakoff, 1996), these conservative "experts" claimed that tough new welfare rules, such as bans on benefits to teen and unwed mothers, were needed to discipline the poor and reinforce traditional family values among them.

By funding multiple experts to reiterate the same basic principles in slightly different forms, conservative donors succeeded in narrowing political debates about welfare. Right-wing think tanks inundated politicians, the media, and other opinion leaders with their streamlined policy briefs and carefully cultivated their ties to them (Callahan, 1999; Domhoff, 2002, p. 81). Apparently, such efforts paid off. In 1996, the mainstream media cited conservative think tanks seven times more than progressive ones and cited the Heritage Foundation's "welfare expert," Robert Rector, an average of more than fifteen times a month (Dolny, 1998). To solidify support for their welfare proposals among politicians, right-wing think tanks organized special briefings and conferences for them. For example, in 1995, the Heritage Foundation sponsored a forum for conservative governors that urged them to support "fundamental changes" in the welfare system and co-hosted a conference highlighting welfare issues for incoming Congressional conservatives (Stefancic & Delgado, 1996, p. 94; Wilson, 1995).

Research fellows for the Hudson Institute, the Family Research Council, the Manhattan Institute, Heritage Foundation, and the American Enterprise Institute upheld the two-parent, heterosexual, married family form as the ideal and promoted various welfare policies to reinforce it. For example, they supported restrictions on benefits for unwed and teen mothers, including bans on benefits, rules requiring teen mothers to live at home and attend school, and "family caps" (also known as "child exclusion" policies) that denied additional benefits for children born to women already receiving welfare. The Heritage Foundation and conservative "pro-family" groups were the main advocates for authorizing federal welfare funds for abstinence and marriage promotion programs in 1996. Abstinence-only sex education programs teach that nonmarital sex and

out-of-wedlock childbearing is morally wrong and likely to be psycholog-
ically and physically damaging, while marriage-promotion programs provide premarital and marital counseling to couples to encourage marriage
and prevent divorce (Reese, 2005; Stefancic & Delgado, 1996, p. 58;
Weaver, 2000, pp. 214-215). Meanwhile, the Institute of American Values
and the National Fatherhood Initiative, co-founded by IAV's president in
1994, promoted the spread of federally funded "responsible fatherhood"
programs. These programs, often administered through child support
enforcement offices, put unemployed fathers to work and teach them to be
more involved in their children's lives (Coltrane, 2001; Weaver, 2000).

The statistics and evidence cited by conservative "experts" in support of these policies are frequently misleading. The rise of single
motherhood is not due to the availability of welfare, as conservatives
claim, but instead to broader economic and social changes, such as
declining labor market conditions for working-class men, women's
rising labor force participation, and greater tolerance for premarital
sexual activity and single motherhood (Hays, 2003, pp. 132-136). Indeed, studies show that rates of out-of-wedlock and teenage childbearing bear no strong or consistent relationship to welfare generosity across U.S. states or internationally (Blau, Kahn, & Waldfogel,
2000; Edin, 2000, p. 114; Glassner, 1999; Lichter, McLaughlin, &
Ribar, 1997). Conservative scholars often portray unwed and teen
welfare mothers, disproportionately black and Latina, as "welfare
queens" who pass on their "bad values" to children and as incapable
of properly raising their children on their own. Yet, research suggests
that many of the effects attributed to "father absence," such as high
rates of delinquency and school dropouts among the children of single and teen mothers, are due to the effects of poverty rather than
"father absence" per se (Coltrane, 2001; Glassner, 1999, pp. 87-105).

Mothers who never marry are more likely to be poor and less likely to
work compared to other mothers, as conservatives are quick to point
out.[2] However, job creation programs, living wages, and work supports
are far more likely than welfare restrictions and "marriage promotion"
programs to promote marriage and combat female and child poverty. Indeed, despite the implementation of many of the policies and programs
described previously, the national nonmarital birth rate rose by almost 2
percent after 1996 (De Lollis, 2001). Counseling programs for couples
and fathers might be empowering for some participants, but they do little
to address social structural barriers, such as employment discrimination

and job shortages, which create obstacles to marriage formation and paternal breadwinning (Curran & Abrams, 2000, pp. 670-675; Folse, 2001). They also discourage women from seeking independence from men and make it difficult for them to avoid abusive ones. This is not an incidental consideration, given that the U.S. Department of Health and Human Services estimates that as many as 34 percent of welfare mothers are current victims of domestic violence (Hays, 2003, pp. 82, 164-165). Most research suggests that abstinence-only sex education is less effective at preventing teenage pregnancy than comprehensive programs that include information about contraception (Brody, 2004).

Along with conservative family policies, right-wing think tanks promoted "charitable choice" policies that expand faith-based organizations' role in distributing welfare. For example, Reverend Sirico, head of the Acton Institute, urged Congress in 1995 to replace the "faceless" federal welfare bureaucracy with faith-based charities that could impress upon unwed mothers the magnitude of their sins (Sirico, 1995). According to their "experts," civic virtue, premarital abstinence, responsible parenting, and religiosity flourished in the absence of federal welfare, when churches played a more prominent role in distributing aid to the poor (Reese, 2005). Such romantic images of the past overlook the gross inadequacies of private charity before 1935 in addressing the needs of the poor (Katz, 1996 [1986]). Marvin Olasky, whose research was sponsored by the Heritage Foundation and Acton Institute, was one of the most prominent authors calling for faith-based welfare initiatives. Through *The Tragedy of American Compassion* (1992), interviews, and other publications, Olasky claimed that "successful anti-poverty programs emphasize ... some level of spiritual involvement" (Acton, 1995). He even urged state officials to "put welfare entirely in the hands of church- and community-based organizations" (Olasky, 1996, p. 47).

Working hand-in-hand with these right-wing think tanks was the Christian right, whose political rise revitalized the Republican Party and shifted it rightward on social issues. The politicization and conservative realignment of evangelical Christians, underway since the 1970s, became more abrupt in the 1980s. The spread of dominion theology encouraged Christians to become more politically active and occupy secular institutions to return the United States to its biblical principles, which include the traditional family and unfettered capitalism (Coltrane, 2001). Republican activists, courting white voters, also mobilized evangelical and fundamentalist Christian voters and lent resources to create and expand Christian right groups, such as the Moral Majority (Diamond, 1995; Himmelstein, 1990).

In the 1990s, the Christian right, organized through such groups as the Christian Coalition, increased their activism within the Republican Party, especially in the South. A 1994 study found that it played a dominant or substantial role in the state Republican Party in thirty-one states and ten out of the eleven former Confederate states (Persinos, 1994). In 1992, more than 40 percent of Republican national convention delegates were evangelical Christians, while an estimated 15 to 20 percent were Christian Coalition members. Their members also made up almost one-fifth of the Republican platform drafting committee (Penning, 1994). The Christian right, drawing support from a wider range of faiths than previously, was both a beneficiary of and political force behind the Republicans' unprecedented Congressional victories in the mid-1990s and the South's electoral realignment. The Christian Coalition distributed about 30 million voter guides in 1994 and 45 million in 1996 (Diamond, 1995; Manza & Brooks, 1999, p. 96; Weaver, 2000, pp. 211-215). By 1996, religious conservatives who attended church at least once a week and claimed that religion guides their life a "great deal" made up 9 percent of all voters and 23 percent of all Republican voters (Knuckey, 1999, pp. 486-487).

Perhaps the most influential Christian right group to promote welfare cutbacks was the Christian Coalition which claimed about 1.7 million members. In 1995 and 1996, it actively lobbied for "pro-family" welfare policies. According to some observers, these policies were given priority over antiabortion policies during those years. Along with other groups, the Christian Coalition "visited and telephoned senators and their staffs" and even "stake[d] out hallways outside the Senate Chamber during the floor debate" on welfare reform (Weaver, 2000, pp. 211-215). The Christian Coalition was joined by the Concerned Women of America, the Traditional Values Coalition, Focus on Family, and Eagle Forum. These groups claimed hundreds of thousands of members and spread their ideas through syndicated newspaper columns, radio commentaries, and popular magazines, such as *Focus on the Family*.

Highlighting the themes that public welfare programs subsidized "immorality" and "illegitimacy," the Christian right echoed the concerns and ideas of right-wing think tanks. Both groups viciously attacked the rights of unwed and teen mothers to receive welfare. They also urged Congress to authorize federal welfare funds for faith-based initiatives and programs promoting abstinence, marriage, and "responsible fatherhood" (Reese, 2005). The religious right and right-wing think tanks engaged in effective coalition work during the 1995-1996 welfare reform debates. For example, representatives of "pro-family" organizations and the Heritage Foundation met informally to develop common policy positions and coordinated phone calls, letters, and visits to Congress (Weaver, 2000, p. 216; DeParle, 1995). Unity among social conservatives around welfare issues made it difficult for politicians, especially Republicans, to ignore their demands.

The extent of social conservatives' influence on the 1996 welfare reform act was striking. The opening paragraph of the 1996 federal welfare reform act proclaimed the promotion of heterosexual, two-parent, married households to be a major goal of the law because this family form was crucial to both a "successful society" and "the interests of children" (cited in Curran & Abrams, 2000, p. 665). To fulfill this goal, Congress allocated $100 million annually for an "illegitimacy bonus," used to reward states for reducing their out-of-wedlock births,[3] and $50 million annually for abstinence-only education and marriage promotion. Congress also declared that the promotion of "responsible fatherhood" was crucial to "successful child rearing" and authorized states to allocate federal welfare funds for "responsible fatherhood" programs. Although Congress rejected social conservatives' proposals for federal "family caps" and bans on benefits to unwed teen mothers, it authorized states to adopt a "family cap" and required unwed teen welfare mothers to attend school and live with their parents. Congress also approved "charitable choice" policies that allow faith-based organizations to compete for government service contracts and to incorporate religious beliefs and symbols in their services (Banzhaf, 1999; Chaves, 2001; Curran & Abrams, 2000; Mink, 1998, pp. 65-70; Reese, 2005; Weaver, 2000).

SOCIAL CONSERVATIVES' INFLUENCE IN THE BUSH ERA

Since 1996, the Christian right and right-wing think tanks pushed for expansions in abstinence, marriage, and "responsible fatherhood"

programs and "charitable choice" policies and gained support for this
agenda among many Congressional representatives, especially Republicans (Reese, 2005). George W. Bush, a born-again Christian,
two-fifths of whose support in the 2000 election came from evangelical Christians, was a strong supporter of these policies (Green, Guth,
Kellstedt, & Smidt, 2001). Shortly after becoming president, Bush
pushed for expansions in charitable choice policies through legislation and executive orders and established an Office of Faith-Based
and Community Initiatives. He appointed Don Eberly, a born-again
Christian and co-founder of the National Fatherhood Initiative, to
lead it (Coltrane, 2001, p. 389; Reese, 2005).

Bush also made marriage promotion a central goal of welfare reform
reauthorization, clearly pleasing social conservatives. In 2002, he proposed spending more than $300 million worth of federal and state funds
over five years for community and religious groups to run "healthy marriage" programs, a proposal given revived media attention in 2004, as
controversies over gay marriage heated up and the presidential election
neared ("Many Injured," 2002; MarriageMovement.org, 2004; Toner,
2002). Bush also made his allegiance to the conservative "family values"
movement clear by appointing Wade Horn, co-founder of the National
Fatherhood Initiative, as the Assistant Secretary for Children and Family
Services and Andrew Bush, another NFI co-founder, as Director of the
Office of Family Assistance (Coltrane, 2001).

EXPLAINING THE INFLUENCE
OF SOCIAL CONSERVATIVES

Social conservatives gained Congressional support for "pro-family" and "pro-church" policies in 1996 partly because of Republican
control of Congress and the growing power of the Christian right
within the Republican Party. Backing these policies provided a way
to increase their political support among traditional white voters that
was less risky than supporting more controversial policy initiatives,
such as restrictions on abortion rights, which might affect middle-
class women. Surveys taken in 1993 showed that most Americans favored a number of the welfare reform policies and ideas promoted by
social conservatives, including family caps and rules requiring unwed teen welfare mothers to live with their parents (Weaver, 2000, pp.
177-184). By 1995, about 69 percent of national survey respondents

agreed with the statement that the "welfare system does more harm than good, because it encourages the breakup of the family and discourages the work ethic" (Weaver, Shapiro, & Jacobs, 1995, p. 611).

Right-wing think tanks and the Christian right effectively appealed to both reactionary sentiments and broadly held moral values to manufacture support for their welfare initiatives. Drawing on racist and classist stereotypes, they portrayed welfare mothers, disproportionately black and Latina, as "unfit parents," irresponsible "breeders," and "welfare queens" (Banzhaf, 1999; Sparks, 2003, pp. 178-179; Schram, 2003, p. 218). In doing so, they helped to channel many white voters' resentments against taxes, changes in the racial status quo, and immigration and concerns about the rise of single motherhood into support for welfare cutbacks. These groups also appealed to religious and "family" values, and the "strict father" model of morality (Lakoff, 1996) that portrays tough rules and regulations as necessary for disciplining the poor. Survey research shows that, although widespread, opposition to welfare spending was most pronounced among politically conservative whites, while support for family caps was significantly higher among whites than blacks and linked to anti-black and anti-Latino prejudice (Gilens, 1999, p. 95; Soss, Schram, Vartanian, & O'Brien, 2003, pp. 237-242; Weaver, 2000, pp. 177-184).

Social conservatives' policy proposals also dovetailed with other powerful demands on Congress. For example, the family cap was consistent with white taxpayers', fiscal conservatives', and mainstream business groups' interests in reducing welfare expenditures, while calls for expanding faith-based welfare initiatives were consistent with corporate demands for welfare privatization. Social conservatives' emphasis on "responsible fatherhood" also echoed liberals' and feminists' calls for greater paternal involvement in children's lives and improving child support enforcement.

Progressives face a huge challenge in countering the influence of social conservatives. To do so, they need to unite and mobilize voters around a coherent policy agenda that meets the needs of most working families, fostering solidarity rather than division among low-income female-headed households and other working families struggling to make ends meet. Simply having good policy ideas will not be enough to win the welfare debate, however. Progressives need to alter the terms of this debate, countering the popular myths about low-income people and welfare programs that are promoted by the right, and effectively linking their own policy ideas to broadly held moral values. Like the Christian right, they also need to actively mobilize voters and put significant grassroots pressure on politicians to respond to their policy demands.

NOTES

1. The twelve foundations were the Lynde and Harry Bradley Corporations, the Carthage Foundation, the Earhart Foundation, the Charles G. Koch, David H. Koch and Claude R. Lambe charitable foundations, the Phillip M. McKenna Foundation, the J.M. Foundation, and John M. Olin Foundation, the Henry Salvatori Foundation, the Sarah Scaife Foundation, and the Smith Richardson Foundation. Of these, the most active were the Mellon-Scaife, Olin, and Smith Richardson foundations (Callahan, 1999).

2. Data from the National Survey of Families and Households, 1987-1988 and 1992-1994, show that unwed mothers are ten times more likely to be on welfare and 70 percent less likely to be working full time than mothers who marry at some point in their lives (Alan Guttmacher Institute, 1999).

3. The bonus, $20 to 25 million, is given annually to the five states that best reduced their out-of-wedlock births without increasing their abortion rates (Banzhaf, 1999; Mink, 1998, p. 70).

REFERENCES

Acton Institute. (1995). A Revolution of Compassion. Grand Rapids, MI: Acton Institute. Retrieved May 19, 2002, from <http://www.acton.org/publicat/randl/interview.php?id=164>.

Alan Guttmacher Institute. (1999). Married Mothers Fare the Best Economically, Even If They Were Unwed at the Time They Gave Birth. *Family Planning Perspectives,* 31(5), 258-260.

Banzhaf, M. (1999). Welfare Reform and Reproductive Rights: Talking About Connections. Presentation for the National Network of Abortion Funds on June 11. Seattle, WA: Feminist Women's Health Center, Retrieved May 23, 2002, from <http://www.fwhc.org/tanf.htm>.

Blau, F. D., Kahn, L. M., & Waldfogel, J. (2000). Understanding Young Women's Marriage Decisions: The Role of Labor and Marriage Market Conditions. *Industrial and Labor Relations Review,* 53(4), 624-647.

Brody, J. E. (2004, June 1). Abstinence-Only: Does It Work? *New York Times,* p. F7. Retrieved July 3, 2004, from LEXIS-NEXIS Academic Universe, News Sources.

Callahan, D. (1999). *$1 Billion for Ideas: Conservative Think Tanks in the 1990's.* Washington, DC: National Committee for Responsive Philanthropy.

Chaves, M. (2001). Religious Congregations and Welfare Reform. *Society,* 38(2), 21-27.

Coltrane, S. (2001). Marketing the Marriage "Solution": Misplaced Simplicity in the Politics of Fatherhood. *Sociological Perspectives,* 44(4), 387-418.

Covington, S. (1997). *Moving a Public Policy Agenda: The Strategic Philanthropy of Conservative Foundations.* Washington, DC: National Committee for Responsive Philanthropy.

Curran, L. & Abrams, L.S. (2000). Making Men Into Dads: Fatherhood, the State, and Welfare Reform. *Gender & Society,* 14(5), 662-678.

De Lollis, B. (2001, November 21). Out of Wedlock Births Not Decreasing As Welfare Reformers Had Hoped. Gannett News Service. Retrieved December 22, 2003, from LEXIS-NEXIS Academic Universe, News Sources.

DeParle, J. (1995, November 12). Sheila Burke Is the Militant Feminist Commie Peacenik Who's Telling Bob Dole What to Think. *New York Times,* pp. 6, 32. Retrieved June 8, 2002, from LEXIS-NEXIS Academic Universe, News Sources.

Diamond, S. (1995). *Roads to Dominion: Right-Wing Movements and Political Powers in the United States.* New York: Gulford Press.

Diamond, S. (1998). *Not by Politics Alone: The Enduring Influence of the Christian Right.* New York: Guilford Press.

Dolny, M. (1998, May/June). What's in a Label?: Right-Wing Think Tanks Are Often Quoted, Rarely Labeled. *Extra!* Retrieved May 26, 2002, from <http://www.fair.org/extra/9805/think-tanks.html>.

Domhoff, G. W. (2002). *Who Rules America? Power & Politics,* 4th Ed. Boston: McGraw Hill.

Edin, K. (2000). What Do Low-Income Single Mothers Say About Marriage? *Social Problems,* 47(1), 112-133.

Folse, K. A. (2001). Child Support/Deadbeat Dads. In Dennis L. Peck & Norman A. Dulch (eds.), *Extraordinary Behavior: A Case Study Approach to Understanding Social Problems* (pp. 144-155) Westport, CT: Praeger.

Gilens, M. (1999). *Why Americans Hate Welfare: Race, Media, and the Politics of Antipoverty Policy.* Chicago: University of Chicago Press.

Glassner, B. (1999). *The Culture of Fear: Why Americans Are Afraid of the Wrong Things: Crime, Drugs, Minorities, Teen Moms, Killer Kids, Mutant Microbes, Plane Crashes, Road Rage, and So Much More . . .* New York: Basic Books.

Green, J. C., Guth, J. L, Kellstedt, L. A., & Smidt, C.E. (2001). Faith in the Vote: Religiosity and the Presidential Election. *Public Perspective: A Roper Center Review of Public Opinion and Polling,* 12(2), 33-35.

Hardisty, J. & Williams, L. A. (2002). The Right's Campaign Against Welfare. In Applied Research Center (Ed.), *From Poverty to Punishment: How Welfare Reform Punishes the Poor* (pp. 53-72). Oakland, CA: Applied Research Center.

Hays, S. (2003). *Flat Broke with Children: Women in the Age of Welfare Reform.* New York: Oxford University Press.

Himmelstein, J. L. (1990). To the Right: The Transformation of American Conservativism. Berkeley, CA: University of California Press.

Katz, M. B. (1996). *In the Shadow of the Poorhouse: A Social History of Welfare in America,* 10th Ed. New York: Basic Books. (Original work published 1986).

Knuckey, J. (1999). Religious Conservatives, the Republican Party, and Evolving Party Coalitions in the United States. *Party Politics,* 5(4), 485-496.

Lakoff, G. (1996). *Moral Politics: What Conservatives Know That Liberals Don't.* Chicago, IL: The University of Chicago Press.

Lichter, D. T., McLaughlin, D. K., & Ribar, D. C. (1997). Welfare and the Rise in Female-Headed Families. *American Journal of Sociology,* 103(1), 112-143.

Many "Injured by the Helping Hand." (2002, February 27). *Los Angeles Times,* pp. A10.

Manza, J. & Brooks, C. (1999). *Social Cleavages and Political Change: Voter Alignments and U.S. Party Coalitions.* New York: Oxford University Press.

MarriageMovement.org. (2004). Media Coverage of the Administration's Healthy Marriage Initiative, January 14, 2004-February 9, 2004. New York: Institute for American Values. Retrieved June 26, 2004, from <http://www.marriage movement.org/hmi/hmi_backgrounder_print.htm>.

Mink, G. (1998). *Welfare's End.* Ithaca, NY: Cornell University Press.

O'Connor, A. (2001). *Poverty Knowledge: Social Science, Social Policy, and the Poor in Twentieth Century U.S. History.* Princeton and Oxford: Princeton University Press.

Olasky, M. (1992). *The Tragedy of American Compassion.* Washington, DC: Regnary Gateway.

Olasky, M. (1996). The Right Way to Replace Welfare. *Policy Review,* 76, 46-51.

Payne, J. (1997). The Smart Samaritan: Five Habits of Highly Effective Charities. *Policy Review: The Journal of American Citizenship,* 83, 48-53.

Penning, J. M. (1994). Pat Robertson and the GOP: 1988 and Beyond. *Sociology of Religion,* 55(3), 327-344.

Persinos, J. F. (1994). Has the Christian Right Taken Over the Republican Party. *Campaigns & Elections,* 15, 21-24.

Reese, E. (2005). *Backlash Against Welfare Mothers: Past and Present.* Berkeley and Los Angeles: University of California Press.

Schram, S. (2003). Putting a Black Face on Welfare. In S. F. Schram, J. Soss, and R. C. Fording (Eds.), *Race and the Politics of Welfare Reform* (pp. 196-221). Ann Arbor: University of Michigan Press.

Sirico, R. A. (1995). Statement of Rev. Robert A. Sirico, President, the Acton Institute for the Study of Religion and Liberty, Grand Rapids, Michigan; and Member, Michigan Civil Rights Commission, pp. 209-215 in *Contract with America-Welfare Reform. Hearing Before the Subcommittee on Human Resources of the Committee on Ways and Means, House of Representatives.* 104th Cong., 1st sess., Part 1.

Soss, J., Schram, S. F., Vartanian, T. P., & O'Brien, E. (2003). The Hard Line and the Color Line: Race, Welfare, and the Roots of Get-Tough Reform. In S. F. Schram, J. Soss, & R. C. Fording (Eds.), *Race and the Politics of Welfare Reform* (pp. 225-253). Ann Arbor: University of Michigan Press.

Sparks, H. (2003). Queens, Teens, and Model Mothers: Race, Gender, and the Discourse of Welfare Reform. In S. F. Schram, J. Soss, & R. C. Fording (Eds.), *Race and the Politics of Welfare Reform* (pp. 171-195). Ann Arbor: University of Michigan Press.

Stefancic, J. & Delgado, R. (1996). *No Mercy: How Conservative Think Tanks and Foundations Changed America's Social Agenda.* Philadelphia, PA: Temple University Press.

Toner, R. (2002, March 12). Bush's Proposal on Welfare Draws Fire From Democrats. *The New York Times,* p. A20. Retrieved July 2, 2003, from LEXIS-NEXIS Academic Universe, News Sources.

Weaver, K. (2000). *Ending Welfare As We Know It.* Washington, DC: Brookings Institution.

Weaver, R. K., Shapiro, R. Y., & Jacobs, L. R. (1995). The Polls—Trends: Welfare. *Public Opinion Quarterly,* 59, 606-627.

Weicher, J. C. (2001, January/February). Reforming Welfare: The Next Policy Debates. *Society, 38*(2), 16-20.

Wilson, P. (1995). Kicking America's Welfare Habit: Politics, Illegitimacy, and Personal Responsibility. Lecture and Seminars No. 540. Washington, DC: Heritage Foundation, Retrieved September 20, 2001, from <http://www.heritage.org/Research/Welfare/HL540.cfm>.

Chapter 15

Safety and Self-Sufficiency:
Rhetoric and Reality
in the Lives of Welfare Recipients

Lisa D. Brush

He beat me so bad I lost the pregnancy. Just pounded on me. I think he wanted to kill me. . . . When I was at home, I was raising *his* daughter, and he could control me. But [when I worked] out in the real world, he got even more possessive. He would leave his job to check up on me. . . . He was possessive, abusive, and didn't want me to work. Just an all-American guy. (Subject 23: white, divorced, age 35; emphasis in original)

PARADOXES OF "SELF-SUFFICIENCY" RHETORIC

The welfare cuts of the past sixteen years are rooted in part in the neoliberal assumptions of exchange theory: Employment is proof of

Author's Note: This project was supported by Grant No. 2000-WT-VX-0009 awarded by the National Institute of Justice, Office of Justice Programs, U.S. Department of Justice. Points of view in this document are those of the author and do not necessarily represent the official position or policies of the U.S. Department of Justice. The research received expedited review and approval from the University of Pittsburgh Institutional Review Board (IRB #001097). Lorraine Higgins designed and ran the community literacy project (funded by the NIJ and the University of Pittsburgh Women's Studies Program) from which the author drew the excerpts of Red's pseudonymous story. Thanks to Danielle Ficco and Lisa Huebner for research assistance, Mimi Abramovitz and Linda Gordon for inspiration, the editors for opportunity, and Amy Elman, Lorraine Higgins, Katie Hogan, Mimi Schippers, and Carol Stabile for comments on various versions of this chapter.

doi:10.1300/5608_16

183

personal responsibility, prerequisite for first-class citizenship, and the cure for every social problem. Indeed, commentators from across the political spectrum posit waged labor as the solution to problems as diverse as poverty, drug addiction, out-of-wedlock births, gender inequality, and domestic violence. In particular, exchange theory predicts the earnings, social connections, and confidence women gain through employment will shift the balance of power within couples in women's favor (Howard & Hollander, 2000). Money, networks, and work experience are all supposed to reduce men's violence against their girlfriends or wives by providing women with means to leave (exit), or means to bargain without leaving (voice), or both (Hirschman, 1970; Hobson, 1990). Wage-earning women presumably can navigate the legal and social service systems designed to help them either to protect themselves while staying in their relationships or to leave abusers without facing penury. Policies that "make work pay" are intended at least in part to create incentives for men to support women's employment. Many welfare-slashing legislators and "street-level bureaucrats"[1] in welfare offices and employment training programs charged with implementing the cuts and sanctions of the 1996 legislation implicitly share the assumptions of exchange theory. Their hopes are high about both outcomes: Increasing women's work will *make batterers think twice* and *enable women to escape* poverty and abuse.

Conservatives have been remarkably successful at translating the neoliberal rhetoric of exchange theory into legislative and practical reality. Policymakers and program personnel alike now focus on moving the poor from welfare to work. The idea is to save tax dollars by turning welfare offices into employment training and job placement programs, enforcing personal responsibility through work and marriage, and promoting "self-sufficiency." Self-sufficiency sounds as though it means relying solely on one's own efforts (rather than the welfare state) to make ends meet. Given the stigma, intrusive surveillance, and miserliness of public assistance, reducing the extent of poor mothers' depending on welfare is not necessarily a bad idea. But expecting program and benefit cuts, sanctions, and work requirements—even when they coincide with significant drops in welfare caseloads[2]—to result in meaningful self-sufficiency for poor women is not only delusional and hypocritical but downright dangerous.

In addition to enforcing wage work as the free-market solution to every conceivable social problem, the new workfare programs seek to establish paternity, enforce child support, encourage marriage, and thus reduce out-of-wedlock births without increasing abortions. "Personal responsibility" in the rhetoric of welfare opponents favors economic support by biological fathers in the context of marriage. Thus, putatively self-sufficient women may justifiably depend on the labor market, friends and family, and of course a male breadwinner.[3] In reality, a growing body of research refutes the neoliberal rhetoric of exchange theory and the salutary effects of self-sufficiency and shows instead a backlash effect of work requirements on abuse (Riger & Staggs, 2004). As feminists have long argued, depending on a male breadwinner is problematic, especially when he is controlling or abusive. The risks are exacerbated if he disapproves of women's employment. Abusers who fear losing power and control over women react to women's increased education, earnings, and potential or actual independence by initiating or escalating control, sabotage, abuse, and physical violence (Brush, 2003b; Raphael, 2000). This is part of why mandatory paternity establishment and marriage promotion are so objectionable: They may increase substantially the risks of abuse.

For abusers interested in controlling women's earnings, abuse may not preclude employment. The abuser may insist that the woman work or otherwise comply with the requirements of welfare reform to forestall loss of his access to her income or noncash benefits, especially housing. Abusers seeking to control their partners resort to battering—specifically, to physical violence—"not as an expression of their power but as an instance of its collapse" (Kimmel, 2002, p. 1353). Contrary to the expectations of exchange theory, in such cases employment does not moderate abuse, and a woman's earnings become yet another realm where the abuser exercises power and control (see e.g., Sev'er, 2002).

Work requirements are a central feature of welfare reform. Paradoxically, the independence effect of women's labor force participation—that is, a woman's enhanced ability to leave a relationship when she has earnings of her own and approaches "self-sufficiency"—appears empirically to be related to an upswing in abuse in general and in violence after separation in particular (Bachman & Saltzman, 1995; Fox & Zawitz, 2001; Hardesty, 2002), at least for a significant group of welfare recipients. Advocates for battered women were able to include a Family Violence Option in the 1996 federal legislation, which allows states to exempt battered women from time limits, work requirements, and cooperation with child support enforcement if work or contact with the father put them at risk for

abuse. However, implementation varies as widely as the state-level welfare programs that resulted from the end of federal entitlements and standards. Moreover, in states where the legislature did not include the FVO in
mandatory welfare reform plans, battered women must vie with others
groups eligible for the limited "hardship exemption" from work requirements.

LISTENING TO REALITY

In order to track some of the paradoxes of self-sufficiency and the
realities of work, welfare, and abuse in the lives of poor women, a
trained graduate student research assistant and I interviewed forty
welfare recipients enrolled in a "work first" program.[4] We then followed them for the first year of their transition from welfare to work.
We wanted to answer two key questions: (1) What are the costs of taking a beating? (2) How do women experience and explain what happens when abuse in their relationships spills over into their work
lives?

We wanted to put abuse into perspective as one of many barriers or
obstacles to women's transition from welfare to work. We also sought
to understand the extent to which welfare recipients felt going to
work aggravated or ameliorated abuse and related symptoms of traumatic stress. We focused on the individual-level economic and emotional consequences of the ways intimate partner violence against
women can disrupt education and employment.

About one in four of the welfare recipients with whom we spoke—
such as the woman featured in the epigraph to this chapter—reported
trying simultaneously to work "out in the real world" and to deal with
control, sabotage, and sometime violent abuse from their current or
former boyfriends or husbands. Compared with their peers, physically abused women earned less, worked fewer weeks, and more frequently worked part-time involuntarily. Women whose partners sabo-
taged their work effort experienced more hardships associated with
poverty (that is, evictions and homelessness, utility shutoffs, hunger
and food insecurity, and the like) than did other respondents. The
women who had ever filed a protective order[5] against an intimate
partner (including one woman who filed during the follow-up period)
averaged a fifty-three cents per hour *decrease* in their hourly wages
over the follow-up period. The women who did not file a protective

order averaged about the same-sized *increase* in their hourly wages (Brush, 2003b, 2004). That means an average difference of roughly a dollar per hour—a sizable cost to taking a beating for women whose hourly earnings are generally in the high single digits (among these forty women, $7.55 per hour at their most recent job).

Listening to poor mothers and welfare recipients describe their experiences confirms the claims of advocates and other observers: Significant numbers of welfare recipients are in or have fled relationships where they were battered.[6] Abuse sometimes obstructs employment. Conformity with the requirements of welfare reform endangers some women.[7] Most significantly, welfare can be a safety net not only in the usual sense as a crucial part of a package of household income, but also as the resource of last resort in safety planning for battered women (Davis, 1999; Raphael, 1999).

In the context of welfare cuts, assumptions about the extent to which work requirements build or threaten women's safety and solvency play out in the lives of women who find themselves trapped by both poverty and abuse. Only a very small fraction (5 percent) of respondents in my study reported the positive effects hoped for by many welfare reformers: "[When I was working, I] would get dressed up and be out at work, not under his control" (Subject 36, white, divorced, age 43). This finding provides slim support for the "independence effect" of employment as a deterrent to abusers assumed by exchange theory.

Consider the far more typical story of Red, a pseudonymous participant in a community literacy project with current and former welfare recipients who was also part of my recent research. Red described a husband who stole her money and belongings. He spent rent money on crack, jeopardizing their housing situation and forcing her to borrow money from her mother. After leaving him, she became involved with a man who provided for Red financially but physically and emotionally abused her. Red recounted the many ways in which he exploited her dependency. She felt trapped. "He still had a key, and he was on the lease, so there was nothing I could do to keep him out. . . . Even though he was often with . . . [an]other woman, he had still been paying my bills," she tells her readers. Red finally split with him after a violent incident she recounted in her narrative.

> I came home from work one day, and he showed up. He parked his police car in front of my place. . . . We had an argument, and

he slapped my face. I called the police, but because he was a police officer, he just got on his radio and told them to disregard the call. I could hear my mother crying as she witnessed this, but all I could see was red. I grabbed his gun and had it at his head. Although she was right next to me, I couldn't see my mother—I could only hear her crying, but that finally made me put the gun down. I put a brick through the window of his police car. Then he left.

This incident was critical. I was trying to hold on to the house. . . . I was working a little . . . , but my life was chaotic. As it turned out, we split up after this incident. I stayed in the house, but he was no longer supporting me. . . . [T]hat was when I first turned to welfare for help.

Although they now see each other occasionally, Red explains that she resists his attempts to control her life financially and otherwise. He wants her to go off public assistance, but she argues that only with the cash and medical benefits she receives can she become healthy enough to support herself once again. Red writes, "I can block out his little comments and work on myself, and welfare makes it possible for me to do what I need to do until I can work a full day." But realistically, it may be difficult for Red to maintain "self-sufficiency" if her benefits are cut before she re-establishes herself.

I told my boyfriend I'll go off welfare when he's ready to marry me, but what I mean is I need welfare for now to help me do what I need for myself. I have applied for SSI, because my doctor has agreed that I cannot work right now. If it doesn't come through, and I don't get better, I don't know what I will do when my time limit is up.

Accounts like Red's suggest it is not surprising that many women stay with, or return to, abusers because of financial dependence. Public assistance itself can encourage a degree of "self-sufficiency" by providing safe housing and other essentials. Arbitrary time limits truncate support in the midst of an unpredictable and lengthy process of leaving an abusive relationship. This is especially true for a woman such as Red, who has multiple barriers to escaping both poverty and abuse, including serious mental health issues, ongoing recovery from drug addiction, and a weak social support network. Moreover, for the respondents in our interview study who noticed that their working precipitated or aggravated abuse, conforming to work requirements could jeopardize their safety.

RISKS AND REALITIES

Welfare cuts and new measures such as mandatory paternity establishment, compliance with child support enforcement, and marriage promotion shred the figurative and literal "safety net" the federal entitlement to income support used to provide. Implementing such surveillance and control measures may inadvertently or deliberately reveal the whereabouts of women and children fleeing abusers. The rhetoric of "a father for every child" and child support enforcement bolsters men's control over women by encouraging biological fathers to insist on visitation rights in return for child support and shared custody arrangements. Marriage promotion efforts shame or sanction poor women into depending on men to "legitimate" their sexuality and fertility—dependence that can undermine the safety as well as the dignity, integrity, and autonomy of women.

The realities of abuse in the lives of welfare recipients expose the contradictions of moralistic, neoliberal antiwelfare rhetoric. The welfare legislation vilifies welfare recipients. At the same time, the Violence Against Women Acts (1994 and 2000) deem battered women worthy of public assistance so long as they present as innocent victims. Of course, the battered woman and the welfare recipient are often the same person (Brandwein, 1999). The realities of her complex situation defy efforts by welfare opponents to justify providing temporary support for the deserving while punishing those who do not "work hard and play by the rules." The risks and realities of abuse reveal the perhaps ironic paradox that conforming to work requirements endangers some poor women. The realities of poor and battered women materially contradict the rhetoric of "safety through self-sufficiency" at the heart of exchange theory.[8]

NOTES

1. Lipsky (1980); see also Hays (2003), Kingfisher (1996), and Monson (1997).
2. See Brush (2003a) and the studies of the "impacts" of welfare reform cited there.

3. See Fraser and Gordon (1994) for an analysis of the rhetoric of dependency in the history of the U.S. welfare state, and Misra, Moller, and Karides (2003) for a recent analysis of media representations of dependency and welfare.

4. We conducted initial retrospective interviews in the summer of 2001. For details on the research project and instruments, see Brush (2002).

5. Orders of protection (usually obtained from a family court judge) provide civil remedies for battering. Because they involve a court appearance and are generally granted in cases of physical violence, restraining orders represent a conservative measure of abuse.

6. Studies with groups of poor women in Chicago (Lloyd & Taluc, 1999) and Worcester, Massachusetts (Browne, Salomon, & Bassuk, 1999) found widespread abuse. So did longitudinal studies with welfare recipients in Allegheny County, Pennsylvania (Brush, 2003b), Michigan (Tolman, Danziger, & Rosen, 2002), and Kern and Stanislaus Counties, California (Meisel, Chandler, & Rienzi, 2003).

7. Qualitative studies of the connections among work, welfare, and abuse in relationships include Bell (2003), Purvin (2003), Raphael (2000), and Scott, London, and Myers (2002). Richie's (1996) interviews with incarcerated women starkly illuminate the extent to which racialized gender expectations "entrap" women of color in risky relationships and survival strategies.

8. The notion of safety through self-sufficiency is an eerie, Orwellian echo of *arbeit macht frei*—labor liberates—the slogan over the entrances to the Nazi labor/death/administration camps at Auschwitz, Dachau, Gross-Rosen, Sachsenhausen, and Terezín.

REFERENCES

Bachman, R. & Saltzman, L. (1995). *Violence against women: Estimates from the redesigned National Crime Victimization Survey*. Washington, DC: U.S. Department of Justice, Bureau of Justice Statistics.

Bell, H. (2003). Cycles within cycles: Domestic violence, welfare, and low-wage work. *Violence Against Women* 9: 1245-1262.

Brandwein, R. (1999). Family violence, women, and welfare. In R. Brandwein (Ed.), *Battered women, children, and welfare reform: The ties that bind* (pp. 3-14). Thousand Oaks, CA: Sage Publications.

Browne, A., Salomon, A., & Bassuk, S. S. (1999). The impact of recent partner violence on poor women's capacity to maintain work. *Violence Against Women* 5: 393-426.

Brush, L. D. (2002). Work-related abuse: A replication, new items, and persistent questions. *Violence and Victims* 17: 743-757.

———. (2003a). Impacts of welfare reform. *Race, Gender and Class* 10: 137-192.

———. (2003b). "That's why I'm on Prozac": Battered women, traumatic stress, and education in the context of welfare reform. In V. Adair & S. Dahlberg (Eds.), *Reclaiming class: Women, welfare, and the promise of higher education in America* (pp. 215-239). Philadelphia, PA: Temple University Press.

———. (2004). Battering and the poverty trap. *Journal of Poverty* 8: 23-43.

Davis, M. (1999). The economics of abuse: How violence perpetuates women's poverty. In R. Brandwein (Ed.), *Battered women, children, and welfare reform: The ties that bind* (pp. 17-30). Thousand Oaks, CA: Sage Publications.

Fox, J. A. & Zawitz, M. W. (2001). *Homicide trends in the United States: Intimate homicide.* Washington, DC: U.S. Department of Justice, Bureau of Justice Statistics.

Fraser, N. & Gordon, L. (1994). A genealogy of dependency—Tracing a keyword of the United States welfare-state. *SIGNS* 19: 309-336.

Hardesty, J. L. (2002). Separation assault in the context of postdivorce parenting— An integrative review of the literature. *Violence Against Women* 8: 597-625.

Hays, S. (2003). *Flat broke with children: Women in the age of welfare reform.* New York: Oxford University Press.

Hirschman, A. O. (1970). *Exit, voice, and loyalty: Responses to decline in firms, organizations, and states.* Cambridge, MA: Harvard University Press.

Hobson, B. (1990). No exit, no voice: Women's economic dependency and the welfare state. *Acta Sociologica* 33: 235-250.

Howard, J. & Hollander, J. (2000). *Gendered situations, gendered selves.* Walnut Creek, CA: AltaMira Press.

Kimmel, M. S. (2002). "Gender symmetry" in domestic violence: A substantive and methodological research review. *Violence Against Women* 8: 1332-1363.

Kingfisher, C. P. (1996). *Women in the American welfare trap.* Philadelphia: University of Pennsylvania Press.

Lipsky, M. (1980). *Street-level bureaucracy: Dilemmas of the individual in public services.* New York: Russell Sage Foundation.

Lloyd, S., & Taluc, N. (1999). The effects of male violence on female employment. *Violence Against Women* 5: 370-392.

Meisel, J., Chandler, D. & Rienzi, B. M. (2003). Domestic violence prevalence and effects of employment on two California TANF populations. *Violence Against Women* 9: 1191-1212.

Misra, J., Moller, S., & Karides, M. (2003). Envisioning dependency: Media depictions of welfare in the 20th century. *Social Problems* 50: 482-504.

Monson, R. (1997). State-ing sex and gender: Collecting information from mothers and fathers in paternity cases. *Gender & Society* 11: 279-295.

Purvin, D. M. (2003). Weaving a tangled safety net: The intergenerational legacy of domestic violence and poverty. *Violence Against Women* 9: 1263-1277.

Raphael, J. (1999). Keeping women poor: How domestic violence prevents women from leaving welfare and entering the world of work. In R. Brandwein (Ed.), *Battered women, children, and welfare reform: The ties that bind* (pp. 31-43). Thousand Oaks, CA: Sage Publications.

———. (2000). *Saving Bernice: Battered women, welfare, and poverty.* Boston, MA: Northeastern University Press.

Richie, B. (1996). *Compelled to crime: The gender entrapment of battered black women.* New York: Routledge.

Riger, S. & Staggs, S. L. (2004). Welfare reform, domestic violence, and employment: What do we know and what do we need to know? *Violence Against Women* 10: 961-990.

Scott, E. K., London, A. S., & Myers, N. A. (2002). Dangerous dependencies: The intersection of welfare reform and domestic violence. *Gender & Society* 16: 878-897.

Sev'er, A. (2002). *Fleeing the house of horrors: Women who have left abusive partners.* Toronto: University of Toronto Press.

Tolman, R. M., Danziger, S. K., & Rosen, D. (2002). *Domestic violence and economic well-being of current and former welfare recipients.* Joint Center for Poverty Research Working Paper 304.

United States Congress. (1994). Violence Against Women Act. Title IV of the Violent Crime Control and Law Enforcement Act. P.L. 103-322.

United States Congress. (2000). Violence Against Women Act of 2000. P.L. 106-386.

Chapter 16

Welfare Reform and the Safety Needs of Battered Women

Christine C. George

The road to safety for women who are victims of domestic violence is neither straightforward nor easy. For battered women, access to independent economic support and the ability to support an independent household is often a critical factor in rebuilding a safe life for themselves and their children (Brandwein, 1999b; Davis, 1999; Lyon, 2000). Poor women without family resources, as well as women who are blocked by their abusers from access to family resources, have used public family assistance as an important resource in their strategies toward building economic independence from their abusers (Brandwein, 1999a). Aid to Families with Dependent Children (AFDC), the federal family assistance program enacted with the New Deal Social Security legislation and expanded in the 1960s civil rights era (Quadagno, 1995), along with food stamps, Medicaid, and other social welfare programs, were integral tools within a system of battered women services built by feminists in the 1970s (George, Sharma, & Sabina, 2004).

Deliberately weakening that tool in 1996, Congress enacted and President William Clinton authorized, as part of their welfare reform agenda, the Personal Responsibility and Work Opportunity Reconciliation Act (PRWORA). The act abolished Aid to Families with Dependent Children and replaced it with Temporary Assistance for Needy Families (TANF). This action, along with the accompanying passage of the Illegal Immigration Reform and Immigrant Responsibility Act of 1996 dramatically restricted access to assistance and limited the scope of assistance. The result for battered women was a serious reduction in available public resources and the elimination of one of the primary tools that had been available to build a safer life.

doi:10.1300/5608_17

Some women are excluded from access to programs altogether, while others have difficulty with eligibility and participation requirements.

During the passage of the PRWORA and in subsequent legislation, advocates were able to add provisions that allowed for exemptions and specialized services for the needs of victims of domestic violence. However, while these provisions have mitigated the impact of the legislation on safety for many women, their limited scope and lack of universality, combined with implementation problems, have left a weakened system of support for many battered women. Congress, in its upcoming deliberations to reauthorize TANF, has an opportunity to address these problems, and commit itself to a strong support system for battered women and their children.

THE DOMESTIC VIOLENCE SYSTEM AND THE ROLE OF PUBLIC ASSISTANCE

Beginning in the 1970s and growing out of the women's movement of that era, grassroots feminist networks and organizations in the United States started developing at the local level a system to serve battered women (Roberts, 2002). Shelters were established and community education and awareness campaigns were launched. Policy advocacy was instituted to change and/or develop both social welfare and criminal justice program policies and laws in state and local government to best support and assist these women. As the system developed and advocacy efforts were successful, the civil and social rights of women to public services and protections were strengthened. The passage by the U.S. Congress of the Violence Against Women Act (VAWA) of 1994 heralded a new level of federal commitment to battered women, expanding and codifying definitions of abuse, strengthening the criminal justice response to abuse, providing new rights for certain immigrant women and children, and providing funding to state and local private-public systems that served abused women. The system of support to domestic violence victims never seemed stronger.

Accessible and responsive public assistance programs were an important component of this maturing system. Although far from adequate, with low monthly stipends and often-unsympathetic implementation, public assistance has been an important lifeline for many abused women seeking to build self-sustaining, healthy, and safe lives

(Brandwein, 1999b). Women leaving their abusers often depart without any financial resources (Brandwein, 1999b). Emergency shelters can provide them succor, but their material needs are also great. They need permanent housing and, in order to achieve that goal, they need immediate money with which to rent an apartment for themselves and their children. Housing is only the beginning of a number of economic tasks. These women need a stable source of income to meet the monthly rent and household expenses, to name a few. If unemployed and able to work, they might need assistance in job readiness training and placement assistance. They also might need access to adequate child care, transportation assistance, and other support services associated with employment. If unskilled or underemployed, they need educational and training opportunities that can lead to even better employment. If unable to work, public assistance can provide economic support while women address various barriers they face toward economic self-sufficiency.

WELFARE REFORM: LIMITING THE LIFELINE

Welfare reform changed the basic philosophy of federal public assistance from a program of family assistance focusing on ameliorating poverty to a work program aimed at reducing welfare dependency (Riger & Staggs, 2004). The PRWORA eliminated many entitlements that poor families headed by single parents had to public assistance and made it less responsive to the needs of abused women seeking its support. Lifetime access to TANF benefits was capped at sixty months. Most noncitizens became ineligible for benefits, as were women with felony drug convictions. Moving women from welfare to work became the main focus of service delivery, as recipients faced new requirements of up to thirty hours a week work activities in order to continue receiving benefits. Women were required to vigorously cooperate with establishing paternity and child support orders—which, for victims of spousal abuse could create unsafe situations—or risk losing their public assistance benefits.

Fearful of the impact on abused women, battered women advocates and welfare rights advocates raised, and continue to raise, a number of concerns about these welfare reform changes. In the final welfare reform package in 1996, after vigorous lobbying by advocates, a number of provisions were included to address the needs of abused women. First, states were allowed some leeway in their implementation of the law, with some of the restrictions offering more flexibility than others. For example, up to 20 percent of the state caseload can be exempt from the sixty-month lifetime restriction without the state suffering a penalty in terms of a reduction in federal funding. One of the allowable reasons for this exemption is family violence. Second, the Wellstone/Murray amendment (the Family Violence Option or FVO) gave states the option to screen recipients for domestic violence and to grant them temporary exemptions from welfare program work and paternity/child support requirements. In addition, under VAWA 2000, some battered immigrants became eligible for some public assistance in certain circumstances.

ADVERSE IMPACT ON POOR, ABUSED WOMEN WITH THE MOST NEEDS

Looking more closely, it is clear that that the women most impacted by welfare reform are likely to be those who most need assistance.

Lifetime limits to assistance. Women can receive TANF for a total of sixty months during their lifetime. At least half of the women receiving welfare are likely to have experienced abuse at some point in their adult life, and 30 percent of welfare recipients report abuse in their current relationships (Tolman & Rafael, 2000; Lyon, 2000). Not surprisingly, many of these women have complex, long-terms problems that are not easily addressed and that often adversely affect their workforce participation and their ability to successfully leave welfare (Lyons, 2000; Taylor and Barusch, 2004).

Immigrant noncitizens. Most noncitizens are barred from TANF, food stamps, and most other federal social welfare programs. Most immigrant domestic violence victims married to lawful permanent residents or U.S. citizens can receive benefits after a minimum of five years from the date of their entry into the United States (if their entry occurred after August 21, 1996) (Asian & Pacific Islander Institute on Domestic Violence, 2002). No other noncitizens are eligible for benefits.[1]

Many immigrant battered women have few economic resources, and issues of language and lack of familiarity with American society and culture put them at a disadvantage as they seek safety (Abuinnab et al., 2001; George, Sharma, & Sabina, 2004). They tend to be economically dependent on their abusers. They cannot easily find work; they tend to have no work permits, making them prey to exploitive employers. Many are continents away from family and friends who might provide support. Unable to access social welfare and other supports, they often fall through the cracks (Legal Momentum, 2004b).

Women with felony drug convictions. TANF bans individuals with felony drug convictions from receiving food stamps or federal cash assistance.[2] Stringent federal and state sentencing laws have resulted in an increasing number of women being convicted of felony drug charges. Many of these women addicts are likely to have experienced physical or sexual abuse in their lives and over half are likely to be in abusive relationships at the time they seek assistance. They need drug treatment, health care, education, job training, counseling, and assistance in order to build a safe life for themselves and their families (Pimlott-Kubiak, Siefer, & Boyd, 2004).

Work participation requirements. TANF requires women to participate in a number of welfare-to-work related activities, and women who fail to meet these requirements lose their welfare stipend. In addition, at the street level, applicants for assistance are often required to look for employment and/or accept substandard employment opportunities. This can block them from accessing subsidized child care and health insurance (Illinois Domestic Violence Advocate, Private Communication, December 8, 2004). Battered women on welfare experience more difficulties in complying with work requirements than women who are not experiencing abuse (Lyon, 2000). A study of participants in a short-term, welfare-to-work program found one-third of the women reporting posttraumatic stress symptoms (Brush, 2000). Compared to other women on welfare, battered women are twice as likely to rate their health as poor, have higher rates of depression, and are nearly twice as likely to report a physical limitation, all factors that can impact on their ability to work and/or participate successfully in welfare-to-work programs (Lyon, 2000; Staggs & Riger, 2005).

Abusive partners also sabotage women's efforts to participate in employment-related activities through a number of strategic activities. They may start fights or inflict visible injuries on their partners just before key job interviews or departure for work. They may harass the women at their workplace, calling multiple times a day or appearing at the workplace unannounced. Studies have found that about 50 percent of battered women who work are harassed at work by their abuser (GAO, 1998).

Child support. The PRWORA includes comprehensive child support enforcement provisions. There are stiff penalties for recipients who do not cooperate with efforts by public assistance agencies to hold nonpaying parents accountable. Most women want to pursue the child support cases, but those with more recent abuse are likely to be at risk (Lyon, 2000). These women are put in the untenable position of having to choose between safety and support (Brandwein, 1999b; Pearson, Griswold, & Thoennes, 2001). Abusers and their victims argue more about child support and visitation than other couples with no abuse. Also the child support and custody process can renew contact between abuser and victim and create an unsafe situation (Pearson, Griswold, & Thoennes, 2001).

Marriage promotion. Although there is no current provision in the PRWORA to promote marriage, some welfare-to-work programs are emphasizing marriage as part of a welfare reduction strategy. Among the new proposals to welfare reform that Congress will be considering this coming session (2005) are those that would strengthen this thrust, incorporating the promotion of marriage into the new law. This would be similar to provisions in the PRWORA which rewards states that have reduced teenage pregnancy and "illegitimacy" rates. Advocates fear any provision promoting marriage as a strategy of welfare reduction would compromise the safety of women (Family Violence Prevention Fund, n.d.). Some advocates report that some local welfare-to-work programs' strategy of promoting marriage as part of welfare reduction reinforces women's denial of family violence, often leading them to postpone addressing the abuse until it has become more dangerous (private communication, Chicago Department of Human Services Homeless Advocate, December 9, 2004).

UTILIZATION OF FAMILY VIOLENCE OPTIONS AND OTHER PROVISIONS FOR ABUSED WOMEN

Currently, the FVO allows states to screen and identify victims of domestic violence, refer those victims to appropriate services, grant waivers to domestic violence victims when welfare requirements are harmful or unsafe, and ensure the protection of the confidentiality of domestic violence victims. Confirming the need for this flexibility expressed by both advocates and local public aid officials, forty-two states and the District of Columbia had instituted some or all the provisions in the FVO by July 2004, another five states implemented some equivalent measures, and only four states have not adopted state-wide provisions (Legal Momentum, 2004a). However, the use of these options on the street level has been problematic in many localities.

In order for women to receive these various services and exemptions, battered women must disclose their abuse to welfare officials. And in turn, the officials have to be responsive to the disclosure and act appropriately. Yet, many women do not disclose or apply for exemptions (Barusch et al.'s report [cited in Lyon, 2000]; GAO, 1999; Pearson, Griswold, & Thoennes, 2001). Key to disclosure are the proactive skills and sympathy of street-level workers; disclosure is three to four times higher if the workers are proactive in encouraging it (Pearson, Griswold, & Thoennes, 2001). Yet, a number of studies have shown that often workers are not only passive, but in fact are unsympathetic or hostile to the needs of domestic violence victims (Levin, 2001). For example, a review of a three-state study found that, even though only those victims with recent and severe abuse were likely to disclose to workers, only 10 percent of those applications were granted (GAO, 1999). In Chicago, immigrant battered women who are eligible for benefits are often turned away by street-level workers, unless accompanied by advocates (George, Sharma, & Sabina, 2004).

Street-level workers' attitudes and capacities. Hagen and Owens-Manley (2002) found mixed attitudes among workers regarding domestic violence. On one hand, workers ranked the lack of physical safety of women and their children as situations in which they would be likely to apply more flexible requirements. On the other hand, workers expressed serious concerns that applicants would use domestic violence as a scam in order to qualify for benefits.

Levin (2001), in exploring why few TANF recipients were being referred to on-site domestic violence case managers, found street-level workers with an antipathy to clients' needs. Levin suggested that the workers might be resentful that their own experiences with abuse were not being addressed. A domestic violence counselor in Chicago who advocates for homeless women with street-level welfare workers echoed this analysis (confidential communication, December 2004).

Gatekeepers, not social workers. Workers are also limited in their ability to provide services. Most state agencies provide specific and in-depth training to caseworkers (Levin, 2001), but the demands of their work also impinge on their ability to provide services to victims. An Illinois Department of Human Services administrator complained that workers were spread too thin and did not have time to build personal relationships with clients (confidential communication, December 8, 2004). Also, the culture of public assistance demands that welfare workers be "benefit police," rather than providers of social services (Levin, 2001). This culture is deeply engrained, reflecting changes in public assistance for which PRWORA was only the culmination (Lewis, George, & Puntenney, 1998). Making the options work for abused women is difficult and will take a concentrated effort and resources to not only train workers but also to create new cultures of service delivery.

WHAT SHOULD CONGRESS DO?

From the standpoint of providing safe options for women and their children, the resources provided by public assistance should be easily accessible with no obstruction from frontline workers. In other words, TANF—the heir to AFDC—should return family assistance to its core mission, focusing on meeting needs and providing support. However, this is unlikely to happen. The sentiments that drove welfare reform to constrict the rights to public assistance are still shaping the U.S. policy agenda.

As the passage of the Family Violence Option and various provisions of VAWA 2000 demonstrate, there is a commitment to providing safety and succor to victims of domestic violence in spite of the broader retrenchment trends in the provision of public assistance. This commitment must be harnessed in the coming session to expand and to strengthen the Family Violence Option and other provisions for abused women. Given the large percentage of abused women among the long-term welfare caseload, addressing violence should be one of the key focuses—not a peripheral option—of TANF.

What could this mean? As a first step, all states should be required to uniformly institute all aspects of the Family Violence Option, therefore providing battered women throughout the nation with the same rights to access economic support and other welfare assistance. Additional steps should include

1. requiring all states to allow access to public assistance by abused immigrant women utilizing VAWA and other domestic violence related immigration provisions;
2. counting participation in domestic violence programs toward TANF work participation;
3. making safety a key consideration in the design of any new TANF provisions and in the evaluation and redesign of current provisions; and
4. providing funding to state public assistance agencies to increase the capacity of their street-level staff to serve abused women.

NOTES

1. Immigrants who had special refugee status and/or have been admitted to the United States on humanitarian grounds still maintained some rights to public assistance for a certain period of time. Twenty states have TANF programs that provide some relief to "qualified" battered immigrants—married to U.S. citizens or legal permanent residents—who have filed under VAWA for adjustment of immigration status.

2. States have the option to provide state benefits if they so choose. Just over half the states have chosen to either eliminate or modify the ban.

REFERENCES

Abuinnab, R., George, C., McCourt, K., Nargang, J., & Speicher, L. (2001, June). A partnership for self-sufficiency. Paper presented at the meeting of the Institute for Women's Policy Research, Washington, DC.

Asian & Pacific Islander Institute on Domestic Violence. (2002, October). *TANF reauthorization and its effects on Asian and Pacific Islander families.* San Francisco: Author. Retrieved 7/17/2004 from <http://www.apiahf.org/apidvinstitute/ResearchAndPolicy/Policypaper.htm>.

Brandwein, R. (1999a). Family violence and welfare use: Report from the field. In R. Brandwein (Ed.), *Battered women, children, and welfare reform: The ties that bind* (pp. 45-58). Thousand Oaks, CA: Sage Publications, Inc.

Brandwein, R. (1999b). Family violence, women, and welfare. In R. Brandwein (Ed.), *Battered women, children, and welfare reform: The ties that bind* (pp. 3-16). Thousand Oaks, CA: Sage Publications, Inc.

Brush, L.D. (2000). Battering, traumatic stress, and welfare-to-work transition. *Violence Against Women, 6*(10), 1039-1066.

Davis, M.F. (1999). The economics of abuse: How violence perpetuates women's poverty. In R. Brandwein (Ed.), *Battered women, children, and welfare reform: The ties that bind* (pp. 17-30). Thousand Oaks, CA: Sage Publications, Inc.

Family Violence Prevention Fund. (n.d.). *TANF (welfare) reauthorization.* San Francisco: Author. Retrieved 12/15/2004 from <http://endabuse.org /programs/ display.php3?DocID=305>.

General Accountability Office. (1998). *Domestic violence: Prevalence and implications for employment among welfare recipients* (HEHS-9912). Washington, DC: Author.

General Accountability Office. (1999). *Welfare reform: Assessing the effectiveness of various welfare-to-work approaches* (HEHS-99-179). Washington, DC: Author.

George, C., Sharma, A., & Sabina, C. (2004). Hardly a leg to stand on: The civil and social rights of immigrant victims of domestic violence. Unpublished manuscript, Loyola University Chicago Center for Urban Research and Learning.

Hagen, J.L. & Owens-Manley, Judith. (2002). Issues in implementing TANF in New York: The perspective of frontline workers. *Social Work, 47*(2), 171-182.

Legal Momentum. (2004a). *Family Violence Option, state by state summary.* Washington, DC: Author. Retrieved 9/05/04 from <http://www.legalmomentum .org>.

Legal Momentum. (2004b). *Immigrant women.* Washington, DC: Author. Retrieved on 11/05/2004 from <http://legalmontem.org/issues/imm/index.shtml>.

Levin, R. (2001). Less than ideal: The reality of implementing a welfare-to-work program for domestic violence victims and survivors in collaboration with a TANF department. *Violence Against Women, 7*(2), 211-221.

Lewis, D., George, C., & Puntenney, D. (1998). Welfare reform in Illinois. In L. B. Joseph (Ed.), *Families, poverty, and welfare reform* (pp. 99-138). Champaign: University of Illinois Press.

Lyon, E. (2000). Welfare, poverty and abused women: New research and its implications. Harrisburg, PA: National Resource Center on Domestic Violence. Downloaded on 12/14/2004 from <http://www.vawnet.org/ NRCDVPublications/ BCSDV/ Paers/BCS10 _POV.php>.

Pearson, J., Griswold, E.A., & Thoennes, N. (2001). Balancing safety and self-sufficiency: Lessons on serving victims of domestic violence for child support and public assistance agencies. *Violence Against Women, 7*(2), 176-192.

Pimlott-Kubiak, S., Siefer, K., & Boyd, C. (2004). Empowerment and public policy: An exploration of the implications of Section 115 of the Personal Responsibility and Work Opportunity Act. *Journal of Community Psychology, 32*(2), 127-143.

Quadagno, J. (1995). *The color of welfare.* New York: Oxford University Press.

Riger, S. & Staggs, S.L. (2004). Welfare reform, domestic violence, and employment. *Violence Against Women, 10*(9), 961-990.

Roberts, A.R. (2002). Myths, facts, realities regarding battered women and their children: An overview. In Albert R. Roberts (Ed.), *Handbook of domestic violence intervention strategies* (pp. 3-22). New York: Oxford University Press.

Staggs, S.L. & Riger, S. (2005). Effects of intimate partner violence on low-income women's health and employment. *American Journal of Community Psychology,* 36(1/2), 133-145.

Taylor, M.J. & Barusch, A.S. (2004). Personal family and multiple barriers of long-term welfare receipt. *Social Work,* 49(2),175-183.

Tolman, R. & Raphael, J. (2000). A review of research on welfare and domestic violence. *Journal of Social Issues,* 56(4), 655-682.

PART IV:
RACE, ETHNICITY, AND IMMIGRATION

Chapter 17

Ever Present, Sometimes Acknowledged, but Never Addressed: Racial Disparities in U.S. Welfare Policy

Susan T. Gooden
Nakeina E. Douglas

Race continues to be a central organizing principle of American society. By noticing race we begin to challenge racism, the state, institutions of civil society, and individuals to combat unequal and unjust legacies. Much of the emphasis placed on concepts of diversity, multiculturalism, and color-blind society plays a significant role in minimizing America's race problem. Opposing racism requires that we notice race, not ignore it, that we afford it the recognition it deserves and the subtlety it embodies (Omi & Winant, 1994). Ignoring race and pretending to be "color-blind" means doing nothing to change the institutionalized racial inequalities and racial discrimination that still pervade American society.

In both the development and implementation of public policy, race serves as a suitable tool for analysis that can provide insight into public policy variations. Race in America has been a component of social structures and plays a significant role in shaping public policy. Public policy plays an important role in the political, economic, and social marginalization of racial and ethnic minorities. Policies that result in the recurring and incessant negative treatment of minorities require policymakers to initiate three remedies. First, the historical context of racial disparities must be well understood. Second, current racial

Authors' Note: The authors express appreciation for research support from the Kellogg Foundation. This work does not necessarily reflect the views of the funder.

doi:10.1300/5608_18

207

disparities must be openly acknowledged. Third, policies and practices specifically designed to reverse these trends must be adopted and vigorously implemented.

EVER PRESENT . . .

The relationship between race and welfare has been important since the inception of welfare policies in the United States (Bell, 1965). One of the earliest systematic examinations of the racial composition of mother's pensions programs in the United States was conducted by the Department of Labor in 1931. This report contained information on approximately half of the aided families across the nation. Of 46,597 families, 96 percent of them were white, 3 percent were black, and 1 percent were of "other racial extraction" (U.S. Department of Labor, 1933). In these early years, blacks were simply not eligible at the same rates as whites. Of particular importance to this analysis, limited provision for black families was particularly obvious in areas in which 19 to 45 percent of the families were black. The most common tactic states employed was to avoid establishing mother's pension programs in localities with large black populations.

The structure of the Social Security Act of 1935, which contained the Aid to Dependent Children (ADC) component, encouraged reliance on the "suitable home" requirements encoded in most state mother's pension statutes. The model state law read, "any dependent child who is living in a suitable family home" will be eligible (Gordon, 1994, p. 274). The definition of a "suitable family home" was highly discretionary.

Many southern states passed additional eligibility criteria targeted directly at black women. During the late 1930s and 1940s, states created seasonal employment policies that cut recipients off the welfare rolls during the cotton picking season (Quadagno, 1994). The accepted rationalization by ADC administrators was that blacks "could get by" with less than whites. This discriminatory administrative interpretation resulted in striking differences in benefit distribution. For example, in the nation's capital city, social workers had two standard budgets for relief benefits, a higher one for whites and a lower one for blacks (Green, 1967). Between 1952 and 1960 formal "suitable home" requirements were strengthened or adopted in Georgia, Mississippi, Virginia, Michigan, Arkansas, Texas, Florida, Tennessee, and Louisiana. The state policies differed substantially in their impact on families, but each in its own way helped to control the growth of the caseload and the increase in public welfare costs.

Although the civil rights movement ushered in much less racism in eligibility determination, a reduction in racism in eligibility determination simultaneously resulted in less public support for welfare programs. In essence, as more black women joined the welfare rolls, public support for such programs declined. Some of the main achievements under the Great Society programs of the 1960s were to expand employment, reduce poverty, and improve opportunities for "nonwhite" citizens. State discriminatory tactics that formally kept black children from receiving benefits were largely eliminated. The federal government strongly denounced such practices, and the states had to comply with federal standards in order to continue receiving federal assistance. Racial discrimination, in terms of access to benefits, had been dismantled.

But, as local agencies were confronted with an unprecedented volume of applications and unprecedented pressure to approve the granting of benefits, "stories of the unusual welfare recipients driving luxury cars and using Food Stamps to purchase filet mignon and of women bearing children solely to obtain AFDC benefits [were] accepted by the public as the norm" (Cottingham & Ellwood, 1989, p. 12). The image provoked by almost exclusively white-serving "mother's pension" programs had been clearly replaced with an image of a minority mother, having more and more illegitimate children, to stay at home and avoid personal responsibility and work.

SOMETIMES ACKNOWLEDGED . . .

The relationship between race and welfare has been more commonly examined in the academic literature since the 1970s. Studies by Larry Orr (1976) and Gerald Wright (1976) suggest that, when controlling for other explanations, welfare benefits are lower in states that have higher percentages of blacks on their welfare caseloads. In particular, numerous studies since the 1990s described the historical relationship between race and welfare (Quadagno, 1994); the role of public institutions in facilitating racial disparities in the treatment of people of color (Gooden, 1998; Lieberman, 1998; Brown, 1999); the politics of race and welfare (see Schram, Soss, & Fording, 2003); and the role of race as a significant factor in state welfare policy choices (Soss et al., 2001).

The Personal Responsibility and Work Opportunity Reconciliation Act of 1996 eliminated AFDC as an entitlement and created a block grant for states to provide time-limited cash assistance for needy families, with an emphasis on immediate employment. These state programs are funded under Temporary Assistance for Needy Families (TANF). States may use their TANF funding in any manner "reasonably calculated to accomplish the purposes of TANF" (U.S. Department of Health and Human Services, 1996). With TANF, U.S. social policy returned to an era of broad state and local discretion to determine eligibility, methods of assistance, and benefit levels.

States with high percentages of black populations have stricter welfare policies. When examining state welfare policy choices in terms of sanctions, time limits, work requirements, and family caps, Soss et al. (2001) found, "As the black percentage of welfare recipients rises from low to high, the probability of strong sanctions increases from .05 to .27, the probability of strict time limits shifts from .14 to .66, and the probability of a family cap climbs from .09 to .75" (p. 387). But it isn't clear which states specifically have stricter policies, the cumulative effect of these policies, or how such states compare to states with low black populations, especially states with very low black populations.

Taking a Closer Look

In order to better understand how blacks in the United States experience welfare, we examined the policies of states with a high black population and compared these policies to states with a low black population. We also examine states within the low black population group that have a very low black population. To conduct this analysis, we examined each state's TANF policy as of 2001 (Finance Project, 2003). According to data from the 2000 U.S. Census, blacks constitute 12.3 percent of the U.S. population. Sixteen states and the District of Columbia have black populations higher than the national average: Alabama, Arkansas, Delaware, Florida, Georgia, Illinois, Louisiana, Maryland, Michigan, Mississippi, New Jersey, New York, North Carolina, South Carolina, Tennessee, and Virginia. As Table 17.1 reports, taken together, nearly 70 percent of all blacks in the United States live in these

TABLE 17.1. U.S. Black and White Population, by State

State	Population	White	Percent of population	Black or African American	Percent of Population
Alabama	4,447,100	3,162,808	71.1	1,155,930	26.0
Alaska	626,932	434,534	69.3	21,787	3.5
Arizona	5,130,632	3,873,611	75.5	158,873	3.1
Arkansas	2,673,400	2,138,598	80.0	418,950	15.7
California	33,871,648	20,170,059	59.5	2,263,882	6.7
Colorado	4,301,261	3,560,005	82.8	165,063	3.8
Connecticut	3,405,565	2,780,355	81.6	309,843	9.1
Delaware	783,600	584,773	74.6	150,666	19.2
District of Columbia	572,059	176,101	30.8	343,312	60.0
Florida	15,982,378	12,465,029	78.0	2,335,505	14.6
Georgia	8,186,453	5,327,281	65.1	2,349,542	28.7
Hawaii	1,211,537	294,102	24.3	22,003	1.8
Idaho	1,293,953	1,177,304	91.0	5,456	0.4
Illinois	12,419,293	9,125,471	73.5	1,876,875	15.1
Indiana	6,080,485	5,320,022	87.5	510,034	8.4
Iowa	2,926,324	2,748,640	93.9	61,853	2.1
Kansas	2,688,418	2,313,944	86.1	154,198	5.7
Kentucky	4,041,769	3,640,889	90.1	295,994	7.3
Louisiana	4,468,976	2,856,161	63.9	1,451,944	32.5
Maine	1,274,923	1,236,014	96.9	6,760	0.5
Maryland	5,296,486	3,391,308	64.0	1,477,411	27.9
Massachusetts	6,349,097	5,367,286	84.5	343,454	5.4
Michigan	9,938,444	7,966,053	80.2	1,412,742	14.2
Minnesota	4,919,479	4,400,282	89.4	171,731	3.5
Mississippi	2,844,658	1,746,099	61.4	1,033,809	36.3
Missouri	5,595,211	4,748,083	84.9	629,391	11.2
Montana	902,195	817,229	90.6	2,692	0.3
Nebraska	1,711,263	1,533,261	89.6	68,541	4.0
Nevada	1,998,257	1,501,886	75.2	135,477	6.8
New Hampshire	1,235,786	1,186,851	96.0	9,035	0.7

TABLE 17.1 *(continued)*

State	Population	White	Percent of population	Black or African American	Percent of Population
New Jersey	8,414,350	6,104,705	72.6	1,141,821	13.6
New Mexico	1,819,046	1,214,253	66.8	34,343	1.9
New York	18,976,457	12,893,689	67.9	3,014,385	15.9
North Carolina	8,049,313	5,804,656	72.1	1,737,545	21.6
North Dakota	642,200	593,181	92.4	3,916	0.6
Ohio	11,353,140	9,645,453	85.0	1,301,307	11.5
Oklahoma	3,450,654	2,628,434	76.2	260,968	7.6
Oregon	3,421,399	2,961,623	86.6	55,662	1.6
Pennsylvania	12,281,054	10,484,203	85.4	1,224,612	10.0
Rhode Island	1,048,319	891,191	85.0	46,908	4.5
South Carolina	4,012,012	2,695,560	67.2	1,185,216	29.5
South Dakota	754,844	669,404	88.7	4,685	0.6
Tennessee	5,689,283	4,563,310	80.2	932,809	16.4
Texas	20,851,820	14,799,505	71.0	2,404,566	11.5
Utah	2,233,169	1,992,975	89.2	17,657	0.8
Vermont	608,827	589,208	96.8	3,063	0.5
Virginia	7,078,515	5,120,110	72.3	1,390,293	19.6
Washington	5,894,121	4,821,823	81.8	190,267	3.2
West Virginia	1,808,344	1,718,777	95.0	57,232	3.2
Wisconsin	5,363,675	4,769,857	88.9	304,460	5.7
Wyoming	493,782	454,670	92.1	3,722	0.8
	281,421,906	**211,460,626**	**75.1**	**34,658,190**	**12.3**

Source: U.S. Census, 2000.

states. The remaining thirty-four states have black populations lower than the national average. Within these states, thirteen have very low black populations, which we define as states in which blacks constitute less than 3 percent of the total population: Hawaii, Idaho, Iowa, Maine, Montana, New Hampshire, New Mexico, North Dakota, Oregon, South Dakota, Utah, Vermont, and Wyoming. Table 17.2 reports each state's policy in the areas under examination.

TABLE 17.2. Selected TANF Policies by State

| State | Lifetime Time Limit for Adult-Headed Families | | Maximum Sanction for Noncompliance with Work Requirements | | Family Cap | Drug Felony Disquali-fication |
	Limit	Months	Sanction	Duration (Months)		
Alabama	Yes	60	Full grant	6	No	Yes
Alaska	Yes	60	$369	12	No	Yes
Arizona	No		Full grant	1	Yes	Yes
Arkansas	Yes	24	Partial grant	URM[a]	Yes	Yes
California	Yes	60	Adult grant	6	Yes	Yes
Colorado	Yes	60	Full grant	3	No	Yes
Connecticut	Yes	21	Full grant	3	Yes	No
Delaware	Yes	48	Full grant	PER[b]	Yes	Yes
District of Columbia	Yes	60	Partial grant	6	No	No
Florida	Yes	48	Full grant	3	Yes	Yes
Georgia	Yes	48	Full grant	PER	Yes	Yes
Hawaii	Yes	60	Full grant	2	No	Yes
Idaho	Yes	24	Full grant	PER	Yes	Yes
Illinois	Yes	60	Full grant	3	Yes	Yes
Indiana	Yes	24	Adult grant	36	Yes	Yes
Iowa	Yes	60	Full grant	6	No	Yes
Kansas	Yes	60	Full grant	2	No	Yes
Kentucky	Yes	60	Full grant	URM	No	Yes
Louisiana	Yes	60	Full grant	URM	No	Yes
Maine	Yes	60	Adult grant	6	No	No
Maryland	Yes	60	Full grant	URM	Yes	Yes
Massachusetts	No		Full grant	URM	No	No
Michigan	No		Full grant	1	No	No
Minnesota	Yes	60	Partial grant	1	No	Yes
Mississippi	Yes	60	Full grant	PER	Yes	Yes
Missouri	Yes	60	Partial grant	3	No	Yes
Montana	Yes	60	Adult grant	12	No	Yes

TABLE 12.2 *(continued)*

State	Lifetime Time Limit for Adult-Headed Families		Maximum Sanction for Noncompliance with Work Requirements		Family Cap	Drug Felony Disqualification
	Limit	Months	Sanction	Duration (Months)	Family Cap	
Nebraska	Yes	60	Full grant	12	Yes	Yes
Nevada	Yes	60	Full grant	PER	No	Yes
New Hampshire	Yes	60	Partial grant	1	No	No
New Jersey	Yes	60	Full grant	URM	Yes	Yes
New Mexico	Yes	60	Full grant	URM	No	No
New York	Yes	60	Adult grant	60	No	No
North Carolina	Yes	60	Full grant	URM	Yes	Yes
North Dakota	Yes	60	Full grant	URM	Yes	Yes
Ohio	Yes	60	Full grant	6	No	No
Oklahoma	Yes	60	Full grant	URM	Yes	No
Oregon	No		Full grant	URM	No	No
Pennsylvania	Yes	60	Full grant	PER	No	Yes
Rhode Island	Yes	60	Partial grant	URM	No	Yes
South Carolina	Yes	60	Full grant	1	Yes	Yes
South Dakota	Yes	60	Full grant	1	No	Yes
Tennessee	Yes	60	Full grant	URM	Yes	Yes
Texas	Yes	60	Partial grant	6	No	Yes
Utah	Yes	36	Full grant	URM	No	Yes
Vermont	No		Partial grant	1	No	No
Virginia	Yes	60	Full grant	6	Yes	Yes
Washington	Yes	60	Adult grant	URM	No	Yes
West Virginia	Yes	60	Full grant	6	No	Yes
Wisconsin	Yes	60	Full grant	PER	Yes	Yes
Wyoming	Yes	60	Full grant	1	Yes	Yes

Source: Finance Project (2003); USDA (2003)

aURM = until requirement met

bPER = permanent

Time Limits

Under PRWORA, states cannot use federal TANF funds to provide assistance to a family which has received federal TANF assistance for sixty months. However, states may use their own funds to assist TANF clients beyond sixty months. States may even elect not to have time limits altogether, as long as they do not use federal TANF funds. Conversely, states may adopt time limits shorter than the sixty-month federal limit, thus imposing a more strict welfare policy. We coded states as strict if they have time limits shorter than the sixty-month federal maximum. We coded states as nonstrict if they use the sixty-month maximum or have no time limits.

The vast majority of all states use the sixty-month federal maximum. However, there are notable differences among high black population states and low black population states. Stricter time limits occur twice as often among states with a high black population. As Figure 17.1 reports, among such states, 23.5 percent (four of the seventeen) have strict time limit policies, compared with only 11.8 percent (four out of thirty-four) low black population states. Examining the very low black population states independently, only 15.4 percent (two of the thirteen) have strict time limit policies.

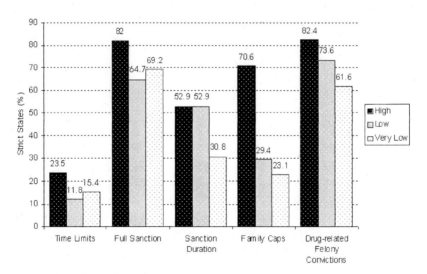

FIGURE 17.1. Strictness of TANF Policies in States with High, Low, and Very Low Black Populations

Sanctioning Policies

Under TANF, caseworkers may issue a financial sanction for welfare clients who do not comply with program rules and work activities without good cause. A welfare client's monthly benefit amount may be reduced, thus decreasing the amount of cash assistance available to that family during the effectiveness period of the sanction. States have considerable discretion in developing sanctions. Stricter states issue a full-family sanction affecting the payment level for the entire family. Other, less strict, states issue a partial sanction typically only affecting the adult portion of the benefit, but leaving the child portion of the benefit intact.

Strict sanctioning policies are more common in states with a high black population. Among the high black population states, 82 percent (fourteen out of seventeen) have adopted the full-family sanction. By comparison, across the remaining thirty-four states that have a low black population, only 64.7 percent (twenty-two out of thirty-four) have such strict policies. This pattern holds among the subgroup of very low black population states, with 69.2 percent (nine out of thirteen) having strict sanctioning policies.

States also have discretion in determining the maximum duration of a sanction. Some states sanction for a specific time period, typically ranging from one to six months. We coded states with a maximum sanction period of three months or longer as strict. Less strict states are those states that have a maximum sanction period of less than three months or states that sanction the welfare client only until the requirement is met. We consider this policy less strict since the welfare recipient can have her benefits reinstated once meeting the requirement, rather than waiting a specific amount of time.

In examining maximum sanction duration among the high black population states, 52.9 percent (nine of the seventeen) have strict sanction duration. This pattern is the same when examining all low black population states together, with 52.9 percent (eighteen of the thirty-four) having strict sanction duration. However, among the thirteen states with a very low black population, only 30.8 percent (four of the thirteen) have a strict sanction duration. The vast majority of states with a very low black population have a less strict sanction duration of one month or until the requirement activating the sanction is met.

Family Caps

Family caps are designed to decrease the number of out-of-wedlock births among welfare recipients, a policy goal of TANF. For example, under AFDC a family of two in Arizona would have received $275. If the family had an additional child, then their cash assistance would increase by $72 per month, to $347 (U.S. GAO, 2001). Although PRWORA is silent on the issue of family caps, states may adopt family caps if they so choose. In most cases, states with family caps do not provide any cash increases when a mother on welfare gives birth. A GAO study estimates that the amount of cash assistance received by families whose benefits were capped was, on average, about 20 percent less than it would have been in the absence of a family cap (2001).

As Table 17.2 reports, nearly half (twenty-two) of all states have a family cap provision. However, the difference between high black population states and low black population states is striking. Among high black population states 70.6 percent (twelve out of seventeen) have a family cap, whereas only 29.4 percent (ten out of thirty-four) of low black population states have a family cap. When examining only states with a very low black population, this drops further to 23.1 percent (three out of thirteen).

Drug-Related Felony Convictions

Federal TANF policies allow states to deny eligibility for TANF and food stamps to anyone convicted of a drug-related felony after August 22, 1996. States have discretion in constructing their policies. For example, states can have a "freeze out" period rather than a permanent ban, or target the ban on selected drug felony categories, such as drug trafficking. We coded a state's policy as strict if they have such provisions.

The vast majority of states (thirty-nine) have a drug-related felony provision of some sort, denying TANF and food stamps to ineligible individuals. However, again we find interesting differences. Among high black population states 82.4 percent (fourteen out of seventeen) deny benefits to individuals convicted of such felonies. This decreases slightly to 73.6 percent (twenty-five out of thirty-four) among low black population states. However, this decreases considerably to

61.6 percent (eight out of thirteen) among states with very low black populations.

In sum, our analysis of state policies shows a clear pattern: States with high black populations have stricter policies than states with low black populations.

- 23.5 percent of states with a high black population have strict time limits, compared to 11.8 percent of states with a low black population.
- Among the high black population states, 82 percent have strict sanctioning polices, compared with 64.7 percent of low black population states.
- States with high black populations have family cap policies at more than twice the percentage of low black population states (70.6 percent versus 29.4 percent).
- Over 80 percent of high black population states deny TANF benefits to convicted drug felons, compared with 61.6 percent among states with very low black populations.

. . . BUT NEVER ADDRESSED

This chapter does not offer a normative judgment on which types of welfare policies should be adopted, but rather highlights a very disturbing pattern. Clients in high black population states are attempting to achieve self-sufficiency under much harsher policies than clients on welfare in states that do not have high black populations. These differences are very real. In essence, welfare policy can be characterized as a "devolution of racial inequities." As Soss and his colleagues correctly conclude,

> Thus, a black woman who conceives a child while receiving welfare is now less likely than a white woman to live in a state that offers additional aid for the child. Likewise, a black client who misses a meeting with a caseworker is now disproportionately likely to live in a state where this single infraction results in a termination of benefits for the full family. White clients committing this same infraction are more likely to live in states that respond in a more lenient fashion. (Soss et al., 2001, p. 390)

Policymakers need to aggressively address the issue of racial disparities in welfare policy. It is simply unsound public policy to operate a time-limited welfare reform program that does not consider the differences white and minority clients receive due to their state of residence, caseworker treatment, types of training services offered, and labor market discrimination, when previous and existing data suggest such troubling patterns occur. Although TANF policy is covered by federal civil rights legislation, a more aggressive approach is needed. Policymakers can start addressing such concerns by (1) promoting racial disparity research and (2) providing cash incentives for states that reduce racial disparities. As is commonly known, the investment of dollars into a particular area of research sends a strong signal of importance. Consider, for instance, the idea of the government promoting marriage among welfare clients. A few years ago, this idea received very little serious attention. However, once the Bush administration made millions of dollars of funding available to research and pilot programs on marriage promotion, such research and programs grew in an incredibly short time period. Likewise, when the National Institutes of Health (NIH) made $60 million available to support health diversity research, including research on racial disparities in health care, these topics evolved in importance as well. Allocating governmental research dollars to seriously examine and reduce racial disparities in TANF policies would elevate this issue's status too.

Since the inception of the PRWORA, states are eligible to receive $200 million in bonuses for high performance. Initially, these bonuses were awarded for annual results in four categories: job placement, job success (retention and earning gains), improvement in job placement, and improvement in job success. Since then, bonuses were also awarded for other program achievements such as a demonstrated decrease in out-of-wedlock births, with no increase in abortion rates, helping low-income working families enroll in food stamps, Medicaid, and the State Children's Health Insurance Program (SCHIP), providing child care for working families, and increasing the proportion of children living in families with married parents. Such high-performance bonuses serve as a powerful incentive for state and local TANF agencies to produce a particular set of desired outcomes. Unfortunately, no performance bonus categories are related to the reduction of racial disparities in welfare programs. Put simply, what gets measured, gets done. Political leaders and policymakers should specifically identify the reduction of racial disparities as a high-bonus award qualifier in order to aggressively direct state and local agencies' attention to addressing this issue.

Despite historical and contemporary evidence of racial inequities in the distribution of welfare benefits, as well as in public policies that determine assistance eligibility, the subject of racial inequities receives minimal attention among policymakers. Reversing this trend requires the above actions. In addition, high-quality research on racial disparities should be accepted as valid. On an anecdotal note, when we have attended professional meetings where racial inequities in public policy are raised, there are typically two types of responses. In many cases, attention immediately turns to the study's design and methodology. The bar for research acceptance is raised in ways not commonly seen when nonracial relationships are examined. In response, very impressive and careful research techniques in examining racial disparities have been employed—advanced statistical methods, paired testing research designs, and well-documented field research, to name a few. Having an informal dual system of standards—one for social science research in general, and another when racial disparities are the subject matter—can function as a delay tactic, both in discouraging further research on racial disparities and in promoting additional delay in the development and implementation of policies specifically designed to correct these inequities.

Another common response is to shift the focus to identifying the cause of such racial disparities, rather than to implement strategies to reverse the outcomes. We should provide additional clarity here. Causal studies are a very important and noteworthy contribution to research on racial disparities in welfare policy. The lack of routine administrative data collection on race and ethnicity promotes ignorance about the source of such disparities (Finegold & Staveteig, 2002). One could logically ask, if we do not know the cause, how can we correct the outcome? But to fail to even attempt to address racial disparities in welfare policy consistently identified by research *until* the cause can be definitively identified is neither responsive nor consistent with the experimental nature of welfare policies, as encouraged under TANF. To illustrate, as previously mentioned, many states adopted family cap provisions, although the ability to link an increase in cash assistance with a decision to have another child is far less conclusive than the data that strongly suggest there are racial disparities in the distribution of welfare benefits. However, many states, especially states with a high percentage of blacks in their population, chose to enact such policies. Yet, when research suggests significant and consistent racial disparities in welfare policy design, the implementation of sanctions, job availability and opportunities, or treatment of welfare clients by caseworkers, to name a few, not a single TANF performance measure, increase in TANF funding base, or bonus award is linked to monitoring or reducing racial disparities. Regrettably, the innovative spirit of welfare reform is notably absent when it comes to aggressively promoting the reduction of racial disparities. Policymakers in federal, state, and local agencies should find these racial disparities unacceptable and work insistently toward their eradication.

REFERENCES

Bell, Winifred. 1965. *Aid to Dependent Children.* New York: Columbia University Press.

Brown, Michael K. 1999. *Race, Money, and the American Welfare State.* Ithaca, NY: Cornell University Press.

Cottingham, Phoebe H. and David T. Ellwood (eds.) 1989. *Welfare Policies for the 1990s.* Cambridge, MA: Harvard University Press.

Finance Project. 2003. *TANF State Plan Summaries.* Retrieved from <http://www. financeprojectinfo.org/WIN/>.

Finegold, Kenneth and Sarah Staveteig. 2002. "Race, Ethnicity, and Welfare Reform." In A. Weil & K. Finegold (eds.), *Welfare Reform: The Next Act.* Washington, DC: Urban Institute, pp. 203-223.

Gooden, Susan Tinsley. 1998. All Things Not Being Equal: Difference in Caseworker Support Toward Black and White Welfare Clients. *Harvard Journal of African American Public Policy,* 4: 23-33.

Gordon, Linda. 1994. *Pitied But Not Entitled: Single Mothers and the History of Welfare, 1890-1935.* Cambridge, MA: Harvard University Press.

Green, Constance McLaughlin. 1967. *The Secret City: A History of Race Relations in the Nation's Capital.* Princeton, NJ: Princeton University Press.

Liberman, Robert. 1998. *Shifting the Color Line: Race and the American Welfare State.* Cambridge, MA: Harvard University Press.

Omi, Michael and Howard Winant. 1994. *Racial Formation in the United States: From the 1960s to the 1990s.* New York: Routledge.

Orr, Larry L. 1976. "Income Transfers As Public Good: An Application to A.F.D.C." *American Economic Review* 66: 359-371.

Quadagno, Jill. 1994. *The Color of Welfare: How Racism Undermined the War on Poverty.* New York: Oxford University Press.

Schram, Sanford F., Joe Soss, and Richard Fording (eds.). 2003. *Race and the Politics of Welfare Reform*. Ann Arbor: University of Michigan Press.

Soss, Joe, Sanford Schram, Thomas Vartanina, and Erin O'Brien. 2001. "Setting the Terms of Relief: Explaining State Policy Choices in the Devolution Revolution." *American Journal of Political Science*, 45(2): 378-395.

U.S. Department of Agriculture. 2003. *Food Stamp Program: State Options Report*. Washington, DC: Food and Nutrition Service, U.S. Department of Agriculture.

U.S. Department of Health and Human Services. 1996. *Major Provisions of the Personal Responsibility and Work Opportunity Reconciliation Act of 1996* (P.L. 104-93). Washington, DC.

U.S. Department of Labor. 1933. *Mother's Aid, 1931*. Children's Bureau. Publication No. 220. Washington, DC: 13, 26-27.

U.S. General Accountability Office. 2001. Welfare Reform: More Research Needed on TANF Family Caps and Other Policies for Reducing Out-of-Wedlock Births. GAO-01-924, September 11.

Wright, Gerald C., Jr. 1976. "Racism and Welfare Policy in America." *Social Science Quarterly* 57: 718-730.

Chapter 18

That Old Black Magic?
Welfare Reform and the New Politics
of Racial Implication

Sanford F. Schram

Welfare was dramatically reformed in 1996. The Personal Responsibility and Work Opportunity Reconciliation Act (PRWORA) abolished the long-standing Aid to Families with Dependent Children
(AFDC) program, originally enacted as part of the Social Security
Act of 1935, and replaced it with the Temporary Assistance for
Needy Families (TANF) block grant. Many procedural safeguards to
accessing assistance were repealed. The TANF program has emphasized time limits and work requirements and allowed states to set
stricter options than specified in the federal law. It has allowed states
greater latitude to use sanctions to reduce benefits and terminate families from assistance. It has given birth to a "Work First" welfare reform regime that puts in place a series of "get-tough" policies designed to reduce the problem of "welfare dependency" (Gais &
Weaver 2002). Welfare has been reformed to have as its main purpose
the promotion of self-sufficiency by enforcing work and family values among the poor. As a result, the number of recipients receiving
what is now called TANF fell from 13,242,000 in 1995 to 5,334,000
in 2002—a decline of 59.7 percent (U.S. Census Bureau 2002, p.
354). Largely for this reason alone, welfare reform has been widely
heralded a "success" (see Schram & Soss 2002).

There are many reasons to question the supposed success of welfare reform, including its failure to improve the living conditions of
most of the families affected by the reforms (see Loprest 2002); however, that is not my main concern in this chapter. Instead, I focus on

doi:10.1300/5608_19

the troubling, even insidious, way in which welfare is part of what we can call a "new politics of racial implication." By the "politics of racial implication," I mean the way in which race both influences and is influenced by welfare reform. In this chapter, I demonstrate that even in what we can call the "post-civil rights" era in which explicit racial discrimination is considered illegitimate, the long shadow of race relations still casts a pall over welfare, and in turn welfare operates to reinforce notions of racial hierarchy.

RACE AND WELFARE IN HISTORICAL CONTEXT

Any consideration of the ongoing relationship of race and welfare necessarily involves understanding it in historical and social context (Ture & Hamilton 1992). As experienced in U.S. society, it is impossible to understand the relationship of race to welfare without also considering its ties to class and gender. Welfare, in the form of cash assistance to low-income families, historically has been a marginal program in liberal-capitalist America for reasons associated with the class, gender, and race biases of the dominant culture. As those biases have changed with a changing society, welfare has changed as well, if not always immediately.

This insight recalls that Frances Fox Piven and Richard A. Cloward (1971) emphasized that welfare has always been a secondary institution calibrated to serve the primary needs of the state and the market in the United States. It was always structured to serve two potentially conflicting goals: (1) to reinforce the work ethic so that the poor would take whatever low-paying jobs the market provided and (2) to offer support to low-income families so as to re-create the conditions for maintaining the state's political legitimacy. Welfare's status as a secondary institution also meant that historically it operated in ways that worked in consonance with the dominant class, gender, and race biases of society.

An overview of welfare's history makes this clear. Mothers' Pensions programs were the precursor of Aid to Families with Dependent Children and were developed to reduce the numbers of children being placed in orphanages because their mothers could not care for them (Crenson 1998). Yet, many of the reformers who championed these pensions explicitly did so in the name of safeguarding "republican motherhood" and fighting back the "race death" that was threatened by growing numbers of immigrant families who were considered then nonwhite (Ward 2000; Berg 2002). In addition, Mothers' Pensions operated more to Americanize immigrant mothers than to assist indigenous blacks, who were largely considered not deserving of such aid (Gordon 1994).

AFDC was added to the Social Security Act of 1935. The Social Security Act was actually titled the Economic Security Act but rather quickly came to take on the name of its most popular program of national old age insurance for retirees—commonly referred to as Social Security (Katz 2001). The other components of the Social Security Act relied on state governments for administration and came to be seen as less important. The legislation is still seen today as forging the cornerstone of the contemporary welfare state in the U.S. federal system of governance.

The Social Security Act gave rise to a two-tiered welfare state that privileges national social insurance over state public assistance programs (Lieberman 1998). In addition, this tiered system tends to reinforce differences in society along class, race, and gender lines with the upper-tier social insurance programs disproportionately benefiting families who were associated with more economically privileged white male workers and the lower-tier public assistance programs relied upon by poorer female-headed families who were disproportionately more likely to be nonwhite.

As Robert Lieberman (1998) has amply demonstrated, none of this is really an accident because of the role of federalism in our policy-making system. Southern congressmen in particular lobbied hard to ensure that public assistance titles be federal programs that accorded states substantial discretion in determining eligibility and setting benefits. They most especially wanted to ensure that public assistance to poor families could be calibrated to the needs of the still ascendant sharecropping system that relied on impoverished black families to work the fields. With substantial discretion, southern states could ensure that these families could be moved on and off the welfare rolls with beginnings and ends of the planting and harvesting seasons. Public assistance, as a second-tier program, administered by the states, could therefore take its place in the political economy of the *ancien regime* that arose in the apartheid of the southern agrarian system. As a result, the main public assistance program that would come to be called Aid to Families with Dependent Children (AFDC) was little more than a federal program that standardized the limited mothers' pension programs already in existence in many states. The top-tier social security program was originally structured to exclude coverage of those in certain occupations, such as agricultural workers and domestics, who disproportionately were nonwhites, and therefore provided access to this privileged program in a way that favored whites. The Social Security Act has been revised many times, but it is still the cornerstone of the tiered U.S. welfare state, and its legacy persists in perpetuating class, race, and gender bias.

As blacks began to gain rights to assistance in the 1960s, AFDC came to be seen as a "black program," making it more politically vulnerable and increasing calls for its retrenchment, which, after years of political gridlock, finally came in the 1990s (Quadagno 1994; Gilens 1999; Neubeck & Cazenave 2001).

The current context is what many call the post–civil rights era (Loury 2002; Williams 2003). This is a time after concern about civil rights and the righting of racial injustices. On the one hand, it is a time for imagining that we as a country are done with the civil rights struggle, that the battle to defeat racial injustice was won and over, and now we can forget about having to have to take race into account when trying to make public policy. On the other hand, it is a time when it is politically incorrect for public policy to explicitly invoke race to legislate either privileges for whites or disadvantages for blacks. It is my argument that in an era of race-blind public policy, racial hierarchy is re-created more by stealth.

CONTEXTUALIZING THE NEW POLITICS OF RACIAL IMPLICATION

In order to understand the relationship of race to welfare today, it must be placed not only in historical but also social context.* Significant changes in race relations in recent decades contribute to the differences between the old and new politics of racial implication (Brown et al. 2003). A number of important factors have led to race still being salient, but in different ways. The most basic factor is the change in demographics. In particular, race is less a black/white issue than in the past. Today it is impossible to talk about race and welfare without recognizing the

---

*This section is based on extensive conversations with Joe Soss.

growing importance of Latinos and immigrants to welfare politics (see Marchevsky & Theoharis 2005).

A second factor is the changes associated with the imbrication of race and gender (Crenshaw 1989). Welfare reform changed a program that largely served single mothers (Mink 2002). Any discussion of race and welfare has to take into account how gender roles have changed and the effect this has had on how black women on welfare are perceived by the public. Today, especially with the large-scale entry of nonpoor women into the workforce in large numbers, skepticism has been growing among the public about the need to support poor women of color via welfare.

Racial politics today is also different for a third reason internal to nonwhites, blacks in particular. This is the emergence of significant class divisions within racial minority groups. These class divisions have increased in large part due to the rise of a minority middle class, leading to within-group tensions/conflicts, and leading to differentiation in the ways white Americans view racial/ethnic minorities (Wilson 1999). The class fracturing of the black population in particular has led to a decline in political insurgency and a growing emphasis on interest group politics. Middle-class political leadership has tended to pursue conventional politics over protest politics.

Yet, as a fourth factor, concomitant with the improvement in the economic well-being of some segments of the nonwhite populations, there has also been a rise of meaningful representation in both policymaking and policy-implementing institutions. Still, this increase in representation has usually been as numerical minorities, often lack seniority and other power resources (Williams 2003). Blacks, in particular, have become a significant voting block for the Democratic Party, but they remain a "captured constituency" that is taken somewhat for granted because they are very unlikely to support the Republican Party whose policy positions they most often oppose. As a result, blacks tend not to be catered to by either national party (Frymer 1999). This paradoxical situation of being included but ignored reinforces a new black-white paradigm at the national level that involves the use of race-coded language as a political tool for denigrating nonwhites as in the case of Republicans and/or of distancing oneself from them as in the case of the Democrats. Under these circumstances, both are seen as having little to lose or a lot to gain in either implicitly denigrating or distancing one's party from the nonwhite population. But it is worth noting that the problem of the captured status of black voters at the national level varies considerably for subnational electoral competition, where they can be a critical voting block in some contested state and local elections. Hispanics, however, have begun to emerge as a "contested constituency," with considerable interethnic divisions across subgroups. These patterns are paired with the continued centrality of working-class white votes (Teixeira & Rogers 2001) and a slight increase in the class polarization of party allegiances overall (Stonecash 2000).

A fifth factor contributing to a different context for the new racial politics is the changing nature of racial differences in public opinion. White/black differences on government action have in recent times hardened in sharp contrast, with blacks much more supportive, not just on "welfare" but also of government intervention to ensure fairness in hiring, housing, etc. (Kinder & Sanders 1997). These differences make it more difficult to develop policies that are seen as fair to both blacks and whites and increase the possibility that an ostensibly race-neutral public policy such as welfare reform will be latently biased in favor of white approaches to addressing problems of poverty while being less sensitive to the circumstances that low-income black families find themselves confronting.

A sixth factor helping to create the conditions for the new politics of racial implication is residential segregation and all the related forms of isolation that follow from it in areas such as education and access to other needed public services (Allard, Tolman, & Rosen 2003). Residential segregation is not new, but the evidence on its persistence shows that it matters not only for access to services and for political coalition building, but also for citizens' racial attitudes and policy preferences. The persistence of segregation has increased the inability of whites to recognize the barriers that confront many low-income black families, thereby increasing the likelihood that policies designed to be consistent with white views will be less likely to address those barriers, even if those policies are racially neutral.

A seventh factor affecting welfare's changing relationship to race is its ties to the neoliberal philosophy that informs economic policymaking in an era of globalization. In this way, issues of race and gender are in this sense imbricated in contemporary issues of class. Today, there is a push to regiment the lower ends of the class structure into an emerging low-wage economy so that the economic system more generally can be competitive and profit in the face of growing global economic competition (Schram 2005a). The United States has led the way in championing the idea that the welfare state has to be retrenched in an era of global economic competition, and welfare reform has been developed and implemented in ways that are entirely consistent with that orientation. The neoliberal emphasis on regimenting the lower orders into the emerging low-wage economy has moved welfare away from its previous emphasis from the 1960s of providing assistance to needy families back to an earlier emphasis on disciplining subordinate populations so that they will be more docile in their willingness to taking menial low-paid work (Piven 2002; Peck 2001).

While the neoliberal disciplinary regime is on the surface race neutral, it operates in a way that reinscribes racial hierarchy. Welfare reform in such a regime takes the existing set of social relations as given and neutrally requires all recipients to meet its requirements. As a result, preexisting patterns of racial disadvantageness are not accounted for so as to re-create them. Welfare functions within a racial order and therefore involves rationalities dependent on that order. As a result, it works to enforce low-wage work disproportionately on nonwhites, who because of the background factors discussed previously are less likely to be in a position to find, get, and hold the better-paying jobs. The neoliberal insistence on scaling back the welfare state and enforcing work in the name of global competitiveness results in recreating racial hierarchy.

The global dimensions of this process are themselves racialized. Welfare reform involves integrating disproportionately nonwhite welfare recipients into low-wage jobs to make local labor markets in the United States more flexible and competitive with other low-wage labor markets elsewhere that are themselves disproportionately nonwhite. Race is an important marker in the global economy for designating who is available for the exploitations of low-wage work.

Welfare's ties to the disciplinary regime of neoliberalism are highlighted in its relationship to mass incarceration of nonwhites over the past few decades. Evidence shows that as incarceration of nonwhites, mostly males, has increased, access to and the value of welfare benefits has declined (Fording 2001; Wacquant 2003). As a more disciplinary regime has come to the fore, welfare has been retrenched in ways that have proven especially dramatic for low-income black communities, forcing them to feel the most draconian effects of these cutbacks and increasing their vulnerabilities for participating in the emerging low-wage labor markets. The old black magic of welfare policy continues on in new form.

WELFARE REFORM AS RACE MAKING

The foregoing historical and social contextualization of race and welfare enables us to see how they continue to interact if in different ways. Today race-neutral policies of the post–civil rights era are at risk of being "socially obtuse" policies that fail to account for the disadvantages that all low-income persons confront and which nonwhite low-income persons are more likely to confront. From this perspective, the "work first" regime of welfare reform becomes one that overlooks that many low-income single mothers of all races and ethnicities have lacked the access to adequate education, training, jobs, community support, etc., needed to make "rapid attachment" to the workforce and end a life of "welfare dependency." A "work first" regime that assumes all single mothers can leave welfare quickly, practice "personal responsibility" and achieve "self-sufficiency" by participating the labor market is destined to fail most single mothers, but is also likely to recreate racial disadvantages simply because nonwhites are less likely to have access to the needed resources and confront more barriers to making such a transition without support.

Under these conditions, the ostensibly race-neutral discourse of welfare reform operates to make race a self-fulfilling prophecy both in the treatment of black clients as individuals and as a group (Loury 2002). At the level of the individual client, even the unbiased caseworkers, who carry out ostensibly race-neutral policies, are implicated in this self-defeating cycle of proving some recipients are less personally responsible than others. Without even saying so, they give welfare recipients an ultimatum: go to work or lose what little social support we offer you. The racially biased results are documented in the available empirical research: nonwhites, who on average have less education and work experience, are less able to comply, more likely to be sanctioned, less likely to find a job before their time on welfare is exhausted, more likely to have to cycle back on to welfare, less likely to get out of poverty, etc. (see Schram 2005b). At the level of black recipients as a group, all these racial disparities operate in public discourse to demonstrate that nonwhites are less deserving. In this way, the stigma of race becomes its own self-fulfilling prophecy and we are encouraged to be suspicious of the very idea of race neutrality. Along with caseworkers, the public is encouraged to think the unthinkable: it was wrong to assume that blacks would do as well as whites. While conservatives claim such race-neutral social policies "assume the best" about blacks—i.e., that they can compete with whites—policies such as welfare reform, with their false neutrality that fails to account for black disadvantage preexisting welfare reform, end up justifying assuming the worst about low-income blacks who need to rely on welfare (Schram 2005a). The emerging research on race disparities occurring in welfare reform indicates that welfare continues to be influenced by race but also helps to reinscribe racial hierarchy.

The concrete practices of welfare-to-work programs starkly illustrate how these programs produce racial disadvantage. Increasingly, welfare policy has focused on targeting resources to address what are euphemistically called "barriers" that prevent recipients from leaving welfare to work (Danziger et al. 2000). Welfare-to-work programs concentrate substantial energy on screening, diagnosing, and treating clients for various personal deficiencies so that they can take jobs and reduce their reliance on public assistance. Yet, as the research reviewed has indicated, one of the most well-documented barriers that a growing number of welfare recipients confront is a racial one: racial discrimination in hiring (Bertrand & Mullainathan 2003). This barrier is not addressed in most welfare-to-work programs.* At best, there are self-esteem and dress-for-success programs designed to get welfare recipients to ingratiate themselves with prospective employers. Recipients who complete these classes and still fail to secure paid employment risk being penalized and even terminated from assistance depending on their time spent on welfare. These programs could, therefore, be interpreted as a perversion of efforts to address the racial barrier confronting welfare recipients. To the extent that these programs can be interpreted as attempting to overcome the racial barrier to employment, they constitute yet another instance in which welfare reform focuses on blaming individuals for the structural problems of society. These programs seek to solve structural

---

*Only California, Delaware, Kentucky, Louisiana, Michigan, and Vermont explicitly list employer discrimination as a good cause for an exemption from sanctions. Other states leave this issue to the discretion of case managers. See Center on Law and Social Policy, State Policy Documentation Project: <http://www.spdp.org/tanf/sanctions/goodcause2.PDF>.

problems by getting victims to change their behavior. We need to recognize that some barriers, maybe the most important ones affecting welfare recipients, are structural and not individual, and a welfare reform program that fails to address relevant structural race biases and then blames individual recipients for failing to overcome those barriers is therefore itself a race-biased policy. As the example of welfare-to-work highlights, welfare reform's failure to account for relevant preexisting racial inequalities makes it an ostensibly neutral public policy that incorporates the race biases of the broader society into its very operations and, as a result, ends up helping to produce racial disadvantage among recipients and the poor more generally. Welfare reform becomes an instance of what Loic Wacquant (2003) calls "racemaking."

This vicious cycle that blames black recipients as individuals and as a group also operates at the level of policy. It is not just that the latent race bias of ostensibly race-neutral policies produces racial disadvantages, but as the welfare population increasingly comes to be seen as a largely nonwhite population, the entire program itself, just like its nonwhite recipients, is at risk of being marginalized to the point where program administrators could not help black recipients even if they recognized this problem. With the darkening of the welfare rolls, welfare risks increasingly being seen as a "black program" for those "other" people who are not conforming to the work and family rules of white middle-class society, making it a program more vulnerable to losing support or being revised to take a more punitive approach. The available research at this level provides evidence of this, indicating that the states with a higher proportion of welfare recipients who are nonwhite are more likely to adopt more draconian welfare reform policies, such as limits on benefits, stricter time limits, and tougher sanction policies for rules violations (Fellowes & Rowe 2004; Soss et al. 2004; Gais and Weaver 2002). The new politics of racial implication creates its own vicious, if implicit, cycle where race continues to influence welfare policymaking, welfare policy reinforces racial hierarchy, and the cycle starts all over again.

CONCLUSION

Some analysts have been at pains to emphasize that welfare reform's "get tough" approach is racially neutral and does not reflect the discriminatory practices of welfare's sordid past (Mead 1998). The foregoing analysis suggests that race continues to play an important, if different, and even more insidious, way of reproducing racial hierarchy through welfare reform today. In the post–civil rights era, explicit forms of racial discrimination are illegitimate. Yet, racially neutral practices that fail to address preexisting inequities end up reinforcing them. And when they are taken as proof that nonwhites have failed to conform to white middle-class standards, these ostensibly neutral practices become the basis for reinscribing notions of racial hierarchy. In fact, that is what is happening in social welfare policy today: race gets recreated via the ostensibly neutral practices associated with welfare reform. The old black magic of racial bias in the development and implementation of welfare policy now operates more by stealth in a particularly insidious way under contemporary welfare reform.

REFERENCES

Allard, Scott W., Richard M. Tolman, & Daniel Rosen (2003). The Geography of Need: Spatial Distribution of Barriers to Employment in Metropolitan Detroit. *Policy Studies Journal* 31: 3 (August), 293-307.

Berg, Allison. (2002). *Mothering the Race: Women's Narratives of Reproduction, 1890-1930.* Chicago: University of Illinois Press.

Bertrand, Marianne & Sendhil Mullainathan. (2003). *Are Emily and Greg More Employable Than Lakisha and Jamal? A Field Experiment on Labor Market Discrimination.* Working Paper 9873. Boston: National Bureau of Economic Research.

Brown, Michael K., Martin Carnoy, Elliot Currie, Troy Duster, David B. Oppenheimer, Marjorie B. Shultz, & David Wellman. (2003). *Whitewashing Race: The Myth of a Color-Blind Society.* Berkeley: University of California Press.

Crenshaw, Kimberle (1989). Demarginalizing the Intersection of Race and Sex: A Black Feminist Critique of Antidiscrimination Doctrine, Feminist Theory and Antiracist Politics. *University of Chicago Legal Forum* 122, 139-167.

Crenson, Matthew A. (1998). *The Invisible Orphanage: A Prehistory of the American Welfare System.* Cambridge, MA: Harvard University Press.

Danziger, Sandra, Mary Corcoran, Sheldon Danziger, Colleen Heflin, Ariel Kalil, Judith Levine, Daniel Rosen, Kristin Seefeldt, Kristine Siefert, & Richard Tolman (2000). Barriers to the Employment of Welfare Recipients. In *Prosperity For All? The Economic Boom and African Americans* (pp. 245-278), Robert Cherry and William M. Rodgers III, eds. New York: Russell Sage Foundation.

Fellowes, Matthew C. & Grethen Rowe. (2004). The Politics of Welfare Reform(ed): How TANF Changed and Did Not Change Redistribution Politics. *American Journal of Political Science* 48:2, 362-373.

Fording, Richard C. (2001). The Political Response to Black Insurgency: A Critical Test of Competing Theories of the State. *American Political Science Review* 95:1, 115-131.

Frymer, Paul. (1999). *Uneasy Alliances: Race and Party Competition in America.* Princeton, NJ: Princeton University Press.

Gais, Thomas & R. Kent Weaver. (2002). *State Policy Choices Under Welfare Reform.* Welfare Reform & Beyond Brief #21. April. Washington, DC: Brookings Institution.

Gilens, Martin. (1999). *Why Americans Hate Welfare: Race, Media, and the Politics of Antipoverty Policy.* Chicago: University of Chicago Press.

Gordon, Linda. (1994). *Pitied But Not Entitled: Single Mothers and the History of Welfare, 1890-1935.* Cambridge, MA: Harvard University Press.

Katz, Michael B. (2001). *The Price of Citizenship: Redefining the American Welfare State.* New York: Metropolitan Books.

Kinder, Donald R. & Lynn M. Sanders (1997). *Divided by Color: Racial Politics and Democratic Ideals.* Chicago: University of Chicago Press.

Lieberman, Robert C. (1998). *Shifting the Color Line: Race and the American Welfare State.* Cambridge, MA: Harvard University Press.

Loprest, Pamela J. (2002). *Who Returns to Welfare?* Washington, DC: Urban Institute, Assessing the New Federalism.

Loury, Glenn C. (2002). *The Anatomy of Racial Inequality.* Cambridge, MA: Harvard University Press.

Marchevsky, Aljeandra & Jeanne Theoharis. (2005). *From Welfare Queens to Working Mamis: Latino Immigrants and the Politics of Citizenship in the Post-Welfare Era.* New York: New York University Press.

Mead, Lawrence M. (1998). Telling the Poor What to Do. *The Public Interest* 103, 97-112.

Mink, Gwendolyn. (2002). Violating Women: Rights Abuses in the Welfare Police State. In *Lost Ground: Welfare, Reform, Poverty, and Beyond* (pp. 95-112), Randy Albelda and Ann Withorn, eds. Boston: South End Press.

Neubeck, Kenneth J. & Noel A. Cazenave. (2001). *Welfare Racism: Playing the Race Card Against America's Poor.* New York: Routledge.

Peck, Jamie. (2001). *Workfare States.* New York: Guilford Press.

Piven, Frances Fox. (2002). Globalization, American Politics, and Welfare Policy. In *Lost Ground: Welfare, Reform, Poverty, and Beyond* (pp. 27-41), Randy Albelda and Ann Withorn, eds. Boston: South End Press.

Piven, Frances Fox & Richard A. Cloward. (1971). *Regulating the Poor: The Functions of Public Welfare* (1993 updated edition). New York: Vintage.

Quadagno, Jill. (1994). *The Color of Welfare: How Racism Undermined the War on Poverty.* Oxford, UK: Oxford University Press.

Schram, Sanford F. (2005a). *Global Welfare Methods: New Approaches to Governance.* Philadelphia: Temple University Press.

Schram, Sanford F. (2005b). Welfare Reform As Racemaking: Toward a New Poverty Research. *Perspectives on Politics* 3: 2 (June), 253-268.

Schram, Sanford F. & Joe Soss. (2002). Success Stories: Welfare Reform, Policy Discourse, and the Politics of Research. In *Lost Ground: Welfare, Reform, Poverty, and Beyond* (pp. 57-78), Randy Albelda and Ann Withorn, eds. Boston: South End Press.

Soss, Joe, Sanford F. Schram, Thomas P. Vartanian, & Erin O'Brien. (2004). Welfare Policy Choices in the States: Does the Hard Line Follow the Color Line? *Focus* 23:1, 9-15.

Stonecash, Jeffrey M. (2000). *Class and Party in American Politics.* Boulder, CO: Westview Press.

Teixeira, Ruy & Joel Rogers. (2001). *America's Forgotten Majority: Why the White Working Class Still Matters.* New York: Basic Books.

Ture, Kwame & Charles V. Hamilton. (1992). *Black Power: The Politics of Liberation.* Reissue Edition. New York: Vintage Books.

U.S. Census Bureau (2002). *Statistical Abstract of the United States.* Washington, DC: U.S. Bureau of the Census.

Wacquant, Loic. (2003). From Slavery to Mass Incarceration: Rethinking the "Race Question" in the US. *New Left Review* 13:1, 41-60.

Ward, Deborah E. 2000. Mothers' Pensions: The Institutional Legacy of the American Welfare State. PhD dissertation, Columbia University, New York.

Williams, Linda F. (2003). *The Constraint of Race: Legacies of White Skin Privilege in America.* University Park: Pennsylvania State University Press.

Wilson, William Julius. (1999). *The Bridge over the Racial Divide: Rising Inequality and Coalition Politics.* New York: Russell Sage Foundation.

Chapter 19

The Politics of Citizenship
and Entitlement: Immigrants, Welfare,
and the Persistence of Poverty

Lynn Fujiwara

The Personal Responsibility and Work Opportunity Reconciliation Act (PRWORA) of 1996 established exclusionary parameters to
systematically bar immigrants from specific welfare benefits based
upon their citizenship status. In many ways welfare reform was just
as much about immigration reform, as principles of "membership"
and "belonging" shaped the provisions that clearly demarcated immigrants as "outsiders" who should find other ways to support their
families regardless of their contributions to this country's economy
and social fabric. As we think about the borders of human security in
our current state of geopolitical globalization, immigrants in the
United States are finding themselves pushed further outside the
fringes of political and economic protection. Welfare reform and its
subsequent legislative revisions further solidified immigrants as outsiders less worthy of public support, and thus devalued for their essential contributions to this nation's economy and unrecognized as
families that continue to shape the cultural terrain of local communities as well as broader political formations.

According to the Congressional Budget Office, nearly half (44 percent) of all budgetary savings through the PRWORA were obtained
through the exclusion of benefits to immigrants (Hing, 1998). At the
time of its passing, PRWORA barred noncitizens from Supplemental
Security Income (cash assistance for the blind, elderly, and disabled)
and food stamps. Likewise states were granted the option to provide
Temporary Assistance for Needy Families (TANF) to immigrants, as

doi:10.1300/5608_20

well as other locally funded benefits. Over the first six years of welfare reform an estimated $23.7 billion of the overall $53.4 billion would be saved due to these immigrant cuts (Hing, 1998). Mass mobilization efforts, along with class-action lawsuits on behalf of veterans denied their veteran status to maintain their welfare benefits, resulted in the restoration of some of the harshest cuts (Fujiwara, 2005). Nevertheless, the cost of welfare reform on immigrant families and communities has been immeasurable. In this chapter, I focus on the political implications of the increasing significance of citizenship in welfare policy that further renders immigrants vulnerable to a myriad of social, emotional, and physical conditions.

DEMONIZING IMMIGRANTS AND THE RACIAL POLITICS OF CITIZENSHIP

How has citizenship become such a defining marker in public assistance debates? By the 1990s the anti-immigrant movement converged with the long-standing antiwelfare movement. The war against the poor was largely based upon racial imagery. By the end of the welfare reform movement two prominent villains were solidified in the popular consciousness of the public as well as politicians: the "welfare queen" (built on a distorted image of single black motherhood) (Hancock, 2003; Mink, 1998; Lubiano, 1992), and the undeserving immigrant (an image of Latina migrants supposedly coming here to reproduce U.S. citizen children). While congressional discussions that centered on the racially constructed "welfare queen" focused on ideas of cultural pathology, cycles of dependency, and irresponsibility, the debates around immigrants centered on assumptions that welfare had become a primary magnet for poor immigrants to choose to migrate to the United States.

First targeted in California's Proposition 187, the "Save Our State" initiative approved by 59 percent of California voters, undocumented immigrants were to be denied health care (including reproductive health care), public benefits, and education. Although federal programs have never been available to undocumented immigrants, with the exception of emergency health care, immunizations, WIC (nutritional assistance for poor women, infants, and children), and education, the construction of "illegal aliens" coincided with the narrative that they were a drain on the public welfare system. PRWORA went a step further to argue that "legal" documented as well as undocumented immigrants constituted a drain on the public welfare system. The story that dominated debates, ascribed to erroneous arguments that the same "overgenerous" system that led to cycles of dependency and irresponsibility for single mothers was also attracting immigrants to the United States, specifically to get on welfare.

The decision to bar immigrants from specific public benefits was established through lines that distinguished between "citizen" and "alien" recipients. As with most immigration policy, lines that appear to be based on citizenship can cover up lines that are based on race. According to legal scholar Frank Wu, "Once citizenship is defined by race, it becomes convenient to refer to the innocuous lines based on citizenship in lieu of the odious lines based on race" (Wu, 2002, p. 91). Drawing purposely confusing lines of eligibility among immigrants, Congress further distorted the demarcations by creating differently qualified and nonqualified categories of noncitizens. Legal permanent residents and refugees constitute the largest group within the qualified category. Nonqualified immigrants include undocumented immigrants, asylum applicants, immigrants formerly considered Permanently Residing Under Color of Law (PRUCOL), as well as those with temporary status such as students and tourists. Through PRWORA, nonqualified immigrants have been barred from most federal, state, and local public benefits. Likewise, immigrants who fall into the qualified category are not necessarily eligible for public benefits. Thus, it was qualified immigrants that became ineligible for SSI and food stamps, unless they could show proof of U.S. veteran status, ten years of employment through social security verification, or prove that they are the wife or child of a U.S. veteran. The legislation is intentionally complex in its creation of new categories of qualifications; differentiating among particular programs, governmental levels, and alien categories; the creation of many exceptions; the insertion of "grandfather" clauses; and the presence of special trans- ition rules (Schuck, 1997). According to Law Professor, Peter H. Schuck,

> This crazy-quilt pattern is not accidental. . . . the federal government has now made a clear comprehensive policy choice, albeit one confusing in its details, in favor of a national policy to discriminate against aliens in its federal programs, and to either require or permit the states to do so in their programs. (Schuck, 1997)

By distinguishing a clear line between legal immigrants and citizens, welfare reform tightened the circle of full membership within the United States. By conditioning access to the safety net on citizenship, welfare reform elevated the importance of citizenship in a nation where its value had been limited largely to exercising political rights, holding some governmental jobs, and obtaining certain immigration privileges (Fix & Tumlin, 1997). Through constitutional protections, legal permanent residents were expected to be treated equally with citizens. PRWORA authorized state and local governments to deny locally funded benefits to legal immigrants, transgressing the long-held constitutional requirement that states treat citizens and legal immigrants alike in terms of public benefits eligibility (Hing, 1998). The power given to the states to determine eligibility for qualified noncitizens coincides with an increasing financial responsibility that falls to states choosing to extend benefits to noncitizens (Fix & Tumlin, 1997). The racial implications of what is referred to as "immigrant exceptionalism," or the process of singling out immigrants for differential treatment (Zimmerman & Tumlin, 1999), was embedded in the exclusionary anti-immigrant narratives that Latinos and Asians were overabusing the welfare system.

THE COST OF WELFARE LOSS: IMMIGRANTS AND POVERTY POST–WELFARE REFORM

The Loss of Supplemental Security Income and the Ensuing Despair

The implications of welfare reform have been astounding. Soon after the PRWORA passed, elderly and disabled immigrants began receiving letters stating that they were going to lose their SSI by September 1997. Panic, despair, and confusion proliferated across immigrant communities, causing community-based organizations and legal services to step in and assist and advocate for immigrants. Most tragic were the scores of suicides primarily by elderly immigrants about to lose their life-sustaining SSI benefits. These suicides began to appear in local and national newspapers as stories of despair and betrayal. Community mobilization efforts launched a nationwide "Immigrant Rights Are Human Rights" campaign in the immediate year after the passing of the PRWORA that resulted in the restoration of SSI to immigrants who were receiving these benefits at the time of the law's passage, as well as to those who were here at the time of the enactment (August 22, 1996) and who become disabled later (Fujiwara, 2005). All immigrants who arrive after August 22, 1996, remain barred from federal SSI benefits.

Food Stamp Cuts and the Marked Increase in Hunger

Although the restoration of food stamps for immigrants was also a part of the Immigrant rights platform, Congress did not restore food stamps in the Balanced Budget Act. On September 1, 1997, most legal immigrants were terminated from federal food stamp benefits. According to the U.S. Department of Agriculture, an estimated 940,000 of the 1.4 million qualified immigrants receiving food stamps lost their eligibility status, of which nearly one-fifth were immigrant children. Some states continued to provide state-funded food stamps for children under eighteen years and adults sixty-five years and older. With another year of public protest by immigrant rights advocates, and several class-action lawsuits on behalf of Hmong and Laotian veterans whose veteran status remained unrecognized by the USDA, and therefore remained ineligible for food stamps, public pressure resulted in more piecemeal restorations. On June 23, 1998, eight months after most legal immigrants were cut from food stamp benefits, President Clinton signed the Agricultural Research Act that restored federal benefits to immigrants who resided in the United States on or before August 22, 1996, and are disabled, older than sixty-five, or younger than eighteen. This act also clearly specified Hmong and Laotian veterans as eligible for benefits based upon veteran status. The restorations went into effect on November 1, 1998. However, the partial restorations impacted only approximately 250,000 of the noncitizens no longer eligible for food stamps, slightly fewer than one in three legal immigrants who lost eligibility due to the welfare law. Thus, over 70 percent of immigrants who were eligible for food stamps pre-welfare reform, as well as most noncitizens who enter the United States after August 22, 1996 (including children) comprise a significant portion of needy immigrants with limited access to adequate food for their families.

Several large-scale studies have examined how immigrant families are faring since welfare reform. The California Food Security Monitoring Project of the California Food Policy Advocates was one of the most immediate studies to examine the impact of food stamp cuts among immigrants. Home to at least 40 percent of the nation's legal immigrant population, in California an estimated 460,000 legal immigrants were receiving federal food stamp benefits. With the implementation of new noncitizen eligibility requirements on September 1, 1997, 241,000 of those recipients were cut from federal food stamp benefits. Although the California legislature partially restored state-funded food stamps to noncitizens under the age of eighteen or over sixty-five, these restorations benefited only about one-fourth of those impacted by the cutoffs.

Through interviews in San Francisco and Los Angeles, in November 1997, 40 percent of the impacted group experienced moderate or severe hunger compared to 33 percent of the control group. By March, 50 percent of the impacted households experienced moderate or severe hunger compared to 38 percent of the nonimpacted group. In San Francisco, one-third (33 percent) of the impacted households with children were experiencing moderate or severe hunger, and were 35 percent more likely to experience this level of hunger than those living in nonimpacted households (Tujague & True, 1998). The study concluded that the alarmingly high rates of food insecurity and hunger among legal permanent residents demonstrated that the immigrant food stamp cuts mandated through welfare reform were actually generating hunger and harming children and adults alike. Several other studies found similar if not more alarming increases in hunger and food insecurity in other states, such as New York and Texas, due to the lack of state-funded food stamp provisions for immigrants (Kasper et al., 2000; Capps et al., 2002).

Chilling Effects for Eligible Immigrants and Temporary Assistance to Needy Families

The complicated nature of TANF has compounded the general loss of food stamps and SSI. Among legal immigrant recipients, between 1994 and 1999 TANF use declined by 60 percent, food stamps by 48 percent, SSI by 32 percent, and Medicaid by 15 percent. For refugees (anyone who entered under refugee status as of 1980 regardless of current immigration status), declines for TANF were by 78 percent, 53 percent for food stamps, and 36 percent for Medicaid (Fix & Passel, 2002). Often referred to as "chilling effects," the drastic drops of immigrant participation in public benefits (even among immigrants who remained eligible) reflects the success of welfare reform in creating so much confusion and panic that immigrants and their citizen children ceased participation rather than fear even harsher government sanction. As I conducted field work on the CalWORKs advisory panel in 1997-1998 in Santa Clara County, the drastic drop in immigrant participation was often referred to as "the disappeared." After the first round of letters were sent to immigrants alerting them of their intake appointments to begin the CalWORKs process, not one immigrant showed up for the "interviews" (which according to policy would have meant that they would all be sanctioned off). Social Service administration staff realized that they would have to do community outreach to convince and coax impoverished noncitizens to utilize the assistance for which they and their children (many citizens) remained eligible.

The Implications for Citizen Children of Immigrant Parents

The concern over citizen children within immigrant-headed house- holds has taken particular attention, given that citizen children in mixed-status families suffer due to their parents' citizenship status. Nearly 75 percent of all children living in immigrant-headed households are U.S. citizens (Fix & Zimmermann, 2001). Among low-income immigrant families with children who are U.S. citizens, 7.8 percent received TANF in 1999 compared with 11.6 percent of low-income citizen families with children. For food stamps 19.8 percent of mixed-citizen households received benefits compared to 27.9 percent of citizen headed low-income households. In 1994 1,342,000 citizen children with immigrant parents received food stamps. By 1998 more than 1 million of these children had fallen off the rolls, with participation declining by 75 percent to 333,000 (Bernstein et al., 2001). Thus, citizen children of immigrant parents are less likely to receive the same benefits as citizen children of citizen headed households.

Additional Barriers to Successful Welfare-to-Work Transitions

In addition to chilling effects due to confusion, fear, and inaccessibility, the welfare-to-work mandate has left many immigrants faced with language and educational barriers, which makes it even more difficult to adhere to strict work requirement rules for TANF assistance. This helps explain the 62 percent drop of legal permanent residents and 76 percent drop of refugee families from TANF in the first years of implementation. In 1999, about 11.7 percent of adult TANF recipients were noncitizens. Among these recipients 69 percent do not have high school diplomas or GEDs (Fremstad, 2002). Limited English proficiency proves to be a major obstacle for immigrants to both negotiate the welfare-to-work system and find and maintain self-sustaining employment. TANF further thrusts immigrants into low-wage service, manufacturing, or agricultural jobs that usually provide no health care or sustainable wages.

CITIZENSHIP POST–WELFARE REFORM: THE PERSISTENCE OF EXCLUSIONARY PRACTICES

Because of the immediate hardships faced by prereform immigrants who lost benefits, less attention has focused on the broader exclusion for future immigrants from safety net programs (Fix & Tumlin, 1997). Immigrants arriving after August 22, 1996, continue to remain ineligible for SSI and food stamps, and are subject to extended bars to other means-tested benefits. Immigrants who arrive post–welfare reform are also subject to harsher sponsorship deeming rules and public charge provisions established through the Illegal Immigration Reform and Immigrant Responsibility Act (IIRIRA) passed within a month of the PRWORA. The new affidavit of support requires sponsors of immigrants to sign legally enforceable affidavits in which the sponsor agrees to provide support to maintain the sponsored alien. Sponsors must now also earn at least 125 percent of the federal poverty level, and states are now required to consider a sponsor's income in federal means-tested programs until the immigrant becomes a naturalized citizen or can prove ten years of employment with social security verification. States are also given the option to consider the immigrant sponsor's income for state-funded benefits.

Some federal means-tested benefits have been associated with public charge provisions that have deterred immigrants from seeking public benefits for which they remained eligible. The public charge provision is a long-standing principle within immigration law. Basically, the public charge provision declares that any individual that may become dependent on the state could be inadmissible, deported, or denied naturalization. The vagueness of its definition and the standards with which this measure is applied generated considerable confusion regarding who is eligible for certain federal, state, or local public benefits and whether noncitizens may face adverse immigration consequences as a public charge for having received public benefits (Park, 2001). Several high-profile cases of immigrants wrongfully denied reentry due to the use of public assistance have resulted in the fear of endangering their opportunities to adjust legal status, become citizens, sponsor their relatives to immigrate, or even acquire re-entry to the United States after visits abroad, if they use any form of public assistance at all.

The drastic decline in immigrant participation in public benefit programs does not coincide with the perpetuation of high poverty levels within immigrant households. Regardless of counterevidence that immigrants contribute more to the nation's economy as taxpayers, consumers, and workers than they take in the form of public benefits, the welfare and immigration legislation of 1996 drew a clear line of differentiation between citizen and noncitizen access to public benefits. It is no coincidence that nearly half of overall budget savings through immigrant exclusions occurred at a time when contemporary immigration reached near-record levels (Fremstad, 2002). Immigrant labor is wanted and desired as demonstrated by President G. W. Bush's campaign to reenact a work-visa program to "legalize" undocumented workers, reminiscent of the Bracero Program of post–World War II. Because of the lack of worker protections within the highly exploitive service, manufacturing, and agricultural sectors, immigrant families remain among the poorest and most vulnerable.

TANF REAUTHORIZATION: ISSUES FOR IMMIGRANTS

Looking at reauthorization nearly ten years post–welfare reform, advocates are concerned over the increasing population of immigrants who have entered since August 22, 1996. Although the many forms of restorations have resulted in some gains, the convoluted system of differently situated immigrant groups has resulted in a general fear, mistrust, and inaccessibility that leads immigrants to avoid the social welfare system altogether, even for their citizen children. Quite simply, given the immense damage inflicted by welfare reform, the subsequent piecemeal restorations are not enough. Since 9/11 significant questioning over civil and human rights violations has occurred regarding unlawful detentions, deportations, and surveillance of immigrants. Immigrant rights have in many ways reached an all time low. The loss of political ground initiated by fundamental shifts in the welfare, immigration, and antiterrorist policies of 1996 paved the way for even more detrimental legislation and enforcement practices (e.g., the U.S.A. PATRIOT Act, and the creation of ICE [Immigration and Customs Enforcement]).

The racial politics that continue to influence major policy decisions have become further embedded in constructions of citizenship that directly impact and target racialized immigrant groups. Because more than 80 percent of the legal immigrant population is from Asian and Latin American countries, welfare reform imposed the greatest burdens among these communities of color (Chang, 1997). While the discourse around welfare reform to exclude noncitizens clearly relied on the imagery of foreigners from Asia and Mexico overabusing an overly generous welfare system, the prevailing logic that ultimately legitimized cuts to immigrants was based upon fundamental "American" principles of citizenship as belonging to the national politic. Citizen has become synonymous with race as a way to formally target the rapidly growing immigrant population. The notion of rights and responsibilities ascribed to citizenship status has led to a pitting of "taxpaying citizens" against noncitizens.

Arguments for immigrant provisions in reauthorization debates need to argue for the undoing of distinctions between citizens and noncitizens. As other researchers argue, welfare reauthorization needs to restore equal access to all immigrants. More reasonable limits need to be established for sponsorship, given that the existing requirements could bar immigrants from eligibility for their entire life. Employment training needs to address language barriers as well as skill and education levels. Generally the devolution to states needs to be reversed on all levels, as states should not be able to differentiate provisions for citizens and noncitizens. Despite the arguments that led to the discriminating lines to bar noncitizens from equal access to public benefits, immigrants are primarily in this country to work. The welfare reform law set an unfortunate course by mandating discrimination based upon citizenship status. This direction in immigration policy has only been further compounded since the politics of 9/11 entrenched nativist assumptions of immigrant threats and national enemies. A course of action to rectify these problematic policies needs to move beyond piecemeal restorations; rather, we need to advocate for the restoration of basic fundamental rights for noncitizens. As more naturalized immigrants obtain the power to vote, now is the time to make known the broader political picture and demonstrate the trend to further disenfranchise important members of the nation's economy and culture by further excluding them from public entitlements.

REFERENCES

Bernstein, J., Broder, T., Capps, R., Drake, S., Fremstad, S., Lessard, G., & Moran, T. (2001). *Immigrant Families: Welfare Reform Restricts Programs That Support Working Families.* Devolution Initiative Series, Technical Paper, No. 123. Battle Creek, MI: W.K. Kellogg Foundation.

Capps, R., Ku, L., Fix, M., Furgivele, C., Ramchand, R., McNiven, S., & Perez-Lopez, D. (2002). *How Are Immigrants Faring After Welfare Reform? Preliminary Evidence from Los Angeles and New York City, Final Report.* Washington, DC: Urban Institute.

Chang, C. (1997). Immigrants Under the New Welfare Law: A Call for Uniformity, A Call for Justice. *UCLA Law Review,* 45 UCLA L. Rev. 205. Los Angeles, CA: UC Regents.

Fix, M.E. & Passel, J. (2002). *The Scope and Impact of Welfare Reform's Immigrant Provisions.* New Federalism Series, Discussion Papers. Washington, DC: The Urban Institute.

Fix, M.E. & Tumlin, K. (1997). *Welfare Reform and the Devolution of Immigrant Policy.* New Federalism Series A, No. A-15. Washington, DC: The Urban Institute.

Fix, M. & Zimmermann, W. (1999). *All Under One Roof, Mixed Status Families in an Era of Reform.* Washington, DC: The Urban Institute.

Fremstad, S. (2002). Immigrants and Welfare Reauthorization. *Focus,* 22(1), Special Issue. Washington, DC: Center on Budget and Policy Priorities.

Fujiwara, L. (2005). Immigrant Rights Are Human Rights: The Reframing of Immigrant Entitlement and Welfare. *Social Problems,* 52(1):79-101.

Hancock, A. (2003). Contemporary Welfare Reform and the Public Identity of the "Welfare Queen." *Race, Gender & Class,* 10(1):31-59.

Hing, B. (1998). Don't Give Me Your Tired, Your Poor: Conflicted Immigrant Stories and Welfare Reform. *Harvard Civil Rights—Civil Liberties Law Review,* 33(1): 159-182.

Kasper, G., Gupta, S., Tian, P., Cook, J., & Meyers, A. (2000). Hunger in Legal Immigrants in California, Texas, and Illinois. *American Journal of Public Health,* 90(10): 1629-1633.

Lubiano, W. (1992). Black Ladies, Welfare Queens and State Minstrels: Ideological War by Narrative Means. In T. Morrison (Ed.), *Race-ing Justice, En-gendering Power: Essays on Anita Hill, Clarence Thomas and the Construction of Social Identity* (pp. 323-363). New York: Pantheon.

Mink, G. (1998). *Welfare's End.* Ithaca, NY: Cornell University Press.

Park, L. (2001). Perpetuation of Poverty Through "Public Charge." *Denver University Law Review.* 78 Denv. U.L. Rev. 1161.

Schuck, Peter H. (1997). The Re-Evaluation of American Citizenship. *Georgetown Immigration Law Journal.* 12 Geo. Immigr.L.J.1.

Tujague, J.L. & True, L. (1998). *The Impact of Legal Immigrant Food Stamp Cuts in Los Angeles and San Francisco.* By the California Food Security Monitoring Project. California Food Policy Advocates, Preliminary Summary. Obtained online at <http://www.cfpa.net/reports/summ.html> on July 2, 2003.

Wu, F.H. (2002). *Yellow: Race in America Beyond Black and White.* New York: Basic Books.

Zimmerman, W. & Tumlin, K. (1999). *Patchwork Policies: State Assistance for Immigrants Under Welfare Reform.* New Federalism Series, No. 24. Washington, DC: The Urban Institute.

Chapter 20

Weaving a Safety Net for Immigrants Post-PRWORA

Susan F. Grossman
Maria Vidal de Haymes
Jami Evans
Lawrence Benito
Choua Vue
Susan Wilkie

In 1996, President Bill Clinton signed into effect the Personal Responsibility and Work Opportunity Reconciliation Act (PRWORA) and significantly changed the face of welfare in the United States (U.S. Department of Health and Human Services, 1996). Prior to PRWORA, most legal immigrants had the same access to public assistance as U.S. citizens. This law significantly affected both legal and undocumented immigrants and their eligibility for public benefits.

According to the 2000 census, the foreign-born population in the United States exceeded 31 million, constituting about 11 percent of the total U.S. population (NILC, 2004). By March 2002, the total foreign-born population was estimated to be 32.5 million, and current trends suggest that the number of immigrants to the United States will continue to increase (Capps, Passel, Perez-Lopez, & Fix, 2003).

Approximately three-fourths of immigrants in 1990 lived in just six states: California, New York, Texas, Florida, Illinois, and New Jersey. This proportion was reduced to about two-thirds by 2000, as a number of other states saw rapid growth of immigrant populations. For example, nineteen states experienced more than a doubling of

doi:10.1300/5608_21

249

their immigrant populations between 1990 and 2000 (Capps et al., 2003).

The influx of immigrants into states that have not previously dealt with meeting the unique service needs of immigrants, particularly in the post-PRWORA climate, creates a need for effective service provision models from states that have traditionally served large numbers of immigrants. Toward this end, this chapter examines one such model, the Outreach and Interpretation (O & I) Project of the Illinois Coalition for Immigrant and Refugee Rights (ICIRR), to better understand the needs of immigrants and refugees and the methods employed to meet those unique needs in the state with the fifth largest immigrant population in the country. Before examining this model, we briefly discuss the impact of PRWORA on this population as well as the economic and social vulnerability of immigrants.

IMMIGRANTS AND THE IMPACT OF PRWORA

At the time of PRWORA's passage in 1996, immigrants represented 15 percent of all welfare recipients in the United States (Capps et al., 2003). In the aftermath of welfare reform, most documented immigrants were restricted from receipt of any federal means-tested benefits for their first five years of residence in the United States. A limited number of immigrants qualified for programs under the partial restoration of access to some programs (primarily food stamps and SSI), but most have been left without a social safety net, contributing to food and housing insecurity. Also under the PRWORA, states were given broader power to determine eligibility of "qualified" immigrants for state-funded programs. Previously, states could not discriminate against legal immigrants in the provision of benefits, but now states can choose to deny, limit, or extend access to locally funded aid such as general assistance. States also retain the option to deny nonemergency Medicaid, social services block grants, and the Supplemental Food Program for Women, Infants and Children (Kilty & Vidal de Haymes, 2000). At the same time, with the loss of eligibility for many federal programs, immigrants have had to turn increasingly to the state and private sector for supports such as health care, rent subsidies, and nutrition programs to replace the benefits previously provided through federal programs.

Even among those eligible for programs such as food stamps, Temporary Assistance for Needy Families (TANF), and public health insurance, many have gone without assistance due to confusion regarding eligibility or misunderstandings about the nature of the affidavit of support signed by their sponsor or fear of being deemed a "public charge," a status that may affect their access to a green card, which is needed for legal employment (Legal Aid Society, 2002). Furthermore, many immigrants are reluctant to seek health care for fear of losing their jobs or losing income for missed time at work to seek health care, fear of being deported if they are undocumented, or because of a simple lack of knowledge regarding how to access health care in the United States (Chavez, 1992).

Prior to August 22, 1996, all legal immigrants had the same access to public assistance as U.S. citizens, including Aid to Families with Dependent Children (AFDC), food stamps, and Medicaid. Since the enactment of PRWORA, foreign-born people's eligibility for public assistance has been purposely restricted through Title IV–Restricting Welfare and Public Benefits for Aliens. As Rosenbaum and Hirsh (2000) note, the policy objective behind the Title IV of PRWORA is ultimately to eliminate individuals who are not U.S. citizens from public benefit programs (cited by Fuenzalida, 2004) . Indeed, Hagen, Rodriguez, Capps, & Kabiri (2003) point out that half of the $45 billion in projected PRWORA savings for the period between 1997 and 2002 was to be from immigrant benefit cuts in a variety of means-tested benefits programs.

Although some of the restrictions on immigrants originally put into place by PRWORA were slightly relaxed in 1997 and 1998 (Rosenbaum & Hirsh, 2000, cited by Fuenzalida, 2004), PRWORA essentially divided the foreign-born population of the United States into different groups whose eligibility for benefits was based upon their legal status. Lawful permanent residents (LPR), refugees, asylees, and undocumented immigrants could have time limits or be barred entirely from eligibility.

Furthermore, the particularly punitive measures of the 1996 immigration laws, the Illegal Immigration Reform and Immigrant Responsibility Act (IIRIRA), the Anti-Terrorism and Effective Death Penalty Act (AEDPA), and the post-9/11 government policy initiatives aimed at increasing national security (e.g., immigration raids conducted under programs such as Operation Chicagoland Skies and Operation Landmark) have led to increased mandatory detention and automatic deportation of many immigrants (American Immigration Lawyers Association, 2003; Tsao, 2003). As a result, many immigrant families have been deprived of loved ones, who often are the primary sources of economic support, and are ineligible to qualify for public support programs because of the 1996 welfare changes.

IMMIGRANT ECONOMIC AND SOCIAL VULNERABILITY

In order to truly understand the impact of welfare reform on immigrant families, it is important to consider their context, which has not changed. While welfare reform has diminished the supports available to these families, their economic and social vulnerability has remained high, thus increasing the gap between needs and resources. This gap is especially problematic given the rapid growth of immigrant communities in recent years. Some of the factors contributing to this gap are described next.

Economic Insecurity

More than 11 million children live with only immigrant parents, and nearly a third of these families are recent immigrants, having come to the United States in the past ten years. These immigrant families, in particular, have a number of characteristics that increase their economic and social insecurity. For example, 65 percent of children of recent immigrants are of low income, despite the fact that 85 percent of these children live with parents who are employed. Recent immigrant, low-income families are more likely to have younger children present in their households than are households headed by low-income, native-born adults (Douglas-Hall & Koball, 2004). The youthfulness of this population, many of whom are below school age, means than many immigrants have a need for child care. The majority of slots in state-subsidized child care, however, are reserved for children whose parents are current or former TANF recipients.

Although most immigrants work, they are concentrated in low-wage jobs that typically do not offer employer-based health insurance. Almost 43 percent of immigrants work at jobs paying less than $7.50 an hour, compared to 28 percent of all workers. Only 26 percent of immigrants have job-based health insurance (Levinson, 2002). This employment pattern, paired with government restrictions on immigrant access to public health insurance, renders these children and families more likely to lack health care coverage than similar low-income, native-born populations. More specifically, nearly half (47 percent) of children living with low-income recent immigrant parents do not have any type of health insurance. In contrast, the percentage of children of uninsured, low-income, native-born parents is 22 percent (Douglas-Hall & Koball, 2004).

Nativity and Citizenship

According to 2000 Census estimates, 37.4 percent of the total foreign-born population of the United States are naturalized citizens. Although 81.6 percent of those who entered the country before 1970 had obtained citizenship by 2000, only 13 percent of those who entered between 1990 and 2000 had become citizens (Malone, Baluja, Costanzo, & Davis, 2003). The latter figure is not surprising since the process of becoming a naturalized citizen usually requires a minimum of five years of residence in the United States. Furthermore, the Urban Institute, based on data from the Census Bureau and the Department of Homeland Security, estimates that 9.3 million undocumented immigrants were living in the United States in 2002 (Passel, Capps, & Fix, 2002). Such individuals have a particularly hard time accessing assistance. Many are too afraid to seek help when it is needed because of their undocumented status.

English-Language Fluency

Language can pose a tremendous barrier for immigrants and refugees trying to access the public benefit system. Findings from the 2000 Census indicate that 47 million U.S. residents (18 percent) five years of age or older spoke a language other than English at home. The number of people in this category grew by 38 percent in the 1980s and 47 percent in the 1990s. Of these households, 4.4 million, encompassing 11.9 million individuals, were considered linguistically isolated in 2000. The U.S. Census Bureau considers a household to be linguistically isolated if it is one in which no person aged fourteen or over speaks English at least "very well" (Shin and Bruno, 2003).

THE ILLINOIS COALITION FOR IMMIGRANT AND REFUGEE RIGHTS AND THE OUTREACH AND INTERPRETATION PROJECT

In 1992, the Illinois Coalition for Immigrant and Refugee Rights was incorporated as a not-for-profit agency committed to "promote the rights of immigrants and refugees to full and equal participation in the civic, cultural, social, and political life of our diverse society" (ICIRR, 2005). The coalition grew out of the six-year efforts of community activists and service providers, who had formed and maintained a committee to discuss and advocate on matters affecting immigrants and refugees that were not being met by public and private agencies. The coalition has maintained its grassroots base but has expanded to include 120 member organizations drawn from across Illinois. These organizations include social service agencies, unions, and faith-based, community-based, and legal advocacy organizations. They represent diverse constituent communities, including varied Asian, Middle Eastern, Latin American, African, Caribbean, and European immigrant-focused organizations (ICIRR, 2005).

In 2000, in response to a number of issues identified by member agencies related to receipt of public benefits and existing barriers, the coalition developed and implemented the Outreach and Interpretation Project. The O & I Project is a partnership between the Illinois Department of Human Services (IDHS), ICIRR, and member agencies serving immigrants in Illinois. As stated on their Web site:

> The goal of the O & I project is to ensure that immigrant families in Illinois are able to thrive by reducing the barriers that low income immigrants and their children face when seeking public benefits and services (nutritional, medical, housing, psychological, childcare, employment) as well as the cash support they need for proper health, well-being and economic self-sufficiency. (O & I Project, 2005)

The O & I project works with thirty-four community-based agencies serving immigrants and refugees from the Caribbean, Asia, Middle East, Europe, Mexico, Central and South America, and Africa in an effort to overcome the identified service barriers for immigrants. Case managers must understand the policy changes and political motivations involved in the shift in welfare, but more pressing is the actual need faced by the individuals they serve and accessing services for their clients. Immigrants have specific needs for service accessibility that state welfare departments are unable to meet because of ineligibility for benefits as well as barriers to effective communication with service providers. Toward this end, member agencies provide easily accessible information and referrals to immigrants, case management services for long-term assistance, and accurate interpretation and translation services for immigrants with limited English ability. O & I agency partners also conduct community outreach activities aimed at informing immigrants about the availability of public and private assistance and the corresponding eligibility criteria for such programs, as well as immigration issues that impact accessibility of services (O & I Project, 2005).

During the nine months for which data are available in fiscal year 2004,* outreach efforts involving print, radio, and TV advertisements totaled 1,040. O & I agencies sponsored 335 public benefit programs, and they participated in 314 community events. Information and referral activities involved 20,027 contacts, and a total of 11,536 active cases were served through case management services. On behalf of these cases, a total of 7,354 applications for various public benefits were initiated. The programs for which the largest number of applications were made included food stamps (2,022), Medicaid (1,974), and Kidcare (1,640). (Kidcare is an Illinois medical program for children who are not covered by Medicaid or other public or private insurance programs and are U.S. citizens or qualified legal immigrants. Recipients may be above the poverty line but must meet the program's low-income eligibility standards.) Finally, 12,356 persons were provided interpretation services, and 13,541 translations were performed (O & I Project, 2004b).

Outreach and Interpretation Project Participants Reflect on Their Efforts to Weave a Safety Net for Immigrants Post-PRWORA

Outreach and Information project case managers from the thirty-four participating agencies meet at least quarterly with ICIRR. These meetings provide a forum to discuss relevant issues and barriers to

---

*The reporting system changed in the 2nd quarter of FY04, so that data from the first quarter are incompatible with the current system.

service, as well as an opportunity for those present to develop strategies for addressing these barriers. The remainder of this chapter looks at the feedback provided by case managers from the thirty-four member agencies at quarterly meetings of the coalition, as presented in their quarterly reports, as well as information provided by member agencies that were present at a retreat on September 21, 2004, which the authors attended. Using summaries from the quarterly reports, as well as content analysis of these reports and meeting notes, we present the key issues identified by participating agencies related to service barriers and issues they face in providing services to their clients in the post-PRWORA climate. We also discuss strategies that have worked as identified by these participants.

Service Barriers and Issues

Agencies were asked to respond to two questions each quarter in the quarterly reports submitted to the O & I Project: "In your experience, what are the three most important barriers that continue to exist between clients and access to public benefits?" and "Please list the top three non-IDHS related activities that you have encountered in your I & R activities and in your case management sessions (i.e., drivers license, food pantries, housing issues, etc.)." Answers to these two questions were summarized each quarter (except for the first quarter when they were not asked).

Consistently, the top two issues related to barriers were either language-related difficulties such as immigrants with limited English trying to access benefits at IDHS offices where interpretation services were inadequate, and IDHS service issues including long waits, insensitivity, and lost papers at offices. The third most frequently cited issues varied across quarters but tended to include problems such as lack of information about public benefits and eligibility requirements, transportation, and immigration status rendering persons ineligible for benefits. Fear, related to immigration status or status as a public charge, as well as misconceptions about eligibility and lack of information about programs, were also frequently reported barriers.

In contrast, problems or barriers that were mentioned less frequently or by fewer agencies (one or two at most in any given quarter) included pride or shame, employer noncooperation, lack of bilingual providers in the community, and client noncooperation with program requirements.

Although much of the work that the organizations do is to help advocate for and guide individuals through the application process in order to secure public benefits for which immigrants and refugees may be eligible, the second question, related to non-IDHS activities the staff of agencies are called upon to provide, addresses the issue of what staff do when they are not able to access public benefits. Responses from member organizations to this question indicate that the majority of activities in these areas involve health-related referrals such as referring individuals to health clinics, job training and employment-related activities, translation and interpretation services, and immigration counseling or assistance with immigration issues and citizenship assistance. Housing-related activities and referral to food pantries are also mentioned frequently by member agencies. In addition, domestic violence counseling is an activity some agencies are involved in, but not as frequently as some of the other services. Less common activities include assistance with social security issues and transportation-related activities.

The Outreach and Interpretation project is principally funded by the Illinois Department of Human Services (IDHS) with the primary goal of assisting immigrant families in accessing public programs, but the staff at the various member organizations also expend a considerable amount of effort in assisting these families in securing resources from private, non-IDHS programs. For example during the three quarters of 2004 for which data are available, 58 percent of information and referral activities, 38 percent of case management sessions, and 43 percent of translation services were non-IDHS in nature. This considerable amount of non-IDHS-related service provision seems to suggest that immigrant families experience substantial needs that are not met by public programs, or that these families are ineligible for some of the relevant public programs (O & I Project, 2004b).

Several cases illustrate these activities. For example, one program described its attempts to help a family relocating to Illinois from another state. Upon arrival, the husband lost the job he had come here to obtain. The wife, at the same time, did not have a place to take their children so that she could go to work. Their funds were so limited that they did not have enough money to feed themselves or to pay their rent. Caseworkers helped them to get food stamps as well as assisted them in obtaining employment and connecting them to a local program that could help with rent (O & I Project, 2004a).

Another agency detailed its efforts to address questions related to eligibility for various programs, deal with confusion over the application process, and listen to the fears of clients related to deportation or losing future opportunities to obtain residency. They described one individual who lost his job and had no income. He refused to apply for benefits, despite the fact that he might qualify because his children were citizens and because he was in the process of obtaining permanent residency and was afraid that an application for public benefits would result in a denial. The worker explained to him that he could apply for food stamps or medical assistance without affecting his residency application, and that he could not be deported if he were to apply (O & I Project, 2004a).

Strategies to Address Barriers

At the Outreach and Interpretation member agency retreat on September 21, 2004, staff from the participating agencies discussed continuing barriers and moved on to identify a number of strategies to address these. Barriers that were recognized by the staff at the retreat were very similar to those identified in the quarterly reports. Again, language, misperceptions/lack of information regarding public programs and eligibility, transportation, and problems with IDHS offices and workers were the most frequently cited barriers to service. For example, coalition members spoke about IDHS workers who were confused about eligibility requirements and were therefore frustrated with immigrant clients whose cases seemed to present additional work. They saw processing their applications and answering questions as an additional burden because of the confusion regarding eligibility issues as well the need to enlist translators. In response to this coalition member, case managers became experts regarding eligibility and would assist welfare workers in responding to client questions and completing applications. Case managers worked to develop relationships with welfare workers in the field offices and also provided in-service training specific to immigrant populations. O & I staff also established monthly meetings with IDHS case manager supervisors to address difficult cases and work toward finding solutions whenever possible. O & I staff have also translated applications and IDHS forms on their Web site. Member agency workers can then access the forms, complete them with clients, and have them ready for the IDHS workers. Other short- and long-term strategies utilized or suggested by the participants to combat the persistent barriers experienced by immigrant families, particularly those associated with IDHS included increasing in-service training for IDHS staff regarding cultural awareness; advocating for the hiring of additional bilingual staff at IDHS offices; developing a Web- or phone-based system to access information regarding the status of applications for public programs; and exploring a community-based application model that would allow workers and clients to apply for benefits in settings other than IDHS offices, similar to the model that has been used in Illinois for the KidCare program, where schools can serve as the point of application for health care benefits. Additional strategies involved updating directories to assist in private program referrals and creating an advocacy team with representatives from the various O & I agencies to develop a sustained advocacy effort to address the persistent barriers to services for immigrant families.

CONCLUSION

The impact of PRWORA on immigrant communities is undeniable. PRWORA has changed eligibility requirements for many immigrants, rendering them ineligible for many supports that had previously been available to legal immigrants. In addition, the popular rhetoric and misperceptions regarding families that utilize public support programs, in this case particularly those regarding immigrant families, combined with the post-9/11 anti-immigrant sentiments, have had a chilling effect on applications for services among those immigrants who do qualify for benefits. Beyond policy and perceptual barriers, language, transportation, and cultural and bureaucratic blunders and mazes add additional burdens to the application process.

The effects of these barriers are visible in a number of ways. Primarily, immigrant families are often left with many unmet needs, and private programs are left to shore up resources for these families. The Outreach and Interpretation Project of the Illinois Coalition for Immigrant and Refugee Rights presents a collaborative community-based model to address the convergence of these factors. While those involved in both the O & I Project and ICIRR have made strides in addressing some of these barriers and generated some promising strategies, many problems remain. It would seem that wider efforts, particularly advocacy at the federal level, may be warranted. Whether a model such as the O & I Project and its advocacy approach could be replicated on a national basis, however, remains unclear. Illinois and Chicago are perhaps unique to the extent that they have fairly well-organized immigrant groups and agencies to address the needs of immigrants and refugees; some of these agencies have been established for many years. Communities experiencing more recent growth in their immigrant and refugee populations may not have such resources to draw from. Nonetheless, if all immigrants and refugees are to truly have a safety net, a number of advocacy, education, and service provision strategies must be advanced. The O & I Project offers one valuable model.

REFERENCES

American Immigration Lawyers Association (2003). Restore fairness and due process: 1996 immigrations laws go too far. *AILA Issue Papers.* Retrieved December 26, 2004, from the American Immigration Lawyers Association Web site at <http://www.aila.org/context/default.aspx?docid=8381>.

Capps, R., Passel, J., Perez-Lopez, D., & Fix, M. (2003). *The new neighbors: A user's guide to data on immigrants in U.S. communities.* Washington, DC: The Urban Institute. Available online from the Urban Institute at <http://www.uran.org/url.cfm?ID=310844>.

Chavez, L. R. (1992). *Shadowed lives: Undocumented immigrants in American society.* New York: Harcourt Brace College Publishers.

Douglas-Hall, A. & Koball, H. (2004, December). *Children of recent immigrants: National and regional trends.* Retrieved December 26, 2004, from the National Center for Children and Poverty of the Columbia University Mailman School of Public Health Web site at <http://www.nccp.org/pub_cri04.html>.

Fuenzalida, J. E. (2004). PRWORA and its impact in immigrant access to public benefits. Paper prepared for Social Work and Welfare, Social Work 507, School of Social Work, Loyola Univesity, Chicago, IL.

Hagan, J., Rodriguez, N., Capps, R., & Kabiri, N. (2003). The effects of recent welfare and immigration reforms on immigrants' access to health care. *The International Migration Review, 37,* 444-463.

Illinois Coalition for Immigrant and Refugee Rights (2005). Mission statement. Retrieved December 20, 2004, from Illinois Coalition for Immigrant and Refugee Rights Web site at <www.icirr.org/abouticirr.htm>.

Kilty, K. M. & Vidal de Haymes, M. (2000). Racism, nativism, and exclusion: Public policy, immigration, and the Latino experience in the U. S. *Journal of Poverty, 4* (1/2), 1-25.

Legal Aid Society (2002, July 11). *Testimony of the Legal Aid Society concerning problems facing immigrant families in the child welfare system: Hearings before the New York State Assembly Committee on Children and Families and the Assembly Legislative Task Force on New Americans.* New York. Retrieved December 15, 2004, from the Legal Aid Society Web site at <http://www.legalaid. org>.

Levinson, A. (2002). *Immigrants and welfare use.* Retrieved November 19, 2004, from the Migration Policy Institute at <http://www.migrationinformation.org/ Feature/display.cfm?ID=45>.

Malone, N., Baluja, K. F., Costanzo, J. M., & Davis, C. J. (2003, December). *The foreign born population: 2000.* Census Brief, C2KBR-34. Washington, DC: U.S. Census Bureau.

National Immigration Law Center. (2004). Comprehensive health care for immigrants: A sound strategy for fiscal and public health (Issue Brief). Available online from the National Immigration Law Center at <http://www.nilc.org/ immspbs/ health/Issue_Briefs/comphealthcare_0404.pdf>.

Outreach and Interpretation Project (2004a). *4th Quarter, FY04 report* [brochure]. Chicago, IL: Illinois Coalition for Immigrant and Refugee Rights.

Outreach and Interpretation Project (2004b). *Aggregate performance chart* [brochure]. Chicago, IL: Illinois Coalition for Immigrant and Refugee Rights.

Outreach and Interpretation Project (2005). About Outreach and Interpretation. Retrieved November 30, 2005, from Illinois Coalition for Immigrant and Refugee Rights Web site at <http:// www.icirr.org/outreach.aboutus.htm>.

Passel, J., Capps, R., & Fix, M. (2004). *Undocumented immigrants: Facts and figures.* Washington, DC: The Urban Institute. Available online from the Urban Institute Web site at <http://www.urban.org/urlprint.cfm?ID=8685>.

Rosenbaum, H., & Hirsch, J. (2000). *Medicaid eligibility and citizenship status: Policy implications for immigrant populations.* Washington, DC: Kaiser Commission on Medicaid and the Uninsured.

Shin, H. & Bruno, R. (2003). *Language use and English-speaking ability: 2000* (Census 2000 Brief, C2KBR-29). Washington, DC: U.S. Census Bureau.

Tsao, F. (2003). *Losing ground: The loss of freedom, equality, and opportunity for America's immigrants since September 11.* Available from the Illinois Coalition for Immigrant and Refugee Rights Web site at <http://www.icrir.org/publications/ losingground03.pdf>.

U.S. Department of Health and Human Services (DHHS) (1996). *HHS fact sheet PRWORA.* Retrieved July 2004 from DHHS Web site at <http://www.acf.dhhs. gov/programs/ofa/prwora96.htm>.

PART V:
LOOKING TO THE FUTURE

Chapter 21

Welfare As We *Should* Know It: Social Empathy and Welfare Reform

Elizabeth A. Segal

WHY CHANGE WELFARE?

By now we are familiar with the provisions of the Personal Responsibility and Work Opportunity Reconciliation Act of 1996, the popular welfare reform effort completed by a Republican-led Congress and a Democratic president. Nine years following passage of this legislation we have witnessed shifts in our nation's approach to public assistance, particularly toward the recipients of such services. Briefly, let us review the foundation of this policy.

The legislation (P.L. 104-193) was based on ten points that served as the rationale and understanding of the Congress. Exhibit 21.1 lists the ten points in their entirety. The backbone of this legislation is *marriage,* and the ten points culminate in the conclusion that the "crisis" facing our nation was out-of-wedlock pregnancies and births. This "crisis" was the impetus for the overhaul of the sixty-year contract originally made as part of the New Deal.

What did this crisis look like? While marriage rates were falling from 9.3 per 1,000 people in 1990 to 8.9 in 1995, birth rates to unmarried mothers was increasing as was the rate of teenage motherhood (U.S. Census Bureau, 2003). The AFDC program, which primarily served single mothers, was seen as the bastion of these trends. Women were marrying less and having children out of wedlock, and legislators viewed AFDC as making this possible. These trends prompted legislators to create PRWORA and to focus almost exclusively on these behaviors. Since passage of PRWORA, the marriage rate has continued to decline, dropping 6 percent more by 2001, while births

doi:10.1300/5608_22

EXHIBIT 21.1.
Personal Responsibility and Work Opportunity
Reconciliation Act of 1996 (P.L. 104-193)

The Congress makes the following findings:

1. Marriage is the foundation of a successful society.
2. Marriage is an essential institution of a successful society which promotes the interests of children.
3. Promotion of responsible fatherhood and motherhood is integral to successful child rearing and the well-being of children.
4. In 1992, only 54 percent of single-parent families with children had a child support order established and, of that 54 percent, only about one-half received the full amount due. Of the cases enforced through the public child support enforcement system, only 18 percent of the caseload has a collection.
5. The number of individuals receiving aid to families with dependent children (AFDC) has more than tripled since 1965. More than two-thirds of these recipients are children. Eighty-nine percent of children receiving AFDC benefits now live in homes in which no father is present.
6. The increase of out-of-wedlock pregnancies and births is well documented.
7. An effective strategy to combat teenage pregnancy must address the issue of male responsibility, including statutory rape culpability and prevention. The increase of teenage pregnancies among the youngest girls is particularly severe and is linked to predatory sexual practices by men who are significantly older.
8. The negative consequences of an out-of-wedlock birth on the mother, the child, the family, and society are well documented.
9. Currently 35 percent of children in single-parent homes were born out-of-wedlock, nearly the same percentage as that of children in single-parent homes whose parents are divorced (37 percent). While many parents find themselves, through divorce or tragic circumstances beyond their control, facing the difficult task of raising children alone, nevertheless, the negative consequences of raising children in single-parent homes are well-documented.
10. Therefore, in light of this demonstration of the crisis in our Nation, it is the sense of the Congress that prevention of out-of-wedlock pregnancy and reduction in out-of-wedlock birth are very important Government interests and the policy contained in part A of title IV of the Social Security Act (as amended by this Act) is intended to address the crisis.

Source: Section 101, P.L. 104-193.

to unmarried mothers inched up 4 percent. Thus, while the goal of the legislation was to reverse those social trends, that has not been the case.

THE IMPACT OF WELFARE REFORM

Instead, PRWORA has been successful in decreasing the number of public assistance recipients. Caseloads dropped significantly following PRWORA. From 1996 through 2003, 60 percent fewer individuals were receiving benefits, a tremendous decline (Administration for Children and Families, 2004a). Thus, although the marriage and out-of-wedlock birthrates have not changed, the number of people receiving public assistance benefits has been greatly reduced. Unfortunately, research on those who have left TANF is not promising. The majority of women who have left TANF are working full-time in jobs that pay between $7 and $8 an hour (Bazelon, 2002). The agency responsible for TANF, the Administration for Children and Families (2004b) reports that of closed cases in 2002, 34 percent of families had non-TANF monthly incomes averaging $866. This comes to about $10,400 annually, well under the federal poverty rate for a small family. There is no mention of the other 66 percent of closed cases. It would seem that the impact of TANF, while serving to decrease the number of people on public assistance, neither leads to economic well-being nor changes the social trends of decreasing marriage and increasing out-of-wedlock births. How did something heralded as "ending welfare as we know it," with its implication of fixing a broken system, miss the mark?

WHAT ABOUT POVERTY?

It is instructive to note what is *not* in this legislation and what was *not* the impetus for change—that is, poverty. Although AFDC was typically included as a major part of the arsenal of the War on Poverty, the crisis that prompted the shift to create TANF was not poverty (Segal & Kilty, 2003). Thus, all the needs associated with poverty, such as low wages, lack of health care, disappearing jobs, inadequate education, lack of affordable housing, hunger, homelessness, lack of child care, sexism, and racism—the corollaries of poverty—were not on the table when welfare reform was discussed. Because poverty was not the national crisis, addressing poverty was not important to leading lawmakers. Instead, what was on the table were the issues of marriage and out-of-wedlock births. The debate over welfare reform in 1996 in essence was a mismatched debate. Supporters of national public assistance for poor women and children were debating poverty, while adversaries of the system were debating personal behavior in the private realms of marriage and pregnancy. It was a mismatched argument that revealed how far away from the War on Poverty we as a nation had moved.

Why was poverty, and why does poverty continue to be, far from the minds of policymakers and not part of the discussions of welfare reform? Why do welfare debates focus on marriage and out-of-wedlock births? There may be several reasons for this shift in perspectives. One might argue that poverty is entrenched and that the failure of the programs of the War on Poverty to fix this social problem led policymakers to look elsewhere for answers. Surely, the correlation between single-parenthood and poverty was clear, and the correlation between teenage pregnancies and poverty has been equally pronounced. The legislation itself points to these facts and builds the case for promoting marriage as the solution to these correlates of poverty, without actually addressing poverty. The thinking was that if women married, and postponed childbearing from their teen years to later years when they would be more likely to marry, then the problem of poverty and welfare dependency would be solved. And we do know, both logically and from statistics, that two-adult families have more earnings than one-adult families. So the solution to welfare dependency became abundantly clear—promote marriage. So why do progressives and welfare advocates and feminists and liberals and leftists all argue that true welfare reform is not marriage? Is not marriage a lasting solution to the poverty of women and children? Typically, yes and no. To the extent that marriage lasts—and the divorce rate of more than 50 percent suggests that it is equally unlikely to last as it is likely to last—there is a financial benefit to families with children. But to rely on the institution of marriage, a highly personal and private decision, to solve the societal problem of poverty, is as likely to fail as all the previous attempts. In addition, promoting marriage ignores other issues such as domestic violence and the social class likelihood that poor women marry poor men. So why is there so much attachment today to this approach? I would argue that, while the frustrations of previous approaches surely contributed to a fatigue with the social programs of the 1960s and 1970s and emphasis on maintaining institutions of the status quo have shifted the argument to the preservation of marriage, those are not the overriding reasons.

SOCIAL EMPATHY

The reason welfare reform has taken the direction it has is because our political leaders and social welfare pundits to a large extent lack social empathy (Segal, 2006). Social empathy is the ability of people to understand the situations and experiences of others and use that knowledge to craft social programs that respond to people's needs. It is the understanding of another's situations and experiences even though one may never have actually lived through such experiences himself or herself. We use insight gained by observing and studying the life conditions of others to develop public policies that realistically respond to people's needs.

Unlike so many current public policy efforts that attempt to direct what policymakers think *should be,* public policies guided by social empathy emphasize what *fits best* given the realities of people's situations. It is neither judgmental nor prescriptive. Public policy based on social empathy is a radical shift from the way we have changed public assistance in this country over the past couple of decades. The 1996 legislation is a clear example of policy built with a lack of social empathy.

TANF Recipients

What did we know about recipients of AFDC in 1995? What were their life conditions that needed to be attended to through public policy? And how have those conditions changed? Table 21.1 lists the major characteristics of AFDC recipients prior to the adoption of PRWORA and compares them to TANF recipients in 2002. Not much has changed, as most adults are single females in their late twenties and early thirties with one or two children between the ages of seven and eight. Although the number with high school diplomas has

TABLE 21.1. Comparison of AFDC and TANF Recipients

Characteristics	Recipients of AFDC	Recipients of TANF
	FY 1995	*FY 2002*
The average family	One adult and two children	Same
	90% had three or less children	
Average age of adult	30.5 years	31 years
Adults with less than a high school diploma	54.6%	42.8%
Length of receipt of benefits	66% for 3 years or less	Average length of receipt was 29 months
Children 5 years old or younger	47%	40%
Average age of children	7.1 years of age	7.7 years of age
Received any direct child support	5%	10.3%
U.S. citizens or legal residents of the United States	99.3%	99.5%
Female adult recipients under 20 years of age	4%	7.5%
Average monthly payment for a family of 3	$381	$355
Race/ethnicity		
white	37.4%	31.6%
black	35.4%	38.3%
Hispanic	19.9%	24.9%

Source: Administration for Children and Families (1995, 2004b).

increased, the vast majority lack any postsecondary education. More may be working, but for very low wages (Acs & Loprest, 2004). And the majority are families of color, with a proportional increase over the years.

Congressional Leaders

So what do the policymakers look like? The current salary for rank-and-file members of Congress is $158,100 per year. Members in leadership positions earn from $175,600 to $203,000. The president's salary is now $400,000 per year. All members participate in retirement and health insurance programs as part of the Federal Employees Retirement System. Most members of Congress are highly educated, male, and white. The average age is fifty-five years old. Table 21.2 outlines the characteristics of members of Congress and adult TANF recipients. Clearly the differences and social distance are great. Members of Congress differ in all demographic, social, and economic categories: gender, race, age, education, income, and employment.

Of course, most Americans are somewhat aware of these differences. We expect our leaders to be educated and accomplished, and that tends to skew their characteristics to being male and white, and in positions of wealth based on historical tendencies. In fact, members of Congress tend to differ from *most* Americans. Only about 15 percent of households earn more than $100,000 (DeNaves-Walt, Proctor, & Mills, 2004) compared to all members of Congress, and less than 1 percent earn more than a million dollars while almost 30 percent of members of Congress do so (Common Dreams News Center, 2004). Only about one-fourth of adults have a bachelor's degree or higher (U.S. Census Bureau, 2003) while almost 93 percent of the members of Congress do (Amer, 2004). The majority of TANF recipients are members of nondominant groups, experiencing life as a person of color in America. Most members of Congress experience life as a member of the dominant culture and class.

TABLE 21.2. Comparison of TANF Adult Recipients and Members of Congress

Characteristics	TANF adults	Members of Congress
Average age	31 years	55 years
Female	90%	14.4%
White	31.6%	87.1%
Black	38.3%	6.9%
Hispanic	24.9%	4.5%
More than a high school education	3.3%	92.7%
Employment rate	25.3%	100%
Millionaires	0	29.2%

Source: Administration for Children and Families (2004b); Amer (2004); Common Dreams News Center (2004).

Social Empathy and Policymakers

It is clear that those making policy decisions do not look like the people for whom those policies are designed. Although a handful may have backgrounds that have some similarities (Senator John Edwards was proud of his working-class background), almost all members of Congress do not share the social, gender, racial, and economic experiences of TANF recipients. In and of itself, that fact does not preclude the making of social welfare policy that is sensitive to the needs and circumstances of recipients. However, the 1996 legislation demonstrates how far removed the legislation was from the reality of people's lives. The vast majority of AFDC recipients lacked education. The 1996 legislation ignored that need. Almost all were single mothers raising children. Although the majority of members of Congress live in two-adult households, most of them are finished with raising children, as evidenced by their age. And as more than 85 percent are men, few, if any, have experienced the same parental role as single women heading households. Because the majority are men who are married with financial stability, it is not surprising that marriage and decreasing out-of-wedlock births would be the focus of the 1996 legislation. Why not? These problems were never the experience of members of Congress.

WHAT CAN WE DO?

To the reader of this book, it is likely that these points are obvious, although the stark comparison in Table 21.2 may surprise many of us. The larger question is, What do we do about this mismatch of experience? It is interesting to note that in 1935 Social Security legislation was shepherded by a poor immigrant in the Senate and a member of the House who had started working in the coal mines at the age of nine and was illiterate until the age of sixteen (Leuchtenburg, 1963). Historians cite their personal experiences with poverty as reasons for their passion in creating the Social Security program. What members of Congress today share the experience of TANF mothers and feel the passion to create social welfare policies that relate to their real needs? Where is the much-needed child care? Where is the discussion about helping women go back to school? What are we doing to create employment opportunities with living wages for women on welfare?

What health insurance is there for the working poor woman? How do we address the impact of racism and sexism? These are all questions that are raised when we analyze public welfare from a social empathy perspective.

So how do we get privileged, well-to-do lawmakers to understand what it means to be a young, undereducated woman trying to raise children without access to resources? That is the most difficult question. Empathy is a critical part of understanding the experience of others, and those with empathy are more apt to become socially involved (Frank, 2001). Empathy fosters people's involvement in social change (Loeb, 1999). Empathy is a critical part of emotional intelligence, the ability to feel, sense, and intuit knowledge and understanding (Goleman, 1994). We need to find ways to help policymakers feel and sense what life is like for recipients of welfare. We can do that through personal testimonies of real people. We need to invite elected officials for firsthand visits and personal time spent with people on welfare. We need to challenge policymakers to try to live their lives more like the people for whom they develop policy. And we need to tell the stories of real people to those who will listen, and ask people ways they might relate. When we see ourselves in other people's experiences, we tap our empathetic natures. Social empathy requires us to think about what other people's lives are like, and then create public policies based on that understanding. It is not moralistic. If policymakers begin to examine and feel what the day-to-day life is for welfare mothers, and take that understanding and apply it to policy, then we really will end welfare as we know it, and for the better.

REFERENCES

Acs, G. & Loprest, P. (2004). *Leaving welfare: Employment and well-being of families that left welfare in the post-entitlement era.* Kalamazoo, MI: W.E. Upjohn Institute for Employment Research.

Administration for Children and Families (1995). *Characteristics and financial circumstances of AFDC recipients FY 1993.* Washington, DC: U.S. Department of Health and Human Services.

Administration for Children and Families (2004a). *TANF fact sheet.* Washington, DC: U.S. Department of Health and Human Services.

Administration for Children and Families (2004b). *TANF sixth annual report to Congress.* Washington, DC: U.S. Department of Health and Human Services.

Amer, M. L. (2004). *Membership of the 108th Congress: A profile.* Washington, DC: Congressional Research Service.

Bazelon, E. (2002, June 17-23). A limit that loses sight of the goal: What will happen when welfare recipients reach the five-year cutoff? *Washington Post National Weekly Edition,* 19 (34), 23.

Common Dreams News Center (2004). *Millionaires fill US Congress halls.* Available at <http://www.commondreams.org/headlines04/0630-05.htm>. Retrieved 11/30/2005>.

DeNaves-Walt, C., Proctor, B. D., & Mills, R. J. (2004). Income, poverty, and health insurance coverage in the United States: 2003. *Current Population Reports,* pp. 60-226. Washington, DC: U.S. Census Bureau.

Frank, R. H. (2001). Cooperation through emotional commitment. In R. M. Nesse (Ed.), *Evolution and the capacity for commitment* (pp. 57-76). New York: Russell Sage Foundation.

Goleman, D. (1994). *Emotional intelligence.* New York: Bantam Books.

Leuchtenburg, W. E. (1963). *Franklin D. Roosevelt and the New Deal.* New York: Harper and Row.

Loeb, P. R. (1999). *Soul of a citizen: Living with conviction in a cynical time.* New York: St. Martin's Press.

Segal, E. A. (2006). *Social welfare policies and programs: A values perspective.* Belmont, CA: Thomson Brooks Cole.

Segal, E. A. & Kilty, K. M. (2003). Political promises for welfare reform. *Journal of Poverty: Innovations on Social, Political & Economic Inequalities,* 7 (1/2), 51-68.

U.S. Census Bureau (2003). *Statistical abstract of the United States: 2003,* 123rd edition. Washington, DC: US Government Printing Office.

Chapter 22

Establishing Respect
for Economic Human Rights

Kenneth J. Neubeck

Do not all people, everywhere, have a human right to food? To shelter? To medical assistance? To work that pays a living wage? To an adequate income and economic security, in the event that they cannot obtain these necessities through work? Welfare reform has been implemented in the United States as if such economic human rights do not exist. I take the position that such rights do indeed exist and urge others who share this position to become involved with and lend assistance to economic justice groups and other organizations that are pressing for recognition of and respect for economic human rights in the United States.

INTERNATIONAL RECOGNITION
OF ECONOMIC HUMAN RIGHTS

In 1948 the United States joined forty-seven other members of the United Nations General Assembly in voting to endorse the Universal Declaration of Human Rights. This historic and globally influential document was framed in the wake of the unthinkable horrors and overwhelming hardships suffered by so many people during World War II. The Universal Declaration identified a set of fundamental rights that all human beings are said to possess, simply by virtue of being members of the human family. Humans, it was held, could not possibly live with dignity and freedom if governments failed to respect these rights.

Besides addressing fundamental civil and political rights, the Universal Declaration spoke economic human rights as well to, which it treated as equally important in terms of human well-being. Respecting economic human rights meant that governments would have to make efforts to extend assistance to those who were unable to meet their basic subsistence needs, including impoverished lone mothers and their children. Article 25 of the Universal Declaration stated, for example, that

> Everyone has the right to a standard of living adequate for the health and well-being of himself and of his family, including food, clothing, housing, and medical care, and necessary social services, and the right to security in the event of unemployment, sickness, disability, widowhood, old age, or other lack of livelihood in circumstances beyond his control.

Article 25 went on to state that "motherhood and childhood are entitled to special care and assistance. All children, whether born in or out of wedlock, shall enjoy the same social protection" (Center for the Study of Human Rights, 1994, p. 8).

The Universal Declaration was intended to express a set of human rights ideals. It is an eloquent statement that calls upon nation-states to recognize and respect the rights that it identifies. Nation-states voting in the U.N. General Assembly to approve the Universal Declaration were not legally bound by the articles it contained. It was a declaration, not an international treaty. But the Universal Declaration did, and still does, carry a great deal of moral force. Since 1948, many of the human rights it identifies have been incorporated into constitutions, influenced judicial decisions, and informed the creation of international treaties and domestic laws. Oppressed populations around the world have drawn inspiration from the Universal Declaration in carrying out their struggles against governmental mistreatment and injustice.

ECONOMIC HUMAN RIGHTS ADVOCACY
IN THE ROOSEVELT ADMINISTRATION

By voting for its adoption in 1948, the United States signaled that it endorsed the human rights contained in the Universal Declaration, including the economic human rights addressed in Article 25. Few today realize, however, that the United States also played a key role in the Universal Declaration's formulation. Indeed, the finished document directly reflected concerns with helping the poor and respecting economic human rights that emerged during the presidency of Franklin D. Roosevelt (1933-1945) (Sunstein, 2004).

As is well-known to most readers of this volume, Roosevelt's Depression-era New Deal package of federal legislation included the Social Security Act of 1935. The act, which authorized important measures aimed at relieving widespread economic deprivation, established the Aid to Dependent Children program, later renamed Aid to Families with Dependent Children (AFDC). This joint federal/state-funded program provided for the payment of cash welfare benefits to lone-mother-headed families that were able to meet a means test. This legal entitlement meant that AFDC benefits could usually be accessed whenever and for as long as impoverished lone-mother-headed families needed them.

In truth, however, for decades many poor families who clearly were eligible for AFDC assistance failed to receive it. Often this was an outcome of state- or local-level practices that subtly discriminated along the lines of skin color and ethnicity (Neubeck & Cazenave, 2001; Reese, 2005). Moreover, "entitlement" to AFDC assistance was neither conceived of as being nor administered by government as a "human right," any more than welfare is treated as a human right today (Mittal & Rosset, 1999). But with the creation of AFDC the Roosevelt administration did commit the federal government, for the first time, to help meet the basic subsistence needs of impoverished lone mothers and children.

In 1941, not long after the New Deal was initiated, Roosevelt delivered a presidential State of the Union address in which he identified "four freedoms" as important goals that all nations should collectively pursue. These included freedom of speech, freedom of religion, and freedom from fear. But Roosevelt also considered "freedom from want" to be an essential goal, the pursuit of which would involve "economic understandings which will secure to every nation a healthy peacetime life for its inhabitants" (Roosevelt, 1941). Roosevelt was moving toward viewing economic security as a human right. He did so in a 1944 State of the Union address in which he advocated the adoption of an "Economic Bill of Rights." This would be a second bill of rights, one that addressed economic rights, which would supplement the civil and political rights already protected by amendments to the U.S. Constitution (Sunstein, 2004).

Roosevelt held that civil and political rights could not in and of themselves protect people in the United States from impoverishment, and that respect for economic rights was necessary as well. (Note, however, at that time important segments of the U.S. population living in poverty, such as African Americans, lacked even civil and political rights protections). As Roosevelt put it, "Necessitous men are not free men." Under his economic bill of rights, all people were to have the right to employment; the right to wages that provided for adequate food, clothing, and recreation; the right to a decent home, education, and health care; and the right to protection from economic fears over which they had no control. In Roosevelt's words, "We cannot be content . . . if some fraction of our people—whether it be one-third or one-fifth or one-tenth—is ill-fed, ill-clothed, ill-housed, and insecure." The adoption of this second bill of rights, he argued, would produce "a new basis of security and prosperity for all—regardless of station, race, or creed" (Roosevelt, 1944).

THE UNITED STATES' ULTIMATE FAILURE TO RESPECT ECONOMIC HUMAN RIGHTS

President Roosevelt died in 1945, but his call for the United States to adopt an economic bill of rights helped to shape some of the human rights provisions contained in the U.N.'s Universal Declaration of Human Rights, to which his widow—Eleanor Roosevelt—contributed a great deal of leadership. While the Universal Declaration was well received domestically and abroad as a statement of human rights ideals, Roosevelt's call for creating an economic bill of rights within the United States gathered no real political traction. Presidential interest in economic human rights did not surface again for over thirty years, not until the administration of President Jimmy Carter (1977-1981). In his first year in office, Carter endorsed a United Nations treaty that would have obligated the United States to take action to implement the economic human rights addressed in Article 25 and elsewhere in the Universal Declaration.

This U.N. treaty, the International Covenant on Economic, Social, and Cultural Rights, was specifically created to put some of the ideals contained in the Universal Declaration into practice. The International Covenant encouraged nation-states to recognize and respect economic human rights, including every family's right to an adequate standard of living. It required those nation-states that ratified it to take immediate and appropriate steps, in keeping with their national resources, to progressively ensure that such economic human rights were realized. President Carter endorsed the treaty in 1977. The U.S. Constitution, however, requires that international treaties also be ratified by the U.S. Senate. For almost three decades now, the Senate has shown no inclination to ratify the International Covenant. The United States thus does not consider itself in any way bound by the treaty's provisions, which would bring its treatment of impoverished families under the mantle of international law and subject to U.N. scrutiny.

When it comes to ratifying international treaties, the United States is clearly an outlier. It has signed only a handful of some twenty international human rights treaties. Recently, the U.S. government has been criticized by other nations for its refusal to endorse the Kyoto Accord aimed at combating global warming, its refusal to be accountable for its actions to the newly established International Criminal Court, and for efforts to define torture of captured enemy combatants as legally permissible. The U.S. government has often objected to international treaties by declaring that its "sovereignty" would be undermined by entering into legal agreements calling for accountability to international norms. While it has refused to ratify the International Covenant on Economic, Social, and Cultural Rights, 151 other nation-states have done so, including many that are far less well equipped than the United States to make progressive inroads into the mitigation of their domestic poverty.

In the 1990s, under the rubric of "welfare reform," the United States effectively underscored its indifference to economic human rights, such as the right of families to an adequate standard of living (Mittal & Rosset, 1999). The hallmark of welfare reform has been the denial of governmental assistance that many impoverished mothers and children need in order to subsist. Under the Personal Responsibility and Work Opportunity Reconciliation Act (PRWORA) of 1996, the individual states have been allowed to systematically discourage ("divert") impoverished families from even applying for AFDC's replacement, Temporary Assistance for Needy Families (TANF). Lone mothers that manage to gain access to the TANF rolls are subject to a variety of rules, including mandatory work requirements, and rule violations are often punished ("sanctioned") by the loss of all or part of a family's cash benefits. Families on the TANF rolls are subject to maximum time limits for cash assistance. Those exhausting the time limits are frequently left mired in poverty, and some struggle without income from either employment or other governmental programs. In some states, the TANF rolls have dramatically declined even during periods of high unemployment and increasing rates of "severe poverty" (defined as household income below 50 percent of the federal poverty line) (Neubeck, 2006).

The U.S. government certainly recognizes the glaring contradiction between the concept of economic human rights and welfare reform under PRWORA. This recognition was rendered starkly apparent during the administration of President Bill Clinton (1993-2001). A Clinton administration representative to the 1996 United Nations World Food Summit took the position that the United States could not possibly join the many nation-states represented there in formally endorsing a declaration on people's right to food. The representative not only refused to endorse a document that treated food as a human right but also claimed that doing so could place the Clinton administration in violation of international law. Clinton had just signed off on PRWORA, which mandated cutbacks in AFDC, food stamps, and the Supplemental Security Income programs, along with the abolition of government benefits for most poor legal immigrants (Mittal, 1997, p. 1).

LEAVING POVERTY MITIGATION TO THE "FREE MARKET"

Not surprisingly, this same resistance to recognizing the existence and legitimacy of economic human rights has been a hallmark of the administration of President George W. Bush (2001-2009). In the view of human rights advocate and scholar David Weissbrodt, in its rejection of a rights-based approach, the Bush administration "endorses freedoms rather than rights, and opportunities rather than entitlements" (Weissbrodt, 2006). Thus, in keeping with the position expressed six years earlier by the Clinton administration representative, a Bush administration emissary to the 2002 U. N. World Food

Conference made the following statement in response to discussions of the need for nation-states to end domestic hunger and malnutrition:

> [T]he U.S. believes that the attainment of the right to an adequate standard of living is a goal or aspiration to be realized progressively that does not give rise to any international obligation or any domestic legal entitlement. . . . Additionally, the U.S. understands the right of access to food to mean the *opportunity* to secure food and not guaranteed entitlement. (cited in Weissbrodt, 2006)

Weissbrodt has recently taken on the task of attempting to understand the reasoning behind such a position (Weissbrodt, 2006). Included in his analysis are two assumptions that have been made by the Bush administration. These assumptions, whose validity is highly in doubt, have been used to reject the claim that people in the United States have economic human rights that the U.S. government is obligated to recognize and respect. The first assumption holds that government need only be concerned with civil and political rights. Protection of these rights, it is said, provides individuals with the freedom they need to successfully pursue their personal economic goals, which could include escaping poverty. Human rights experts, in contrast, believe that civil, political, and economic rights are interdependent and cannot be unlinked in this way. For example, Nobel Prize-winning economist Amartya Sen has pointed out that "economic unfreedom, in the form of extreme poverty, can make a person a helpless prey in the violation of other kinds of freedom. . . . Economic unfreedom can breed social unfreedom, just as social or political unfreedom can also foster economic unfreedom" (Sen, 2000, p. 8).

The second questionable assumption made by the Bush administration holds that by reducing government intervention in the nation's market economy, and by removing barriers to and encouraging greater international free trade, the economic marketplace will create the new jobs and incomes necessary to reduce poverty. Reliance on market forces, not government antipoverty programs, is said to be the most effective way to lift the poor out of their plight. In effect, the Bush administration has rejected respect for economic human rights in favor of giving individuals the "freedom" to compete for economic security, while simultaneously reducing the governmental protections available to those who meet with little or no success.

In recent decades, however, the "power of the market" has led to a shortage of living-wage jobs. Combined with a series of tax cuts that have primarily benefited the wealthy, this job shortage has produced a widening gap between the affluent and the poor, while decreasing economic security for growing numbers of middle- and working-class people (Sklar, Mykyta, & Wefald, 2001). Welfare reform has left impoverished lone-mother-headed families, among the most vulnerable and needy components of the U.S. poverty population, to struggle on their own against the vagaries of the market. Mothers are being torn between the need to ensure that their children receive quality care and being forced to compete with the growing numbers of other people who have no choice but to take low-wage, often dead-end, jobs. In its rejection of economic human rights and its energetic support of welfare reform, the Bush administration is continuing an already well-established trend wherein the U.S. government accepts increasingly less responsibility for the welfare of this nation's needy (Katz, 2001).

The Social Security Act of 1935 made cash welfare benefits a matter of entitlement for impoverished lone-mother-headed families, and at least two presidents have called for the United States to recognize and respect economic human rights, including the right to an adequate standard of living. However, any legal entitlement to cash assistance that impoverished lone-mother-headed families had was effectively scrapped by 1990s welfare reform. PRWORA institutionalized the idea that escaping poverty is poor families' own "personal responsibility," and impoverished lone mothers now are told to end their so-called welfare "dependency" and become "self-sufficient." In the view of the Bush administration, this transformation is best accomplished through lone mothers' increased labor market participation or their acquisition of husbands.

Such thinking ignores the fact that the U.S. labor market has never been kind to poor people, and that it has long put up special barriers to success for poor women and people of color. That is why so many lone-mother-headed families are impoverished and are likely to remain so. Moreover, a significant number of the lone mothers who are forced to look to welfare have been involved in deeply injurious partner relationships. Notwithstanding government prodding, they may have good reason to avoid rushing into new relationships and to expect that these will result in marriage. Advocates of marriage as an antipoverty measure also seem to overlook the growing numbers of two-partner-headed families that have below-poverty-level incomes from employment. Married or not, it is increasingly the case that two adult low-wage earners cannot support a family above the poverty line.

A NEW MOVEMENT TO RESPECT ECONOMIC HUMAN RIGHTS IN THE UNITED STATES

A rationale of "political realism" has led many national antipoverty groups to accept welfare reform. It is no longer seen as "realistic" to contest its fundamental premises. Instead, most groups have been trying to persuade Congress to tinker with some of the existing provisions of PRWORA, with the hopes of making existing welfare reform policy a little more flexible and its impact less draconian. Thus, for example, a great deal of energy has been expended to persuade Congress not to increase the mandatory TANF work requirements for lone mothers to above thirty hours per week. There has also been lobbying activity directed against states' use of TANF funds for "marriage promotion" programs, rather than for direct benefits and services for lone-mother-headed families. But bowing to political realism allows the playing field and the rules of the game to be determined by those who show little demonstrable concern for the suffering endured by impoverished lone-mother-headed families. Do not such families have economic human rights? Do not mothers and children have a right to live their lives with the same dignity and freedom as those who are making the political decisions that dictate their "welfare"?

Of late, a growing number of activists and scholars are answering these questions with a resounding "Yes." More and more interest is being expressed in establishing respect for economic human rights in the United States, rights called for by the Universal Declaration and championed by presidents Roosevelt and Carter. Across the country, the fight against poverty and welfare reform is increasingly being undertaken from a human rights perspective. For example, the notion that welfare reform is in and of itself a human rights violation is being pressed by grassroots groups, with leadership being provided by such organizations as the Kensington Welfare Rights Union (www.kwru. org) and the Human Rights Project of the Urban Justice Center (www.urbanjustice.org). Efforts have been launched to document the adverse impacts of welfare reform and to bring them to world attention, while calling for the United States to cease its shameful economic human rights violations.

Human rights advocates are increasingly insisting that the U.S. government, which freely chides other nations for human rights violations, put its own house in order. They are now framing a wide range of domestic problems in human rights terms, including the treatment of the poor (U.S. Human Rights Network, 2003; LaMarche, 2004; Urban Justice Center, 2002). In 2004, more than fifty civil liberties and social justice groups started working together to promote collective action in the United States and to make human rights training, educational resources, and organizing tools more widely available (www.ushrnetwork.org.). Even so-called establishment institutions have taken note of this important trend. The Ford Foundation, for example, has been supportive of the U.S. human rights movement and its participants' concern that the United States be held accountable to international human rights standards, including respect for economic human rights (Ford Foundation, 2004).

Twenty years ago, in a survey of the state of human rights as practiced by the United States, Robert Justin Goldstein commented that the U.S. government had "an economic-social human rights record that in terms of distributive equity is perhaps the very worst in the Western industrialized world" (Goldstein, 1987, p. 430). Welfare reform clearly contributes to this shameful record of economic injustice, and has added both impetus and urgency to the rising crescendo of demands that the U.S. government finally begin to own up to its domestic human rights responsibilities. For starters, the U.S. Senate could join 151 other nations in ratification of the International Covenant on Economic, Social, and Cultural Rights.

REFERENCES

Center for the Study of Human Rights (Ed.). (1994). *Twenty-Five Human Rights Documents* (2nd ed.). New York: Columbia University Press.

Ford Foundation. (2004). *Close to Home: Case Studies of Human Rights Work in the United States.* Retrieved December 28, 2004, from <http://www.fordfound. org/publications/recent_articles/close_to_home.cfm>.

Goldstein, R.J. (1987). The United States. In Donnelly, J., & Howard, R.E. (Eds.), *International Handbook of Human Rights* (pp. 429-456). New York: Greenwood Press.

Katz, M.B. (2001). *The Price of Citizenship: Redefining the American Welfare State.* New York: Metropolitan Books.

LeMarche, G. (2004). From the Front Lines: A Review of Recent Reports on Human Rights. *American Prospect* (October 1). Retrieved December 28, 2004, from <http://www.prospect.org>.

Mittal, A. (1997). The Politics of Hunger. *Earth Island Journal,* 12 (Spring). Retrieved December 28, 2004, from <http://www.earthisland.org/eijournal/>.

Mittal, A., & Rosset, P. (Eds.). (1999). *America Needs Human Rights.* Oakland, CA: Food First Books.

Neubeck, K.J. (2005). *When Welfare Disappears: The Case for Economic Human Rights.* New York: Routledge.

Neubeck, K.J., & Cazenave, N.A. (2001). *Welfare Racism: Playing the Race Card Against America's Poor.* New York: Routledge.

Reese, E. (2005). *Backlash Against Welfare Mothers: Past and Present.* Berkeley: University of California Press.

Roosevelt, F.D. (1941). Four Freedoms Speech. *Congressional Record,* 87, 44-47.

Roosevelt, F.D. (1944). State of the Union Message. *Congressional Record,* 90, 55-57.

Sen, A. (2000). *Development As Freedom.* New York: Anchor Books.

Sklar, H., Mykyta, L., & Wefald, S. (2001). *Raise the Floor: Wages and Policies That Work for All of Us.* Boston: South End Press.

Sunstein, C.R. (2004). *The Second Bill of Rights: FDR's Unfinished Revolution and Why We Need It More Than Ever.* New York: Basic Books.

Urban Justice Center, Human Rights Project. (2002). *Human Rights Violations in Welfare Legislation: Pushing Recipients Deeper into Poverty.* Retrieved December 28, 2004, from <http://www.urbanjustice.org/projects/index.html>.

U.S. Human Rights Network. (2003). *Something Inside So Strong: A Resource Guide on Human Rights in the United States.* Retrieved on December 28, 2004, from <http://www.ushrnetwork.org/page2.cfm>.

Weissbrodt, D. (2006). International Law of Economic, Social, and Cultural Rights: A U.S. Perspective. In Howard-Hassmann, R., & Welch, C. (Eds.), *Economic Rights in Canada and the United States.* Philadelphia: University of Pennsylvania Press.

Chapter 23

Welfare Reform and the Power of Protest: Quantitative Tests of Piven and Cloward's "Turmoil-Relief" Hypothesis

Eric Swank

A placid poor gets nothing, but a turbulent poor sometimes gets something.

Frances Fox Piven and Richard Cloward,
Regulating the Lives of the Poor

In 1982 I was a teenager in a southern California high school. In being a liberal kid who worried about the future, the political environment did not look so good. Ronald Reagan occupied the White House, and corporations kept getting massive tax breaks and greater deregulation. The rest of us were treated to less funding for education, cuts to public housing, attacks on unions, etc. While these policies were furthering economic disparities and enormous public debt, most of my white, middle-class classmates seemed oblivious to these ominous patterns. Discussions about growing inequalities were almost nonexistent as were references to progressive solutions to this problem. When the topics of poverty, racism, or sexism were broached, one routinely heard some cliché on the virtues of capitalism, reverse discrimination, or that "we can't do anything about it." Moreover, with media outlets and many adults gushing over Reagan, the Moral Majority, and Lee Iacocca, the few progressives in school felt alienated, stifled, and marginalized.

In trying to find some inspiration, or at least some solace, I craved information on the "good old days" of the 1960s. I scanned my school's library for books on hippies, women's lib, or black power. One day

doi:10.1300/5608_24

I mustered up enough gumption to visit the University of California San Diego library. When I entered the building, I was initially intimidated by the vastness of the eight-story edifice. Somehow I overcame this trepidation and began wandering the stacks in awe. During my forays I was often excited; these manuscripts offered me virtual access to progressive activists and gave me visions of how a more equitable America could be achieved.

On one of these trips I discovered *Regulating the Poor* by Frances Fox Piven and Richard Cloward. Although the historical details of the book were a bit overwhelming at the time, the book's major premise captured my imagination. I met the argument that "liberal" welfare policies are not fundamentally driven by a compassion for the poor or some benevolent concerns of a caretaker state. Instead, I heard that welfare programs inherently serve the interests of corporate elites. It was argued that the private sector never provides enough living-wage jobs and the state works as a buffer that keeps the poor people "in their place." In effect, when the economy booms AFDC checks are just enough to keep the unemployed apathetic, quiet, and resigned to their subordination (but not large enough to motivate the working poor onto welfare). Conversely, when economic conditions worsen and large segments of poor people forsake obedience and deference, the welfare system is flexible enough to expand its boundaries in order to co-opt any radical impulses among the angry poor. According to Piven and Cloward (1971, p. 3),

> Relief arrangements are ancillary to economic arrangements. The chief function is to regulate labor, and they do that in several ways. First, when mass unemployment leads to outbreaks of turmoil, relief programs are ordinarily initiated or expanded to absorb and control enough of the unemployed to restore order; then, as turbulence subsides, the relief system contracts, expelling those who are needed to populate the labor market.

Although Piven and Cloward never contend that protest is the sole cause of elite largesse, the rest of this chapter will focus on the theoretical claim that "relief policies are designed to mute civil disorder" (1971, p. 245). This scope is limited for several reasons. First, this emphasis on working-class disruptions is unique since most mainstream models locate policy change in economic capacities, party dynamics, voting, or interest group lobbying. Second, the politics of protest is one of the few political tools available to non-elites (i.e., people of moderate incomes rarely can retain lobbyists or make large contributions to political candidates, but they can get friends to join a demonstration). Subsequently, in having a deficit of conventional political tools, poor people can utilize the more confrontational tactics of class struggles and withdraw their daily cooperation with the organizations that belittle and exploit them. Third, the power of protests seems potentially feasible to me. It is possible that corporate profits can become vulnerable if enough workers obstruct the normal practices of business (through foot-dragging, boycotts, strikes, sit-ins, etc.). In these unique cases of vulnerable profits, companies may turn to the state for assistance. In such situations, politicians may be convinced that it easier to spend a little more on welfare than it is to raise the minimum wage, stop corporate downsizing, or halt urban renewal (incremental modifications are much less burdensome to elites than radical transformations in labor or property relations).

The ensuing text focuses on empirical tests of the "turmoil-relief" hypothesis. Piven and Cloward relied on archival and qualitative evidence, but this chapter sees how their assertion fares in quantitative studies. Although some may find these positivistic approaches as too mechanical in their notion of causation, or too crude in their measures of social processes, these studies have the advantage of using systematic samples. In addition, their computations can weigh the relative impact of different variables and control for the effects of other mitigating factors.

THE EMPIRICAL REPORTS AND RESEARCH DESIGNS

All of these studies had to measure and operationalize the key variables of "turmoil" and "relief." Since *Regulating the Poor* never precisely defines these terms, researchers had to be creative. In looking for indicators of "turmoil," researchers often quote the following passage: "as protests, demonstrations, riots, and other forms of disorder reached unprecedented heights between 1965 and 1968, the relief rolls climbed 58 percent" (p. 245). Subsequently, researchers generally decided that events such as riots, protests, and strikes are suitable representations of turmoil (i.e., Isaac & Kelly, 1981; Schram & Turbett, 1983; Swank, 1983; Hicks & Misra, 1993; Jaynes, 2002).

Although Piven and Cloward simultaneously address all of these events in their book, the literature has mostly divided into riot or social movement studies. These distinct lines of inquiry are due to methodological concerns. In most eras protests and riots emerge concurrently, and this appearance of multicolinearity can wreak havoc in the interpretation of findings for some multivariate techniques (see Swank & Hicks, 1984; Fording, 1997; Jaynes, 2002).

While most studies look at riots or protests, some works look beyond the concept of collective events (events usually entail noninstitutional gatherings in which people publicly challenge the existing social order). Instead of focusing on direct-action settings, these works explored the organizational capacity of poor people to make turmoil (Zylan & Soule, 2000; Andrews, 2001; Chen & Phinney, 2004). Rather than demarcating the number of riots or protests for a region, they identified the number of unions or radical groups that may endorse protests or riots. Another set of studies have deemed a lower-class mobilization as the percentage of poor people who vote in state elections (Hill et al., 1995; Johnson, 2001; Soss et al., 2001; Avery & Peffley, 2005). Although voting is not the sort of contentious act that Piven and Cloward envisioned, these authors contend that lower-class voting boosts the political clout of the poor and reflects the extent to which they are already mobilized into a cohesive political force.

Likewise, *Regulating the Poor* never explicitly defines the terms "relief" or "government payments." To the chagrin of those who desire great specificity, Piven and Cloward broadly applied relief to a wide array of different means-tested, social insurance, and labor law programs (i.e., ADC, Medicaid, social security, unemployment compensation, private pensions, collective bargaining rights). In responding to such breadth, some works utilize aggregated measures for several welfare programs (e.g., Isaac & Kelly, 1981; Swank, 1983; Hicks & Misra, 1993) while others adhere to specific means-tested programs (e.g., Betz, 1974; Jennings, 1980; Chamlin, 1992). Different elements of these programs have been studied as well. Numerous studies have looked at the expansion and reduction in the size of welfare rolls (e.g., Albritton, 1979; Schram & Turbett, 1983; Fording, 1997) while some assessed budgetary allocations for welfare programs (e.g., Welch, 1975; Button, 1977; Jaynes, 2002), the generosity of welfare benefits (e.g., Colby, 1981; Hill et al., 1995; Johnson,

2001), or the type of eligibility rules initiated (e.g., Zlyan & Soule, 2000; Soss et al., 2001; Avery & Peffley, 2005).

RIOTS AND WELFARE

Although riots might serve as a situational excuse to appropriate consumer products, riots can also be viewed as a political response to closed power structures. That is, when economic immiseration spreads, and conventional political avenues ignore input from the disenfranchised, riots can be conceived as an alternative political tactic. Regardless of the reasons behind rioting, numerous bivariate studies have established a link between urban riots and the "relief explosion" of the 1960s (Betz, 1974; Welch, 1975; Button, 1977; Jennings, 1980; Chamlin, 1992; Fording, 1997).

In using either the city or state as a unit of analysis, eight of nine studies suggest that "spontaneous incidents of collective violence" during the 1960s created immediate increases in the amount of welfare spending for municipalities (Betz, 1974; Welch, 1975; Button, 1977) and the growth of welfare rolls (Jennings, 1980; Colby, 1981; Schram & Turbett, 1983; Chamlin, 1992). Numerous tables and scatter-plots reveal that AFDC and general assistance (GA) expenditures increased most rapidly during the period of the most frequent and severe riots during the 1960s (Betz, 1974; Jennings, 1980; Isaac & Kelly, 1981; Schram & Turbett, 1983). Likewise, welfare grew faster for the cities that encountered riots. Button (1977) noted that cities with riots experienced a 2.7 times greater funding increase for welfare than cities without riots, and Betz (1974) showed that the slow growth of 3 percent a year in city welfare budgets during the early 1960s was jettisoned by growths of 21 to 56 percent for cities that had protests in 1964, 1965, or 1966.

In the only case of counterevidence on this topic, Albritton (1979) found that welfare rolls did grow faster for cities that had riots (78 percent growth as compared to 67 percent), but this difference was not large enough to produce a statistically significant F-score. Critics have noted that this anomaly could be due to a small sample size (forty-nine cities) and its cross-sectional approach which failed to explore yearly changes in welfare practices.

The significant link between riots and federal welfare spending remained intact for all of the multivariate studies on this topic (Button,

1977; Isaac & Kelly, 1981). One work that looked at the funding of Community Action Programs found that the number of riots was a better predictor of spending patterns than were any of the deprivation indexes, congressional power measures, local government characteristics, and neighborhood racial breakdowns (Button, 1977). In a time series analysis that stretched from 1947 to 1976, Isaac and Kelly (1981) found that national, state, and local spending on several "antipoverty" programs were always swayed by the frequency and severity of riots (regardless of effects of previous welfare spending, the gross national product, the political party that occupied the executive office, and the unemployment rate).

In other multivariate studies, the connection between riots and the number of welfare recipients is undisputed (Jennings, 1980; Colby, 1981; Isaac & Kelly, 1981; Schram & Turbett, 1983; Swank & Hicks, 1984; Chamlin, 1992; Fording, 1997). In finding moderate associations, some works conclude that riots are one of several factors that swell welfare rolls. For instance, Isaac and Kelly (1981) found that the frequency of riots was one of two factors that consistently predicted changes in AFDC rolls from 1947 to 1976 (the other variables included GNP, unemployment rates, party in control, and the lagged effects of earlier welfare budgets). Other works suggested that the measures of riots netted the largest coefficients in their multivariate models (Jennings, 1980; Schram & Turbett, 1983; Chamlin, 1992). When looking at the annual growth of AFDC rolls for each state, Jennings (1980) found that the number of major riots accounted for 31 percent of the variance in the dependent variable while the next best variables accounted for only 10 percent of the variance (even when controlling for the degree of interparty competition, the percent of Democratic vote, union density, percent unemployed, per capita income, and poverty rates). Similarly, Chamlin (1992) found that riots accounted for almost 50 percent of the variance in the annual growth rate of AFDC programs for 1960 to 1970 (control variables include poverty levels, unemployment, tax revenue, and percent black).

Only a few studies have looked at the effects of riots on welfare benefit levels (Colby, 1981; Isaac & Kelly, 1981). Their findings are illuminating since both studies concluded that riots had no effect on the size of welfare checks. Hence, riots seem to inspire greater access to welfare programs but do very little in boosting the actual per capita benefits received by poor people. Thus governmental responses to riots seems to spread aid to more people, but this aid is not enough to end the recipients' poverty.

SOCIAL MOVEMENTS AND WELFARE

While the intensity and breadth of progressive mobilizations varies, the past century has seen the growth, dissipation, and rebirth of numerous social movements (unionism, welfare rights, women's liberation, antiwar, environmentalism, gay and lesbian rights, etc.). In selecting their samples, some studies created composite protest counts for several working-class mobilizations (Swank, 1983; Hicks & Misra, 1993), while most of the research delineates the role of the civil rights demonstrations in the expansion of welfare programs during the 1960s and early 1970s (Swank & Hicks, 1984; Andrews, 2001; Jaynes, 2002; Santoro, 2002). Finally, some works have turned to substitute measures for direct protest counts. In finding their proxies, some of these works traced the capacity of poor people to make social unrest. Thus some works explored welfare dynamics in light of the number people who joined social justice groups (Andrews, 2001; Chen & Phinney, 2004) or the percentage of poor people who vote in governmental elections (Hill et al., 1995; Soss et al., 2001).

The impact of protests stood out in all these works. The role of protests was statistically significant but relatively modest for several of these studies (Swank, 1983; Swank & Hicks, 1983; Santoro, 2002). One thirty-year study on AFDC caseloads found that the number of civil rights protests were but one of many significant predictors (Swank & Hicks, 1984). Another work by Swank (1983) showed that both the magnitude of lower-class protests and the number of strikes in seventeen industrialized countries predicted the spending on direct income transfer payments. Likewise, Santoro (2002) showed that the number of black-led protests during the late 1950s and early 1960s contributed to the adoption of Equal Employment Opportunity policies. However, when extending this analysis to later decades, he found that public opinion and conventional policy process took over once the social movement stopped creating "dramatic events."

Other regressions found larger protest effects (Hicks & Misra, 1993; Jaynes, 2002). In computations that controlled for matters of tax revenues, characteristics of the local government, and demographic qualities of the community, the total number of civil rights protests for both 1954 to 1968 and 1969 to 1984 presented the biggest impact on city spending for "free" health care, public housing, and cash payments for the poor (Jaynes, 2002). In another comprehensive study, Hicks and Misra (1993) found that employee strikes and working-class protests were some of the biggest factors that swayed the overall welfare spending for eighteen highly industrialized countries. That is, when analyzing "first world" data from a twenty-three-year period, welfare spending was consistently swayed by the number of employee-initiated strikes and working-class demonstrations even after they controlled for total government revenues, the degree of "left control" in the legislative bodies, the number of state employees, unemployment rates, the consumer price index, and the nation's GNP.

The works that used proxy measures for confrontational tactics during the 1960s presented similar results (Andrews, 2001; Chen & Phinney, 2004). One study for the state of Mississippi found that federal War on Poverty dollars flowed faster to the communities that had larger membership rolls in their local wings of two major civil rights groups (Andrews, 2001). Likewise, having a larger constituency in the local NAACP branch also contributed to greater access to housing for the poor (Chen & Phinney, 2004).

While the link between the 1960s social movements and welfare policies is well established, work that explores this relationship during the past two decades is more exploratory and less conclusive. Several Clinton-era case studies suggest that disruptive practices lessened the strictness of workfare rules (Krinsky, 1999; Reese, 2002) and brought better shelters for homeless people (Cress & Snow, 2000). However, the quantitative world has yet to study the way 1990s protests may have altered the trajectories to state welfare reforms. In lieu of precise protest measures, some quantitative works have stretched the meaning of turmoil to the somewhat dubious measures of "union density" (Zylan & Soule, 2000) or "low-income voter turnout" (Hill et al., 1995; Johnson, 2001; Soss et al., 2002; Avery & Peffley, 2005).

These voter studies have provided less consistent results. Three of the five studies contend that greater electoral mobilizations of the poor impeded the implementation of the most draconian versions of welfare reform (Hill et al., 1995; Johnson, 2001; Avery & Peffley, 2005). In a pooled data set for 1978 to 1990, Hill et al. (1995) found that enormous lower-class class electoral turnouts yielded less cuts to welfare spending. However the effects of poor people's voting faded some when Republicans controlled the U.S. Senate or presidency. Similarly, a study with 1990 data found that electoral participation among the poor was one of the major predictors in difference between statewide levels of AFDC benefits (Johnson, 2001). Finally, Avery and Peffley's (2005) post-PRWORA study found that states were less likely to adopt stringent work requirements, harsher time limits, and family caps if the lower class hit the ballot box (even when controlling for nine other variables).

CONCLUSION

To Piven and Cloward, the cyclical nature of welfare policies is driven by the changing needs of corporate elites. To them, welfare programs excel at suppressing rebellions and ensuring a constant supply of cheap workers. During times of labor force stability and little worker resistance, access to welfare is restricted to ensure a steady pool of desperate low-wage employees. Conversely, during periods of greater economic misery and wider working-class defiance, stability and compliance is reestablished by easing access to means-tested programs. In effect, widespread political challenges are muted and quelled by extending aid to more people at the bottom tiers of the economic system. As order is restored, welfare programs again contract and expel welfare recipients back into low-paying service jobs.

In taking these empirical studies as a whole, there seems to be little doubt that "relief" and "turmoil" are connected. Although methodologists may bicker about the reliability and validity of each work, study after study concurred that "the relief rises of the early 1960s coincided with the rise in public disorder" (Piven & Cloward, 1971, p. 245). In fact, fourteen of the sixteen studies on the 1960s found that riots or protests led to larger welfare rolls and greater welfare expenditures for countries, states, and cities.

These works provide sharp insights, but future research should seek greater theoretical breadth. It is clear that turmoil often leads to the liberalization of welfare policies, but political leaders may also turn to authoritarian responses to collective outbursts. Elites can try to delegitimize poor people's movements by stigmatizing and ostracizing their participants. Or in a more direct form of repression, government officials may outlaw organizations, incarcerate leaders, and insist on continual police harassment of activists. Although these side effects of turmoil were rarely discussed in these articles, two of these studies concluded that the riots of the 1960s did inspire greater police budgets (Welch, 1975; Jaynes, 2002).

While Piven and Cloward themselves highlighted the impact of disruptive tactics, they and others recognized the importance of other sociopolitical conditions. In putting forth a state capacity argument, some studies suggest that governments seem more responsive to "turmoil" when they have larger tax revenues (Welch, 1975; Chamlin, 1992; Hicks & Misra, 1993; Zylan & Soule, 2000) and smaller medical, police, or military budgets (Swank & Hicks, 1984; Hicks & Misra, 1993; Zylan & Soule, 2000).

Some authors also contend that social movement success partially hinges on the support of sympathetic power holders, dissident elites, or friendly political insiders (Jenkins & Brents, 1989; Jaynes, 2002). Nevertheless the consequences of specific political alignments are far from settled. Some studies argue that governments are more responsive to protests and riots when there is high interparty competition and neither party holds a large majority of gubernatorial votes or state senate seats (Schram & Turbett, 1983; Hill et al., 1995; Fording, 1997; Avery & Peffley, 2005). Likewise, divisions between the legislative and judicial systems seem to make for larger welfare programs (Fording, 1997) as do the extremely rare cases in which one segment of the capitalist class actively lobbies on behalf of more lenient welfare eligibility rules (Jenkins & Brents, 1989). However, other works offer an opposite take on elite struggles. Rather than seeing elite division as a facilitator of protest powers, they insist that welfare budgets are more likely to expand when members of the Democratic Party dominate legislative bodies and the governors' seat (Button, 1977; Jennings, 1980; Swank, 1983; Hicks & Misra, 1993). Conversely, welfare polices seem to move in a more punitive direction when Republicans monopolize most of the elected positions (Zylan & Soule, 2000; Soss et al., 2001).

Since social movements often enhance their effectiveness when they garner the approval of unaffiliated bystanders, it seems wise to look at the way public perceptions alter the outcomes of poor people's movements (Giugni, McAdam, & Tilly, 1999). In revealing the importance of community attitudes, some works conclude that the impact of working-class challenges are in part mediated by public impressions of poverty, racism, and the role of government in society (Welch, 1975; Button, 1977; Hill et al., 1995; Fording, 1997; Hicks & Misra, 1993; Andrews, 2001; Johnson, 2001; Santoro, 2002). Of these studies, some works conclude that the effects of riots are magnified when a large segment of the local middle class align themselves with the Democratic Party (Welch, 1975; Button, 1977) or when many state residents label themselves as liberals (Fording, 1997). Likewise, the potency of poor people's mobilizations is amplified when large segments of the local population maintain liberal stances on racial integration (Johnson, 2001), affirmative action (Santoro, 2002), and other political issues (Hill et al., 1995). Conversely, the leverage of poor people's movements is hindered when fellow citizens organize reactionary countermovements which seek to maintain historical hierarchies and the status quo (Hicks & Misra 1993; Andrews, 2001; Santoro, 2002).

Expanding welfare budgets may also be a result of both protests and downward business cycles. In noting this relationship, welfare budgets sometimes expand when protest combines with shrinking gross national products (Swank & Hicks, 1984), burgeoning unemployment rates (Schram & Turbett, 1983; Chamlin, 1992; Hicks & Misra, 1993; Hill et al., 1995; Fording, 1997), losses of real income for most employees (Hicks & Misra, 1993; Hill et al., 1995), and the growth of poverty (Welch, 1975; Button, 1977; Hicks & Misra, 1993; Andrews, 2001). Finally, welfare rolls seem to shrink when protest and unemployment become less common (Soss et al., 2001; Avery & Peffley, 2005) and when companies seek new workers for their service industry jobs (Zylan & Soule, 2000). However, it should be noted that many works conclude that economic crises play a necessary but not sufficient role in liberalizing welfare politics.

In the end, the ideas of this chapter should offer some hope. While most of this compilation illustrates some troubling aspects of recent welfare reforms, it is important to remember that America is not forever doomed to enacting more punitive welfare rules. Conservative elites may have currently grabbed the reigns of power, but this condition may be temporary. Bursts of confrontational activism can force the political pendulum in a more liberal direction, so it is the imperative of poor people and lefties to move beyond the voting or lobbying approaches to change. Instead, we must support and foster poor people's movements that are willing to partake in confrontational tactics when need be.

REFERENCES

Albritton, R. (1979). Social amelioration through mass insurgency? *American Political Science Review,* 73: 1003-1013.

Andrews, K. (2001). Social movements and policy implementation. *American Sociological Review,* 66: 71-89.

Avery, J. & M. Peffley. (2005). Voter registration requirements, voter turnout, and welfare eligibility policy. *State Politics & Policy Quarterly,* 5: 19-38.

Betz, M. (1974). Riots and welfare. *Social Problems,* 21: 345-356.

Button, J. (1977). *Black Violence: The Political Impact of the 1960's Riots.* Princeton, NJ: University of Princeton Press.

Chamlin, M. (1992). Intergroup threat & social control: Welfare expansion during the 1960's & 1970's. In A. Lisla, *Social Threat and Social Control* (pp. 210-242). New York: SUNY Press.

Chen, A. & R. Phinney. (2004). *Did the Civil Rights Movement Have a Direct Impact on Public Policy?* Ford School of Public Policy, Ann Arbor: University of Michigan.

Colby, D. (1981). Black power and state welfare policy. *Review of Black Political Economy,* 11: 465-476.

Cress, D. & D. Snow. (2000). The outcomes of a homeless mobilization. *American Journal of Sociology,* 105: 1063-1104.

Fording, R. (1997). The conditional effects of violence as a political tactic. *American Journal of Political Science,* 41: 1-29.

Giugni, M., D. McAdam, & C. Tilly. (1999). *How Social Movements Matter.* Minneapolis: University of Minnesota Press.

Hicks, A. & J. Misra. (1993). Political resources and the growth of welfare in affluent capitalistic democracies. *American Journal of Sociology,* 99: 668-710.

Hill, K. Q., J. E. Leighley, & A. Hinton-Anderson. (1995). Lower-class mobilization and policy linkage in the United States. *American Journal of Political Sciences,* 39: 75-86.

Isaac, L. & W. Kelly. (1981). Racial insurgency, the state and welfare expansion. *American Journal of Sociology,* 86: 1348-1386.

Jaynes, A. (2002). Insurgency and policy outcomes. *Journal of Political & Military Sociology,* 30: 90-112.

Jenkins, J. & B. Brents. (1989). Social protest, hegemonic competition and social reform. *American Sociological Review,* 54: 891-909.

Jennings, E. (1980). Urban riots and welfare policy change. In H. Ingram and D. Mann (eds.), *Why Policies Succeed or Fail* (pp. 59-83). Beverley Hills, CA: Sage.

Johnson, M. (2001). The impact of social diversity and racial attitudes on social welfare policy. *State Politics & Policy Quarterly,* 1: 27-49.

Krinsky, J. (1999). Work, workfare and contention in New York City. *Critical Sociology,* 24: 277-305.

Piven, F. F. & R. Cloward. (1971). *Regulating the Poor: The Functions of Public Welfare.* New York: Vintage Books.

Reese, E. (2002). Resisting the workfare state. *Race, Gender & Class,* 9: 72-96.

Santoro, W. (2002). The civil rights struggle for fair employment. *Social Forces,* 81: 177-206.

Schram, S. & J. Turbett. (1983). Civil disorder and welfare explosion. *American Sociological Review,* 48: 408-414.

Soss, J., S. Schram, T. Vartanian, & E. O'Brien. (2001). Setting the terms of relief. *American Journal of Political Science,* 45: 378-395.

Swank, D. (1983). Group protest and the growth of the welfare state. *American Behavioral Scientist,* 26: 291-310.

Swank, D. & A. Hicks. (1984). Militancy, need and relief. *Research in Social Movements, Conflicts & Change,* 6: 1-29.

Welch, S. (1975). The impact of riots on urban expenditures. *American Journal of Political Science,* 19: 741-760.

Zylan, Y. & S. Soule. (2000). Ending welfare as we know it. *Social Forces,* 79: 623-653.

Index

Page numbers followed by the letter "t" indicate tables.

Order a copy of this book with this form or online at:
http://www.haworthpress.com/store/product.asp?sku=5608

THE PROMISE OF WELFARE REFORM
Political Rhetoric and the Reality of Poverty
in the Twenty-First Century

_____ in hardbound at $49.95 (ISBN-13: 978-0-7890-2921-8; ISBN-10: 0-7890-2921-9)

_____ in softbound at $34.95 (ISBN-13: 978-0-7890-2922-5; ISBN-10: 0-7890-2922-7)

Or order online and use special offer code HEC25 in the shopping cart.

COST OF BOOKS_____

POSTAGE & HANDLING_____
(US: $4.00 for first book & $1.50
for each additional book)
(Outside US: $5.00 for first book
& $2.00 for each additional book)

SUBTOTAL_____

IN CANADA: ADD 7% GST_____

STATE TAX_____
(NJ, NY, OH, MN, CA, IL, IN, PA, & SD
residents, add appropriate local sales tax)

FINAL TOTAL_____
(If paying in Canadian funds,
convert using the current
exchange rate, UNESCO
coupons welcome)

☐ **BILL ME LATER:** (Bill-me option is good on
US/Canada/Mexico orders only; not good to
jobbers, wholesalers, or subscription agencies.)
☐ Check here if billing address is different from
shipping address and attach purchase order and
billing address information.

Signature_____

☐ **PAYMENT ENCLOSED:** $_____

☐ **PLEASE CHARGE TO MY CREDIT CARD.**

☐ Visa ☐ MasterCard ☐ AmEx ☐ Discover
☐ Diner's Club ☐ Eurocard ☐ JCB

Account # _____

Exp. Date_____

Signature_____

Prices in US dollars and subject to change without notice.

NAME_____

INSTITUTION_____

ADDRESS_____

CITY_____

STATE/ZIP_____

COUNTRY_____ COUNTY (NY residents only)_____

TEL_____ FAX_____

E-MAIL_____

May we use your e-mail address for confirmations and other types of information? ☐ Yes ☐ No
We appreciate receiving your e-mail address and fax number. Haworth would like to e-mail or fax special
discount offers to you, as a preferred customer. **We will never share, rent, or exchange your e-mail address
or fax number.** We regard such actions as an invasion of your privacy.

Order From Your Local Bookstore or Directly From
The Haworth Press, Inc.

10 Alice Street, Binghamton, New York 13904-1580 • USA
TELEPHONE: 1-800-HAWORTH (1-800-429-6784) / Outside US/Canada: (607) 722-5857
FAX: 1-800-895-0582 / Outside US/Canada: (607) 771-0012
E-mail to: orders@haworthpress.com

For orders outside US and Canada, you may wish to order through your local
sales representative, distributor, or bookseller.
For information, see http://haworthpress.com/distributors

(Discounts are available for individual orders in US and Canada only, not booksellers/distributors.)

PLEASE PHOTOCOPY THIS FORM FOR YOUR PERSONAL USE.
http://www.HaworthPress.com   BOF06